Return on or before the
last date stamped below.

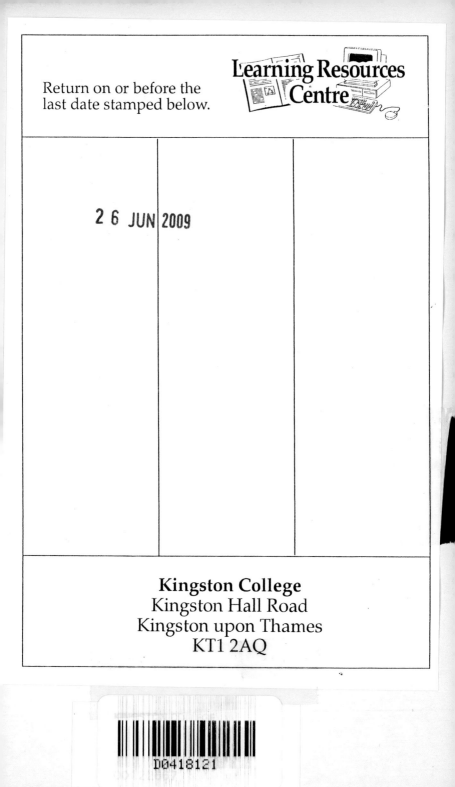

Learning Resources Centre

2 6 JUN 2009

Kingston College
Kingston Hall Road
Kingston upon Thames
KT1 2AQ

D0418121

The Young Vic Book

Theatre Work and Play

Ruth Little

KINGSTON LEARNING RESOURCES CENTRE COLLEGE

Methuen

Published by Methuen 2004

10 9 8 7 6 5 4 3 2 1

Copyright © 2004 by Ruth Little

The right of Ruth Little to be identified as the author of this work has been asserted by her in accordance with the Copyright, Designs and Patents Act 1988

Published in 2004 by
Methuen Publishing Ltd
215 Vauxhall Bridge Road
London SW1V 1EJ
www.methuen.co.uk

Methuen Publishing Limited Reg. No. 3543167

ISBN 0 413 77110 5

A CIP catalogue for this title is available from the British Library.

Designed by Helen Ewing

Typeset by SX Composing DTP, Rayleigh, Essex

Printed and bound in Great Britain
by Mackays of Chatham plc, Chatham, Kent

This book is sold subject to the condition that it shall not, by way of trade or otherwise, be lent, resold, hired out or otherwise circulated in any form of binding or cover other than that in which it is published and without a similar condition, including this condition, being imposed on the subsequent purchaser.

KINGSTON COLLEGE
LEARNING RESOURCES CENTRE

Class No. 792.0942 LIT

Acc. No. 00122667

Date Rec. 12/04

Order No.

Contents

Illustrations

Acknowledgements

This book was built on a foundation laid by Craig Higginson, to whom I am indebted for his research and interviews with theatre practitioners. Its guiding spirit is provided by Sue Emmas and her team in the Teaching, Participation and Research Department at the Young Vic, in particular Hannah Quigley and Claire Newby. Their energy, commitment and enthusiasm for their work with young people and the local community are a constant source of inspiration. My thanks, too, to all the directors, teachers, designers and technicians who have shared their ideas so generously with me, especially Kate Wild, Tom Wright, Titania Krimpas, Nizar Zuabi, Joe Hill-Gibbins, Rae McKen, Poonam Brah, Phil Gladwell, Alison Poynter and Stuart Morley. And above all, thanks to David Lan and Rufus Norris, who gave up valuable time to discuss in detail their work as directors and the ideas behind it. Methuen editor Elizabeth Ingrams offered invaluable advice and guidance, and Sarah Preece and Sue Emmas were wise and careful readers. My thanks to them, and to everyone at the Young Vic.

Grimm Tales © 1996, Carol Ann Duffy, adapted from *The Brothers Grimm* and dramatised by Tim Supple and the Young Vic Theatre Company. Published by Faber & Faber Ltd.

More Grimms Tales © 1997 by Carol Ann Duffy, adapted from *The Brothers Grimm* and dramatised by Tim Supple and the Young Vic Theatre Company. Published by Faber & Faber Ltd.

Extracts from *A Raisin in the Sun* by Lorraine Hansberry copyright © 1958 by Robert Nemiroff, as an unpublished work. Copyright © 1959, 1966, 1984 by Robert Nemiroff. Used by permission of Random House, Inc.

Preface

Long before I took over the Young Vic, I had thought of it, almost without thinking, as one of the most remarkable spaces around. Over the four years I've been Artistic Director, I've spoken to a number of directors who say 'Of all the theatres in London, that's the one I'd want to run'. The main reason, I guess, is the auditorium with which everyone falls in love at first sight. But there is another reason to love the Young Vic: the relationship it has created with its audience.

Quite late in rehearsals of *'Tis Pity She's a Whore*, my first Young Vic production, Tim Supple, then Artistic Director, came to talk to my company of actors and stage management. He told us that the response we'd get from the Young Vic audience would be unlike anything we anticipated. It would be noisier, less polite, more direct; a large part of it would be young; there'd be many local people for the majority of whom this would be their first time inside any theatre. He described the enormous effort his team put into wooing the Young Vic folk who don't ordinarily think of themselves as 'theatregoers' – anything but.

Despite all he said, when, a week or so later, we came actually to meet the challenge of a Young Vic audience, we were unprepared: for its vivacity, for its spontaneity, for the amount that they, consciously and unconsciously, gave us back. The charge was terrific. We were all exhilarated. I've been addicted ever since.

What makes this audience what it is?

Though I trained as an actor, most of my life in the theatre has been as a writer. I've taught in drama schools, and I've been involved in many projects with young directors and writers, especially at the Royal Court and the National Theatre Studio. In my experience, almost all of the so-called 'education' work theatres do is clearly separated from that theatre's 'real' work, i.e. the putting on of shows on that theatre's main stage. It had never occurred to me that there was any other way of doing it. At the Young Vic we put on shows. That's our *raison d'être*. But we believe – i.e. we've discovered – that you have to put almost as much work into making your audience as you do into making the work the audience sees. We're after the best possible total experience. We think it is our job to take responsibility for it. So our work with young people – school students, young directors, whoever they are – is quite simply part of making that audience. Consequently it's at the heart of what we are, of everything we do.

The whole point of going to all the trouble of having a subsidised theatre is that it should do the difficult, the adventurous – it should make contact with people in profound, surprising, disturbing, even unpopular ways – but with such skill and inventiveness that you can't help but pay attention. Our Teaching, Participation and Research Department doesn't push a particular political line. Far from it. What we do is art, we do plays. We're not social workers. We're encouraged to believe that the theatre is good for young people because it stops them stealing cars and sniffing glue. But rebelliousness – or 'rebellion' to give it its proper name – is itself a creative act, often highly imaginative and original. Every teacher knows that. Young people are perfectly capable of stealing cars in order to get to a theatre – as I have often, perhaps fancifully, explained on a number of occasions.

So this book is about ourselves and our audience. I hope it's the story of a love affair – from our point of view, anyway. The ideas that have grown up at the Young Vic are, I think, precious and, to some extent, unique. That's our reason for recording them here.

Let me personalise it. Much, if not all, of the work we do with young people is conceived and guided by my associate artistic director Sue Emmas. She is the inspiration behind this book and has developed a programme of such breadth and depth that only a fraction of it can be recorded here.

All our theatre-making work with young people that Sue and her team have led has one justification: if you allow the experience of being in a theatre, of working with theatre-makers, to affect you, it will change you and you will enjoy the process of being changed. It's as simple as that.

David Lan

INTRODUCTION

In developing their craft and extending the range of their creative responses, professional actors can draw on an array of games, exercises and rehearsal techniques. From Stanislavski and Strasberg to Peter Brook, Augusto Boal and Keith Johnstone, theatre practitioners and their students have gathered the fruits of their experience over many decades and presented these summaries to actors training for or developing professional careers. The nature of the work varies widely; it tends to exist within a particular philosophical approach to theatre and theatre craft, and it often assumes a long-term professional and creative commitment on the part of the practitioner. These methodologies inform many of the teaching practices in drama schools and actor-training centres. They are all rich, probing and challenging guides to mature artistic practice.

But how can teachers, directors and workshop leaders draw on these ground-breaking approaches to inform and inspire their own work with young non-professionals in the classroom, college, theatre or the community? Why play one game rather than another? How does any exercise really work? What might the participants learn or discover by performing it – about a play, about themselves? How can individual games and exercises be combined to form a coherent, meaningful, experiential approach to performance, creativity and self-expression, rather than an *ad hoc* series of orchestrated gestures? The answers lie, in part, in reconnecting the two-dimensional study of drama with the three-dimensional practice of theatre-making.

The aim of this book is to draw on and distil those elements of the acting craft applicable and pertinent to the bodily exploration of plays, and to combine these with simple, illuminating games and exercises anchored to particular texts. The result, it is hoped, is a manual which offers specific, concrete and strategic examples of theatre-making, and which is intended to inspire and encourage teachers and directors to tackle challenging classical works with young people simply because both the plays and the participants have so much to offer.

The history of the Young Vic is a history of engagement with and inspiration by young people. When the company was set up Frank Dunlop in 1969, its remit was to give younger members of the National Theatre Company opportunities to present both classics and new work to young audiences. The Young Vic was intended as an experimental theatre 'university' for young people aged from five to twenty-five, providing education in theatre and functioning as 'a centre for work of a National standard available to students and young people whose incomes or inclinations make existing theatre expensive or forbidding'. Over three decades the work with young people has developed philosophically and functionally, but the abiding aim has been to define and sustain a coherent, resourceful and flexible practice.

The Young Vic's education work has evolved directly out of the core of the company's practice over thirty years: the aim of producing great plays which can be enjoyed, appreciated and responded to by all audiences, and in particular young audiences. The work with young people at the Young Vic is systemic; it runs through every part of the company and the building, and springs from a simple set of principles that create consistency within its diversity. Perhaps the best way to help young people understand plays is to invite them into the process of theatre-making. Games and exercises are the tools with which they and their teachers can strip down a play to expose and explore its complex fragile machinery and then build it up again in a performance context so that it works effectively, efficiently and meaningfully for them as individuals and as a group.

The primary material for performance and process work at the Young Vic is the classics – old and new. The company's original remit – to produce lively and innovative versions of the classics for younger theatre audiences and to provide training opportunities for younger theatre practitioners – is still reflected in the way the company works today. The Young Vic's work has demonstrated that classical drama and contemporary classics provide environ-ments for exploration which are at once challenging and secure; they are talismans we carry with us into the future, which tell us about ourselves and our suffering in terms that never grow old.

Their specific cultural attitudes can be tested, challenged and reinterpreted in a contemporary context. They offer characters of stature and authority, language which is often rich and potent, and, perhaps most importantly, they present lasting accounts of fundamental and universal human dilemmas.

Behind every influential teacher/practitioner there is another, whose pioneering work generates a host of new approaches and adaptations and amalgamations of existing ones. The Teaching, Participaton and Research programme at the Young Vic has grown up around the commitment and curiosity of individual practitioners, especially Sue Emmas, Tim Supple and Barbara Houseman. But its roots are in the founding principles of the Young Vic, and, beyond that, in the practice of Peter Brook and, before him, Jean Vilar. The work is constantly evolving, according to the needs and interests of teachers and their students.

Young participants in drama workshops, and their teachers, are on the whole pursuing quite different aims from those of professional actors. They are often simply looking for ways to animate literary and dramatic works, and for ways to contribute creatively to that exploration. A good play, according to Robert Lepage, 'gives permission', and a good teacher, it seems, needs no further encouragement. The TPR programme at the Young Vic seeks to provide participants with long-lasting and adaptable tools to express their ideas confidently and imaginatively and to take that confidence and imagination out of the classroom and into the rest of their lives. The broader aim is to encourage them, ultimately, towards direct participation in a culture of their own making.

The aim of this book is not to turn young people into professional actors, but to help them discover that they can be *active* – they can use their bodies and their minds to investigate the world in ways that will continue to develop and prove relevant and useful when they are adults. The Young Vic's work with young people takes place outside the framework of the curriculum, with its clear and specific targets, although it is hoped that the approaches outlined here might usefully be adapted and applied to the curriculum, and not just to dramatic texts.

Anyone who works with young people – or any people in fact – may find it very useful to build up a body of games and exercises which can be developed throughout a working life to suit the needs of different educational and interactive situations. Improvisation, text work, character objectives, finding action for images – these are all instruments the teacher/practitioner can bring to the unique combination of problems and questions posed by a play. Whether they are used or not will depend on the nature of the play and the nature of the investigation. From the classroom to the community group, from corporate training sessions to working in the health and criminal justice systems, play *works* – as long as it is anchored firmly to something outside itself, which it can open up and inform unexpectedly, lastingly, and enjoyably. This book thus offers the ingredients which might go towards making up a workshop, rehearsal or exploration session, rather than providing complete or prescriptive workshop outlines. Working with young people, and responding to the fluency of their imaginations, as well as to the conditions which may inhibit or affect their interaction, demands openness, resourcefulness and flexibility. Circumstances and moods can shift suddenly and unexpectedly within a group or between individuals; it is generally more useful to have a number of possibilities available to you than a rigid plan of action.

Theatre games and exercises, like all areas of teaching, begin simply and become increasingly complex and challenging as they progress and as the skill and awareness of the participants increase. Though they can be used spontaneously to energise or synthesise a group, they bear most fruit when they surround and apply to specific objectives beyond the game or exercise in question. The teacher should be aware of and work steadily towards these objectives, but the participants should not be inhibited in their response by being told in advance why they are carrying out certain tasks. The aim is to get young people to use their bodies and their senses as well as their minds; to work empirically towards a 'felt' understanding of the play in question; to be free of self or peer-group censorship or goal-orientated striving. Analysis and evaluation are important, but they should come *after* the sessions of play and exploration have yielded their fruits.

The games and exercises in workshops are stimulating in themselves, but they are always presented in the context of the broader and deeper exploration of the theatre practice which accompanies them. By immersing young people in the skills and crafts of theatre-making from an early age, and by offering them insight into and hands-on experience of the collaborative nature of theatre across all its roles and departments, the directors and workshop leaders hope to spark their imaginations and their aspirations and to generate a lasting sense of ownership of those skills and insights. By this means theatre may become part of their landscape, and theatre buildings such as the Young Vic home to a diverse and engaged community of developing practitioners who recognise that through the fusion of its diverse elements a theatrical experience becomes something more than the sum of its parts. Lighting designer Paule Constable, who worked with Artistic Director Tim Supple on a number of productions at the Young Vic, believes 'it is vital that our work encompasses the opinions and voices of younger generations . . . We should take responsibility for *why* we make theatre and debate the issue of what its function is. And we should attempt to create an environment where we encourage ourselves and others to see our work in terms of a collective process rather than purely in terms of product.'

The first chapter of the book places the participatory work in the context of the Young Vic's history, its geographical and cultural location, and its development as a centre for practical exploration of theatre-making by young people in the diverse local community. The origins of the work with young people in director George Devine's notion of the theatre 'school'; its development under the banner of theatre-in-education work in the seventies and eighties, and its emergence as the current programme in 1996 are described as an introduction to the particular production-based approaches to working with young people which follow. The games and exercises defined here form one of the many strands of work which characterise the TPR programme.

The emphasis in subsequent chapters is on breaking the exploration of a play down into manageable units and practical exercises which will create a focused group and ultimately involve everyone, not just the confident. At the same time, these approaches underline the active, three-dimensional nature of theatre. Particular productions raise specific questions which the accompanying work seeks to answer. The main emphasis in the work with schoolchildren which grew out of the Young Vic's productions of *Grimm Tales* and *More Grimm Tales*, for example, is on strong and simple storytelling. The work associated with *Doctor Faustus* focuses on dramatic language and finding forms for the abstract ideas of the play, and was influenced by the voice and text work of Barbara Houseman at the Young Vic. The sessions with young people which sprang from the production of Lorraine Hansberry's *A Raisin in the Sun* ultimately concentrate on social issues and their impact on character and identity. The 1950s musical *Simply Heavenly* raises the challenge of giving structure and voice to the vibrant world of a musical drama, while the workshops on *Peribanez* raise questions about adding specific and convincing detail to dramatic images and social codes. The workshops become lenses through which the concerns of the play are magnified and explored.

In short, the aim of this book is to inspire teachers and directors to reveal theatre practice with assurance; to dig deeper in their explorations, and to instil confidence and curiosity in young people and in those who want their work with young people to be as illuminating, memorable and meaningful as possible. At the Young Vic these approaches, like the plays they seek to reveal, come to life in the mouths, bodies and minds of the young people for whom they're intended. Reanimated and recontextualised production by production, added to and adapted season by season, they're the tools with which we tune our own practice and, hopefully, they will continue to open doors for young people of all backgrounds to the range of opportunities available to them as the theatre-makers of tomorrow.

Chapter 1

A 'DISPOSABLE' THEATRE – THE YOUNG VIC GROWS UP

*Perhaps there is something in the air of Southwark which
encourages the transaction between reality and imagination.*

Peter Ackroyd

The Young Vic and its two boroughs

The Young Vic is situated near the south bank of the Thames on
the border of the boroughs of Lambeth and Southwark. It stands
on the same road as the Old Vic and the Royal National Theatre
Studio; the Royal National Theatre and the Globe Theatre are
nearby. To visitors and tourists, the area is alive with cultural
activity and leisure pursuits; its bars and cafés brimming with
people and its public buildings busy day and night.

And yet the area surrounding the theatre remains one of the
most disadvantaged in Britain. Lambeth and Southwark are
currently ranked as the fourth and fifth most deprived boroughs
in London (after Hackney, Tower Hamlets and Newham). Nearly
10 per cent of children in Southwark live in households where no
adult is in employment. Lambeth and Southwark are among the
most densely populated boroughs in the UK (the population
density of 99.2 people per hectare in Lambeth compares to an
average across England and Wales of 3.4). According to recent
research conducted by Lambeth and Southwark Councils, in 43
per cent of the schools more than 25 per cent of the pupils were
eligible for free school meals (indicating that the parents or
guardians receive income support). A recent attempt to hand most
of the functions of the Southwark local education authority over
to the private sector was a disastrous failure, and the schools and
colleges in the area have often struggled to improve educational
standards and raise the aspirations of young people against the
pressures of economic deprivation.

The paradox, however, is nothing new. Since Roman and Saxon times (and until the second half of the twentieth century), the area's position on the south bank of the river has made it the trading and traffic centre of London and the home to one of the country's largest immigrant populations. It has always accommodated the contradiction of having some of the wealthiest and most influential people in the country living and working alongside some of the poorest and most disadvantaged.

Lambeth and Southwark are two of the most culturally and ethnically diverse boroughs in Britain. Over 100 languages are spoken by the young people who go to school there and over one third of the population is of a black, Asian or minority ethnic background. After English, the most frequently spoken languages are Yoruba and Portuguese. One quarter of the local population has come from Africa and the Caribbean in the last two or three generations and around 5 per cent from the Indian subcontinent. The area also houses refugees from countries including Vietnam, Somalia, Eritrea, Angola, Azerbaijan and Kurdistan. It is a cosmopolitan and heterogeneous area and its streets hum with the stories of its diverse inhabitants.

The Young Vic began its life as an offshoot of the Old Vic, the former home of Lilian Baylis's Old Vic Shakespeare Company and, later, the first residence of the Royal National Theatre under Laurence Olivier. The first 'Young Vic Company' was established by George Devine shortly after the Second World War. It was part of the Old Vic Theatre School, set up by Devine, Michel Saint-Denis and Glen Byam Shaw, and it was the first company in Britain that aimed at producing classics for young people aged between nine and fifteen. The company became an influential training ground for young actors, but was axed with the withdrawal of its funding in 1951. (Devine later went on to found the English Stage Company at the Royal Court.)

The inspiration behind the second Young Vic Company came from Frank Dunlop, who joined the National Theatre as an Associate Director and Administrator in 1967. Dunlop's proposed programme of work was intended to give younger members of the National Theatre Company the chance to present classics to a young audience. 'Here,' Laurence Olivier said, 'we think to develop plays for young audiences, an experimental workshop for authors, actors and producers; a kind of Young Vic like that in which I and all my generation were able to cut our teeth on the big classic roles without being too harshly judged for it.' But Dunlop wanted also to explore a new kind of theatre for the new generation – one that was unconventional, classless, open, welcoming, circus-like and cheap; a 'disposable' theatre, according to his 'lieutenant' Vi Marriott, 'as good as the RSC or National Theatre but cheap and attractive. It was a tribute to George Devine, and the Old Vic Theatre School in a way.' 'Our brief,' said founding member Denise Coffey, 'is to be the equivalent of a paperback book. The contents and the value are the same but you can get it cheap.'

Dunlop believed the best way to attract a new generation of theatregoers was through doing the classics as well but as cheaply as possible: 'We felt this would keep the other work at the National alive and continually provoked and prodded.' In this he was indebted to influential French actor and director Jean Vilar, who expressed a taste for uncluttered stages and simplicity of setting in large spaces. His battle cry was 'an elite theatre for all'. He insisted that theatre should be as indispensable to life as bread and wine: 'If you deprive the public of Molière, Corneille and Shakespeare – that public we call "the public at large", the only one that counts; then without a doubt a certain quality of spirit within it will be weakened.'

The Young Vic was built in 1970 as a temporary structure designed to last for only five years. For Dunlop, it was the programme of work that mattered; the building itself need only be accessible, functional and unimposing. Dunlop shared entirely Vilar's essentially socialist and unequivocal attitude towards theatre buildings: 'A thousand seats at one hundred francs are better value than 300 at 400 francs. An auditorium where you can embrace your neighbour, eat and drink and piss where you like is worth more for our dramatic literature than theatres for the elite and the bourgeoisie.'

The Young Vic auditorium was built as a shallow octangle along the lines of Shakespeare's Globe with no proscenium arch to separate the thrust stage from the audience. The auditorium was one of the most successful results of the line of development in theatre design championed by Tyrone Guthrie, Lilian Baylis's successor at the Old Vic. The Young Vic seats around 450, which means the stage is large enough to encompass whole battle scenes but small enough for the slightest gesture to register. Five rows of seats and a balcony circle the auditorium. David Lan, the Young Vic's current Artistic Director, is passionate about the space: 'In its ramshackle way, the Young Vic achieves an ideal that very few theatres even aspire to – the Bouffes du Nord in Paris is one other example: a single space in which actors and audience are combined in a perfect, relaxed but urgent tension.' In 1984, a rehearsal room was converted into a 'black box' studio space seating sixty to ninety people.

Dunlop recalls: 'We asked for a cross between the Elizabethan Fortune Theatre, Guthrie's Assembly Hall and a circus.' His aim was to involve the audience in every production, since he was, he insisted, 'in the theatre for social reasons'. The originating ethos at the Young Vic was one of playful irreverence; the architects described part of the acting area as a 'long tongue pointing out at the audience', while the banisters on the lobby staircase end in two carved hands – one grasping a walking stick and the other an ice-cream cone (Dunlop claimed 'the caff's nearly as important as the play to this audience'). The building was intended to 'yield' to the varying needs of artists, technicians and staff as well as the audiences that soon began to stream through the doors. It was, in Dunlop's view, an immediate antidote to the 'dusty splendour' of the West End; he was never in sympathy with the 'dreary middle-class vision of theatre'.

Dunlop recognised that the challenge he faced was 'to find a way of catching the teenage rhythm'. In the first five years of the Young Vic's history, eleven new plays for young people were produced – a number of them written by actor/playwright Denise Coffey. They were directed by members of the permanent company including Roland Joffe (now better known for his work in film) and Jeremy James Taylor (who founded the National Youth Music Theatre). The local community was also drawn in to the theatre – attracted not only by the free concerts, but also keen to participate in regular lectures and workshops (Coffey ran one every Saturday), and to take advantage of the unusually low ticket prices. Because there was no education department, all members of the company took part in the work with local residents and young people. Young audiences also came to the theatre from outside London to see work inaccessible or unavailable to them elsewhere. In addition to plays by Shakespeare, Sophocles, Beckett and Pinter, Dunlop put on music by Stravinsky, and a free concert by The Who, a rock musical from America called *Stomp* and a radical swiss production of *Romeo and Juliet*, in which a naked young actor sat on the laps of audience members. 'The worst possible sin,' Dunlop insisted, 'is to be boring.' Dunlop's cheap and cheerful approach worked; in 1976 playwright Tom Stoppard praised the Young Vic's 'astonishing success in creating the youngest and liveliest audience in London'.

Dunlop's successor, Michael Bogdanov, invested a great deal of money in work for young people, which included workshops for twelve- to sixteen-year-olds, a puppet-theatre company and a Theatre-in-Education (TiE) programme that would mount productions in the Main House and tour to schools in and around London. Like many theatre practitioners during that decade, he chose to concentrate on the community work involving the area of Lambeth and Southwark. Bogdanov's own productions for young people included *The Magic Drum* and *Hiawatha* and a TiE version of *Pygmalion*.

The Young Vic's third artistic director, David Thacker, also developed a strong youth theatre which nurtured the talents of many aspiring actors including Joseph Fiennes, while concentrating on high-quality productions of plays by Ibsen and Arthur Miller in particular. Miller's plays were both revived and premiered at the Young Vic, which the US playwright came to think of as the London home for his work: 'After a few days of rehearsal one knows that only the most intense and truthful work will be good enough.' Thacker brought outstanding actors such as Vanessa Redgrave, Ian McKellen and Willard White to the Young Vic and staved off financial crisis while generating a renewed commitment to younger audiences.

Thacker's audacious successors, Tim Supple and Julia Bardsley, restructured the whole company so that all its activity – administrative, technical, front of house, education work, etc. – was led by the work onstage. They believed the principles and attitudes behind the productions should lead every other activity in the building, no matter how small. They felt that the 'young' in Young Vic should mean not only young but radical and alternative. Supple argued that theatre works best when it is 'disturbed, disturbing, uncertain, not readily tied in with morality'. The company's artistic strategy began to bear real fruit in 1994, when

Supple and designer Melly Still created a landmark Christmas production of *Grimm Tales* in an arresting adaptation by Carol Ann Duffy. In 1995 the Evening Standard described the auditorium as 'the best performance space in the whole of London'. Supple's own Christmas shows, including productions of *Grimm Tales* and *The Jungle Book*, were supported by critically acclaimed productions of *Arabian Nights* (directed by Dominic Cooke, 1998), and by Katie Mitchell's productions of *The Maids* (1999) and *Uncle Vanya* (1998), co-productions with the Royal Shakespeare Company which saw the Young Vic becoming one of the company's official London venues. Sue Emmas, who joined the company in 1991, presented innovative experimental work by such companies as Primitive Science, Theatrerites and Strathcona in the Young Vic Studio and developed an original education programme to run alongside these productions. Meanwhile, watershed funding from the Arts Council's Arts for Everyone (A4E) scheme in 1996 provided the impetus for the company to develop, define and put into practice a set of principles underlying the present and future work with young people. Emmas brought together a team dedicated to the provision of an increasingly wide range of projects and partnerships with individuals, institutions and community groups across the Young Vic's two boroughs.

When Supple left the company in 2000, he was succeeded by David Lan. Lan is a playwright, adapter and, more recently, a director. His first involvement with the Young Vic had come through adapting *Uncle Vanya* for Katie Mitchell's 1998 production, and his second through directing *'Tis Pity She's a Whore* (1999, with Eve Best and Jude Law). What struck and excited Lan most about the Young Vic while working on *'Tis Pity* was the audience: 'It has a much larger percentage of young people than you get in other theatres, and it's very varied in terms of the social, cultural and economic mix.' Jude Law describes the Young Vic as 'my ideal theatre. As an actor the proximity of the audience creates energy. As a member of the audience it thrills me.'

The audience is a result not only of its productions but also of the far-reaching participatory work that goes on around those productions in schools, colleges and the local boroughs of Lambeth and Southwark generally. What makes this audience almost unique, according to Associate Artistic Director Sue Emmas, is that 'it *really* is representative of the whole range of people who live in this county – whatever their age or social or ethnic background'. Lan responded to the fact that Lambeth and Southwark 'are so very varied. There are extremely wealthy people living near extremely poor people. There are some tremendously powerful cultural amenities which are on the whole inhabited by middle-class people, whereas the local people, by and large, service them. The tensions are powerful, the contradictions are great stimulants to thought. Being able to get a broad range of that population into the theatre is tremendously important.'

Since his arrival, David Lan has directed *Julius Caesar* (2000), *A Raisin in the Sun* by Lorraine Hansberry (2001), *Doctor Faustus* (2002, with Jude Law) and an acclaimed production of D.H. Lawrence's *The Daughter-in-Law* (2002). Other significant productions since his arrival have included Peter Brook's *Le Costume*; *Hamlet* (with Adrian Lester); *Six Characters Looking for an Author* (directed by Richard Jones); David Rudkin's *Afore Night Come* (directed by Rufus Norris under the Direct Action Scheme with the RNT Studio, which aims to produce the work of young directors in the main house); and Norris's Christmas production of *Sleeping Beauty*. The Young Vic also housed the final four parts of the RSC's Histories cycle in 2002 (*Henry VI, Parts I–III* and *Richard III*) and the RSC production of *Macbeth* (directed by Greg Doran, with Antony Sher), and presented Josette Bushell-Mingo's production of Langston Hughes' *Simply Heavenly* (2003). Other productions during 2003 included Lope de Vega's *Peribanez* (directed by Rufus Norris), Tanika Gupta's adaptation of Harold Brighouse's 1915 classic, *Hobson's Choice* (directed by Richard Jones); an adaptation of *Romeo and Juliet* by the young Icelandic company Vesturport; and Trevor Nunn's Christmas production of David Almond's children's classic *Skellig*.

Lan intends to present great plays at as high a standard as possible that will also appeal to and stimulate the Young Vic audience in all its diversity. 'There's a slogan we dreamed up when I started here which was: "The Young Vic is great plays for great audiences." That's an aspiration. I guess I hadn't ever thought very deeply about the work of creating an audience, of building an audience – and the fact that that was so deeply embedded here was something I found exciting and rather moving.' Having experienced the potential power of theatre during apartheid in South Africa, he is well aware that it needn't be merely a leisure activity for the affluent. But his other primary goal is to reinvent the Young Vic as a theatre that will support and promote the work of young directors. 'Just as the Royal Court is known as the theatre for new writing, I would like the Young Vic to be known as the theatre for young directors.' With this end in mind, he and Sue Emmas have initiated a number of new schemes designed to help young directors with varying degrees of experience – whether they are just starting out or whether they have already received some critical recognition but haven't yet ventured on to the main stage. This work is constantly evolving in response to the creative and professional needs of the growing number of emerging directors associated with it.

David Lan recognises the importance of the building's location in generating the energy of its productions: 'For four or five hundred years it has been part of the city where the theatres are ... That is exciting and invigorating.' But he acknowledges too the crucial role which young people and the local community play in ensuring that the life and work of the company remain relevant and inspiring in the twenty-first century. The Young Vic is still very much a theatre in which younger artists are supported in the production of lively and innovative versions of the classics for a younger audience. One of the most influential aspects of this work is the theatre's unique range of workshops and creative projects that go under the title 'Teaching, Participation and Research'.

Theatre-in-Education

We wanted to keep reinventing the work we did with young people and to look for better and different ways of engaging them in the theatre – not because theatre would be good for them or because it would help them with their exams, but because we thought it may be exciting for them and it may be exciting for us.

Tim Supple

The growing importance of Theatre-in-Education across Britain during the 1970s was part of a wider political aspiration of theatre in general. Ever since theatre had withdrawn from the Elizabethan thrust stage in the aftermath of the Civil War, confined itself to the private houses of the aristocracy and then re-emerged during the Restoration as high art for the 'cultured' middle classes within the picture frame of the proscenium arch, working-class people not only avoided the theatre like the plague but they were also more or less quarantined from it. Tireless evangelists like Lilian Baylis at the Old Vic had started to bring working people out of the music halls and vaudeville theatres and into the *proper* theatre, where they were encouraged to sit through Shakespeare and Puccini because it was *good* for them; but even here the notion of high art in the theatre still persisted more or less unchallenged.

From 1955, however, when the Royal Court under George Devine produced *The Good Person of Setzuan* and Joan Littlewood, a year later, directed and starred in *Mother Courage* at an arts festival in Devon, the anti-bourgeois influence of Brecht began to make itself keenly felt. Littlewood shared Brecht's belief that theatre should have 'an awareness of the social issues of the time', but she did not share the establishment's idolatry of his work (which was expressed in Kenneth Tynan's sneering review of her production). In the rowdy, populist work she presented at the Theatre Royal, Stratford East, Littlewood held Jean Vilar's torch high, and underlined the 'chemistry' and inclusiveness of the live event.

By the 1970s, the notion of high art, or 'art for art's sake', had been largely discredited by many theatre artists in Britain. It had been replaced by pop art – the art of the people, manifest in the theatre as Vilar's vision of a 'public service': 'Our ambition is . . . to share with the greatest number that which up until now had to be reserved, or so it was thought, for an elite.' Vilar had sought an equilibrium 'between the poet, the poet's work, the general public, the actors and technicians.' In 1968, Peter Brook warned of the spreading infection of the 'deadly' or moribund theatre, which principally inhabited commercial stages and which failed to elevate, instruct or entertain, while driving audiences away or, worse, numbing them to the charge of live theatre. The emergence of oppositional community and fringe groups in the sixties and seventies such as 7:84, Welfare State International, Monstrous Regiment, Joint Stock, Portable Theatre and Nancy Meckler's Freehold presented a lively challenge to the perceived conservatism and narrow aesthetic intention of mainstream theatre (Frank Dunlop himself had founded a company called Pop

Theatre in Edinburgh before coming to the Young Vic). Much of the work was made by and for young people, who came increasingly to be seen as the audience of the future, and whose interests and appetites could be both whetted and fed by a new kind of 'irreverent, inelegant and vigorous' theatre practice. Harold Hobson noted in 1969: 'William Gaskill is probably right when he says that the chief thing that is wrong with theatre audiences is not that they are bourgeois, but that they are old.' New audiences meant young audiences. In the same year, Roger Chapman, Educational Drama Organiser at the Octagon Theatre, Bolton, pointed out that 'there is hardly a repertory company in the country without an assistant director employed with specific responsibility for young people . . . There is growing interest in the exploratory nature of the work.'

In the search for a theatre practice of renewed vigour and significance, Western directors and actors looked to practitioners such as Brazilian director Augusto Boal, who urged that theatre should be put in the hands of the people, to stimulate debate about political issues and give them the tools to make choices which might change their lives. His Theatre of the Oppressed took theatre out of its conservative, proscenium-arch picture frame and brought it to the 'real' people who walked along the pavement outside or worked in factories and on farms; it raised questions about people's everyday lives, dealt with social issues and acted as a tool for educating citizens about class, cultural identity and industrial politics.

Theatre-in-Education (TiE) adopted this democratising principle of removing theatre from middle-class stages, and delivered it through games, exercises, experiment and discussion to young people in the classroom and beyond. Instead of concerning itself with a study of Jacobean theatre, for instance, TiE would create a public forum out of an event like the miners' strike in the early 1980s. Actors might run a workshop in which different scenarios were investigated – where, for example, one actor would be a striking miner, one would be a miner who refused to strike, another would be a striking miner's wife and a fourth would be a member of the National Coal Board. The young people in the classroom would be drawn into identification with the different characters and ideas, and they would be encouraged to get involved in the debate by acting out certain scenarios between themselves. 'Drama is such a normal thing,' said educationalist and drama teacher Dorothy Heathcote in 1976. 'All it demands is that children shall think from within a dilemma instead of talking about the dilemma . . . You can train people to do this in two minutes, once they are prepared to accept it.' Theatre would be used to investigate the consequences of the different and difficult decisions that those characters had to make; the intention was as much to nurture creative, sceptical and analytical systems of thought in young people as it was to educate them about certain social issues. A report on primary education in Scotland claimed that 'by identifying himself with other people, real or imagined, by acting out situations within his experience or imaginative range, by expressing in movement and speech the feelings of himself and others, [the child] is enlarging his experience, and learning in ways that are natural to him'. TiE would take theatre into the streets and the classrooms and, by making it provocative and politically relevant, create a new audience for the future – one that was representative of *all* the people living in Britain. Thirty years on, however, this aspiration still has a long way to go.

Although the Arts Council under Margaret Thatcher's government tended to make education work a prerequisite for funding, there were often too few resources – and not enough of a philosophical commitment on the part of the theatres – to ensure that the education work played a fundamental part in the identity of the building. 'If you mentioned the word "education" among theatre professionals,' says Sue Emmas, 'you'd get a number of reactions – enthusiasm, scepticism, veiled distrust, overt disinterest. The 1980s saw the gradual marginalisation of urgent and energetic TiE work into what were often far less urgent and energetic education departments in theatres.' Playwright Leo Butler recalls: 'When I was at school, we had theatre-in-education groups coming in, and I remember really patronising dramas that had no drama and were about just one issue.' Much TiE work strove to make itself 'relevant' to the lives of young participants, but the attempts were too often self-conscious and unconvincing. Young playwright Neela Dolezalova, whose first play was written at sixteen and produced at Soho Theatre in 2002, was frustrated by the worthiness and generalisations of some TiE work: 'I've seen a few plays about young people, and they tend to be "teenage drama" about teenage angst . . . A lot of young people feel they're made to look stupid on stage.'

In recent years, however, theatre practitioners and teachers have begun to reconsider the meaning and possible applications of theatre in education, and a new enthusiasm is developing for work which brings young people into direct contact with the processes and principles of theatre-making, as much for their own sake as for their relevance to the curriculum. Most professional directors, themselves hungry for training opportunities and experience, no longer feel that working with young people will marginalise them as 'youth theatre' directors, and most no longer feel apologetic about directing productions for younger audiences. Poet and playwright Benjamin Zephaniah insists that 'there's nothing like watching kids when they have a piece of theatre that really connects with them. The joy on their faces, the way they talk about it when they're leaving the theatre or the gym or wherever it's performed . . . That's live theatre, man. This is not dead.' The perspective shift that has accompanied the new approach is based on the recognition that young people are as interested in the mysteries and mechanics of making and presenting theatre as they are in the ideas and issues that plays explore. Theatre is not seen simply as a tool for social engineering but as a valuable and productive activity in itself, capable of involving, challenging and delighting those who come into immediate contact with it. The philosophy lies at the heart of and informs the Young Vic's entire programme of work.

Beyond TiE: young people at the Young Vic

In the early days of the Young Vic there was no Theatre-in-Education staff and the company had no education department. But Frank Dunlop's motivating desire was to 'get things over to people'. 'When people say I'm a populist, what I am is a teacher . . . I was going to be a teacher until I realised theatre is a more exciting form of education.' In the early 1970s, the Arts Council encouraged the company to take productions out to young people in community centres as part of an education programme. In response, according to Donald Sartain, former Young Vic Administrator, Dunlop argued that 'we could attract youngsters to the theatre, and he was proved right'. Drama critic Irving Wardle had argued in 1969 for the need for a 'theatre centre' in London, 'where a continuous reciprocal contact could develop between adult artists and creative youth'. Between 1978 and 1980, Michael Bogdanov, who had a strong reputation in children's theatre, introduced a community and education programme which took Young Vic actors into local schools and impromptu playing areas; he developed youth theatre workshops at the Young Vic, and established a puppet-theatre company and an education programme for main house productions. Bogdanov noted at the time that 'none of these things existed before, so it's very much an exercise in realigning the building and policy'.

When David Thacker joined the company in 1984, he recognised that 'young people want to see adult theatre, but they want it in a non-alienating environment'. The Young Vic Studio was given over to a new youth and education unit. Together, Sue Emmas and the unit's director, Nick Stimson, set up workshops and activities to support current productions and help participants with their school work. In the mid-1990s the company began to seek ways to bridge the apparent gap between theatre, theatre for young people, youth theatre and educational activity. There was a desire to involve all of the crafts of theatre in the work with young people, and a belief that the investigative principles of TiE could be applied directly to the exploration of classical plays as well as contemporary work, and combined with a renewed commitment to teaching and transmitting all the skills of theatre-making. In this way, even those who had been traditionally excluded or overlooked in the provision of training in the dramatic arts could gain access to the range of creative and technical professional opportunities that existed. All theatres, in David Lan's view, 'have a training remit. Everybody's learning all the time. Otherwise you die. It's important for theatres, like any other institution, to have new people coming in so the people who work there are provoked and surprised.'

The shift away from Theatre-in-Education practices towards a more inclusive, participatory model was made possible in 1996 with the award of Arts for Everyone (A4E) funding by the Arts Council. Supple and Emmas wanted to bring young people aged five to eighteen closer to the experience of making and watching theatre. Supple felt that 'theatres were putting themselves in a position of being servants to other aspects of social needs – so they were *serving* education, or *serving* the development of our youth, or having a social function. And in my opinion that's not healthy for theatres, because I think they need to remain totally artistic in their ambitions . . . For me the subject of an independent education department goes against the gut. It suggested two things I don't like. Firstly, that there should be any separate departments in theatres – and I don't think there should, because I think theatres should consist of groups of people who work together in order to create something they share. And secondly, in my experience, it seemed to lead to a difference in quality between the main productions and the productions for young people.'

Emmas considers that 'what has made the Young Vic's education work unique is that since Tim Supple's arrival it has become not only integral to the identity of the building but central to its creative life too'. The company refers to its work with young people and their local community as Teaching, Participation and Research. TPR work grows show by show out of the theatre's current production and is carried out by the core creative team for each show. Teaching is redefined as a two-way process which aims not only to stimulate the minds and imaginations of young participants but also to give them the tools to contribute to the creative life of the company and its developing artistic practice. Emmas points out: 'We try to engage with the participants in a workshop as creatively as we would if we were in a professional rehearsal or workshop situation.'

Emmas decided to separate the TPR work as much as possible from the association with school work and the predetermined content of the curriculum. Instead, she proposed that the creative work that came out of the building should determine the kind of work they would do with schools and young people: 'Each production was to be taken as a fresh opportunity to explore different working methods.' The work would evolve as the theatre's artistic programme and philosophy evolved. The following principles emerged from this process:

- The work with young people is an integral and integrated aspect of the company's identity.
- The spirit of the work with young people is essentially

investigative and experimental. Practitioners often discover more about their own process by teaching others.
- The TPR work concentrates on the schools, colleges and residents of the local community.
- All of the TPR work with young people and the local community is free.

TPR work is based on an evolutionary model and provides different entry points for young people: via their schools (through invitation and ongoing connection); independently (through self-selection and personal interest); and through research (involving young people who have made a more substantial commitment to theatre arts). The aim is to encourage the widest possible range of participants, and to offer ongoing creative and professional development at a number of levels.

As Sue Emmas points out, the TPR philosophy affects every aspect of the life of the company: 'There's been such support and such an integral understanding of the importance of the work from the people who have worked here, and I don't think that kind of thing exists everywhere. The artistic directors have always lent their weight, time and imagination to it – and that's made a great difference too. You find the artistic director three days after press night running workshops onstage with schoolchildren about the process of putting a production together.' Young people are welcomed and encouraged into the theatre, not only through the workshops and productions on offer, but through the provision of free seats made possible by the Funded Ticket Scheme (supported by local businesses, which brings substantial school groups to the theatre free of charge) and the Two Boroughs Scheme (which allows local residents who have not attended the Young Vic to see their first play free).

The programme is divided into three strands which define the company's broad aims in its work with young people and the local community:

Teaching

Initially the most substantial strand of the programme, this refers to the work in schools and colleges (including workshops in classrooms and on school stages); and schools' workshops on the

Young Vic main stage. All of the Young Vic's workshops are based on the exchange of ideas and information and on the relationship between inspiration, collaboration and investigation. School and college workshops are developed out of rehearsal methods in use in the current main house production. Members of the creative team go into schools and work with young people to offer insight into the rehearsal and production process. Participants are invited to see the show before or after their workshop and encouraged to maintain links with the theatre. These explorations of the plays are dynamic and interactive, and the responses and discoveries of the young people are often fed directly back into Young Vic productions.

It was during Tim Supple's production of *Grimm Tales* that this area of the TPR work was first conceived. During a series of schools workshops early in the rehearsal process, the acting company experimented with different ways of telling and performing the stories in order to develop the most appropriate and effective theatre language for presenting them. 'I thought – well, we're going to do this show, and the Young Vic needs there to be a certain number of young people there, so let's discover what we're actually doing here, rather than just reeling it out. For me it was about watching both the actors and the children – I was watching the children watching the actors, and I was watching the actors watching the children, and then we would discuss it afterwards. It provided a spirit that I have wanted to preserve in all my work since.'

Using improvisation, the company collaborated with the children in devising simple, immediate and effective versions of the original stories together. 'Hold their attention,' Frank Dunlop had urged, 'and young people are the most truthful, exacting audience. They spot phoniness a mile off.' Supple acknowledged that young audiences and participants may have an immediate, unselfconscious response to theatre, and he encouraged their open, often noisy reaction to his work. He welcomed them to the building and refused to censor or patronise them. He shares this attitude with David Lan and it has in part been responsible for the unprecedented success of the Young Vic's Christmas shows: 'You don't want to simplify or reduce what's in the play because you're playing to younger people. You don't need to. Younger people are fantastically sophisticated and quick. And if you can hold on to them something extraordinary happens; it's a kind of miracle when that happens, it's a kind of mystery. And if you're not trying to do that through the play itself then you might as well give up.' Head teacher Ros Lines describes the Young Vic's approach: 'They treat [the children] as individuals who can think for themselves and be creative. They really listen to and value their comments. And it's not something they do superficially . . . sometimes they make changes to what they're doing in their rehearsals or production. So they have that quality. They give the children that importance. Another thing that's valuable is that they don't just send people from their education department but they send actors and directors and people directly associated with the performance . . . I don't know any other theatre group that does that.'

Following on from these initial investigations, on-stage work-shops bring school groups and their teachers to the theatre to demonstrate and give young people hands-on experience of the technical and design elements of a production (including stage management, lighting, sound, wardrobe, props, etc.). They give the young people a feeling of close connection with the main house production, and reveal the complex cues and collaborations involved in creating a single stage impression, while demon-strating the range of professional roles and technical skills used in theatre-making. They take place on the set of the current show, and always use the same props and technical effects as the production itself. In this way, participants are able to explore practical solutions to the problems raised by plays.

The teaching strand also includes the placement of over fifty young people a year on work experience. Each works with the company for two weeks and is exposed to as wide a range of activities as possible (stage management, front of house, adminis-tration, box office, marketing, etc.). There are workshops, forums and theatre visits for teachers (who meet regularly and informally at the theatre), post-show discussions and the provision of production-based resource packs. In all, some 10,000 people visit the theatre for free every year, and they are welcomed with free ice creams, pre- and post-show tours and discussions with the actors, production crew and other staff members. Helen Everett, Head of Drama at St Francis Xavier College, is enthusiastic about the Young Vic's 'radically different' approach: 'One major difference is the seriousness with which they take teachers like myself. We feel empowered and benefit enormously from the exposure to the workshops, the meetings with some of the best theatre practitioners around . . . the teachers are made to feel part of the company by being invited to areas not open to the general public, and our views are taken seriously and they affect some of the Young Vic's decisions.'

Participation

Teaching work in schools was enhanced initially by professionally produced experimental and devised work in the Studio, intended in part to give young people access to original and sometimes controversial new approaches to theatre and performance. But the team saw new possibilities in the idea of taking young people out of the classroom and bringing them into a busy producing theatre, to explore and sample at first hand the complex ecology of the building, and to discover for themselves the range of creative and professional opportunities available to them as theatre artists.

As the work progressed it became clear that participants were keen to stage their own work, using the technical and professional resources of the theatre. During the rehearsals of *A Servant to Two Masters,* young people, in partnership with the production's assistant director, developed short scenes in response to Goldoni's play. With subsequent productions this approach was expanded and when the company produced *Julius Caesar* in 2000, with David Lan directing, the main stage show was accompanied by a fully resourced, one-hour version of the play. These parallel productions are informed by the work taking place alongside them in the main house, but they stand alone in the sense that the participants bring their own cultural and creative concerns to them. When they worked on D.H. Lawrence's *The Daughter-in-Law,* for example, the young participants, who came from predominantly Afro-Caribbean backgrounds, found and explored new cultural resonances not present in the original. The parallel plays often have their own cultural and emotional focus; they're generally not plays on the curriculum, so the participants approach them without preconceptions and recontextualise them according to their own interests and concerns. 'They get to play characters of real stature in the security of a classical play,' Emmas says. 'This can transform their perspective on their own lives – they can be imaginative, expressionistic, symbolic.'

The participation work comprises all projects with young people outside schools and educational contexts. It includes:

- 'See Theatre', a programme which encourages young people who have taken part in Young Vic projects to see a range of theatre independently of their schools or colleges at venues across London. Free tickets are provided; participants are invited to bring a friend, and to discuss their responses with Young Vic staff. Again and again participants and their teachers and parents point out that these opportunities would not be available without the theatre's assistance. The programme encourages young people to take pride in their critical responses, to fight their corner, to assess the vastly different ways in which directors may approach plays, and to consider themselves part of the theatrical community to whom the plays are addressed
- Backstage passes, which allow young people with an interest in the technical side of theatre to spend an evening with the stage manager during a performance, observing the relationship between on-stage and backstage activity in the context of a professional production
- Shadowing: an extension of the backstage pass, which allows a number of young people to spend more time during the run of a show observing and contributing to the roles of technicians, designers, choreographers, composers, etc. Each participant shadows one member of the creative team, gaining detailed insight into his or her craft and having the opportunity to question the practitioner about any aspect of the work and the associated career path

Participation work also includes special projects in the neighbouring boroughs. Several thousand young people have already taken part in these projects, which involve working with disabled children, local and community groups and organisations, and participating in arts festivals. The philosophy, according to Helen Everett, is one of 'respect, empowerment and social inclusion . . . the young people feel that they truly have found a theatre where they belong.' 'We give what we can give', says Emmas, 'in terms of resources, expertise and experience to the people we are working with.' She points out that 'everything has constantly evolved, nothing has stood still, so that every time we approach something we're still trying to learn from it, we're still trying to develop it. The work's never got into a rut. We try not to repeat ourselves, and nothing's taken for granted.'

Research

'In theatre,' Brook insists, 'research means doing, it's not sitting around a table, it is exploring through doing. And from then onwards the only difference between experiment and research and doing a production is that in experimental work you don't have to deliver the result.' One of the more recent manifestations of the TPR programme, the final stage in a process of increasing immersion in professional theatre practice, is the research work intended to develop this practice by providing opportunities for interested and committed practitioners to explore their chosen craft and develop their confidence and professional skills in their own space, on their own terms. The research programme at the Young Vic both feeds into and is informed by the teaching and participation work, but represents a distinct form of endeavour – in effect a fulfilment of this associated work – through which young theatre-makers who have absorbed a more comprehensive understanding of the theatre arts are able to put their interests and experience into practice as young directors. The aim is to encourage confidence in working with actors and other theatre artists, to open up the rehearsal process to scrutiny both from within and from without, and to provide a protected working environment where young directors can take risks and begin to sharpen their individual creative edge.

As Helen Manfull points out in her study of influential women directors, *Taking Stage*, 'several of them knew from childhood that the theatre was to be their lifetime pursuit', but 'very few of them knew they wanted to be directors'. Directing is such an inclusive activity; it demands a practical and imaginative insight into all of the theatre arts, and its interpretative, communicative and leadership skills cannot be suddenly forged and delivered whole at an early age. At the Young Vic, emerging directors (usually in their twenties and thirties) are supported in the recognition that they need the same opportunities to play, take risks and make discoveries as those given to schoolchildren and young people in the community through the teaching and participation programme.

When he arrived at the Young Vic as Artistic Director in 2000, David Lan recognised that 'although there are various training schemes and so on, there isn't a place that devotes a large quantity of its time to trying to work out the implications of what being a director in your twenties or thirties in this country means now. We know that directing is difficult, but the fact that it's difficult doesn't really matter – it's fine that it's difficult. But what isn't good is that, more often than not, theatres aren't prepared to take a risk on the few people they think really are interesting and good.' The evolving Directors Programme includes the Jerwood Young Directors Award, which each year gives three directors the opportunity to work with professional actors over five weeks in a rehearsal space, and the Young Directors Forum, an informal community of some 250 emerging directors, who are supported in an ongoing programme of process or laboratory work in the Studio by a substantial grant from the Genesis Foundation. Directors may also be invited to assist the Artistic Director or visiting directors or to direct Studio or main house productions or Direct Action co-productions with the Royal National Theatre Studio.

Teaching, Participation and Research initiatives aim both to establish and maintain longer-term connections with participants; the objective is to inspire and sustain a lifelong interest in theatre and theatre arts: 'You start to see young people who are perhaps thirteen or fourteen,' Emmas says, 'who you have worked with for a long time and who know a great deal about theatre . . . and most of them come from backgrounds that you might not have associated with theatregoers – but they *are* theatregoers, because they've been given that chance and developed that appreciation and love for theatre. So that's really quite moving, actually, to see those people who were once six or seven and are now gangly adolescents, choosing to come back of their own volition.'

There are currently some five thousand young people on the Young Vic's contact list, and the company works with around two hundred schools and local groups each year. From this growing pool of participants, the Young Vic constantly renews itself as both a laboratory of theatre practice and a venue for ambitious, curious and enthusiastic young audiences. 'The minute you see the TPR work operating,' claims Lan, 'it becomes obvious that that is how theatres, all theatres, ought to be. I mean, the whole point of going to all the trouble of having a subsidised theatre is that it does the difficult, the adventurous – it does the bold work of making contact with people in profound and surprising ways. So it's obvious that you've got to do the work to build the audience if you want a younger audience and a more representative audience, and if you want to resist the pressures to go for the expected, the easily assimilated.' The impact of the programme is summed up by Helen Everett: 'I always remember a conversation between two sixteen-year-old students as they waited for a play to begin. They were discussing how sometimes members of the audience gave them funny looks and one of them said, "Yeah, when they do that I just look right back at them and think to myself – Don't look at me like that, this is my theatre and I belong here!"'

Chapter 2
WARM-UPS AND GAMES

The Young Vic's exploration of theatre with young people is based on principles that have developed over a number of years and passed through the hands of many theatre practitioners. At its heart is the notion of involvement and exposure: involvement in every aspect of the exploration of a play; and exposure to the most inspiring and challenging work – to the techniques used to bring it to life in the classroom or rehearsal space, and to the many interlocking roles and skills which are necessary in fulfilling the performance potential of a playtext.

Plays are animated, not simply by reading them aloud, but by incorporating all of what Peter Brook calls the 'languages' of theatre: 'In the theatre, there are infinitely more languages, beyond words, through which communication is established and maintained with the audience. There is body language, sound language, rhythm language, colour language, costume language, scenery language, lighting language.' Even in an empty space, each of these languages can be used in its most rudimentary form to give substance, shape and detail to the physical expression of a play. Together they flesh out its latent potential, while providing a range of creative roles for young people and encouraging resourcefulness and imagination in their approach to the material.

All of the exercises and explorations that follow are located within the context of the broad aims of the company's work, which is to engender a sense of ownership and participation in all of the creative processes and skills involved in bringing a play to the stage, and to encourage an enthusiasm and appetite for live performance in audiences of all social, cultural and economic backgrounds. No distinction is made between a classroom or community workshop on a play, and a rehearsal or on-stage exploration of the making of a piece of theatre. Plays are seen as blueprints for performance, which come to life in the mouths and bodies of actors and in their collaboration with technical and backstage crews.

All of the Young Vic's theatre-making work with young people grows out of the current production. This way, the problems raised by particular plays can be explored against the background of actual solutions found by professional companies and tested in performance. Participants are encouraged to seek their own solutions to these problems in the knowledge that every production of a play is an interpretation – hopefully a fruitful, meaningful and memorable one – but ephemeral all the same, and a product of the particular conditions which surround its presentation. Every play produces a different dynamic and raises a different set of questions. For this reason the Young Vic encourages and enables young people to see plays at a wide range of theatres, to develop the curiosity and insight which will allow them to contribute to the flow of ideas generated by investigations of plays.

Nothing illuminates the process of theatre-making more sharply than working on stage in a professional theatre with the support of its various production departments. But even in a bare room it is possible to generate some of the conditions of a production, or at least an awareness of the range of roles and skills employed in producing a play. Participants will be both the actors and the audience to their own work, and they can be actively involved in other ways as designers, directors and stage managers. You don't need a full lighting rig to explore the principles of stage lighting. You can do it with a torch, a candle or a few lamps. You can make sound effects with your own body and whatever materials are available in the rehearsal room. You can design a set and costumes on paper, using the simplest and most suggestive images and gestures to envisage a three-dimensional landscape for the play.

Theatre-making sessions encourage young people to act professionally and responsibly, to be aware of the enmeshed responsibilities of working in a collaborative environment and of the issues which this generates (i.e. health and safety, the need for focus, tolerance, punctuality, etc.). Participants discover the importance of self-discipline and teamwork for themselves and through their encounters with experienced theatre practitioners.

Inviting young people to take responsibility for their actions and creative choices is never risk-free, and group work can always be disrupted by unfocused participants. Groups and group chemistry vary enormously. Teachers/directors should always be prepared for sessions in which a seemingly straightforward game or exercise leads to general disorder. It may be better to end a session, or divert it entirely to simple and contained exercises in small groups than to try to wrestle a group into order.

However, the group dynamic which develops during workshops often absorbs disruptions, and even young people who are literally running up the walls can be given constructive tasks within the group or independently of it. If participants feel they are being given opportunities for genuine creative input, they will be more likely to expect and encourage support, collaboration and attention from their peers.

Another important element in assessing the efficacy of workshops is monitoring, evaluation and feedback. Feedback forms and recorded face-to-face sessions, audio and videotaped discussions, and letters of response from pupils and teachers form part of the archive for every production at the Young Vic.

Workshops and rehearsals often start with physical (and if relevant, vocal) and ensemble-building warm-ups and games. Then they move to more specific and detailed investigation of aspects of the play, usually through exercises, improvisations and scene work. The Young Vic's aim is to encourage individuals to acknowledge their role in a group, and to give them the skills to work together as a team. Different games and exercises work in different ways to achieve this, and the choice of material will depend largely on the nature of the play in question and the particular problems associated with story, language, action and production that it raises. Theatre workshops and rehearsals look for solutions to problems; they are practical in their intentions and have particular outcomes in mind, though the means used are playful and imaginative rather than scientific and purely rational.

Clive Barker, who developed an influential method of actor training outlined in *Theatre Games*, sees theatre games and practical investigations as 'a springboard for exploring the nature of drama and theatre'. They put the young person at the centre of the exploration and encourage active participation and contribution at every point. Local teacher Helen Everett believes this 'child-centred' approach 'empowers young people by truly valuing and respecting their work and ideas and by giving them a sense of belonging and being a valued part of the theatre'.

The aim, where possible, is to act rather than to discuss; to free young participants from the pressure of providing the 'right' answer to questions posed by plays, and to acknowledge at every stage their original, instinctive and uncensored input. This approach is fulfilled in the Young Vic's parallel play programme, which takes the process a step further and gives young people the opportunity to produce in the Studio their own version of the current main stage production. At every point in the process, the teaching and participation work at the Young Vic seeks to illuminate theatre practice for young people, to inspire their involvement as audiences and practitioners throughout their lives, and to offer them a range of skills and a confidence in their application which may help them to achieve their potential in society.

Directors bring ideas generated by the current production into the workshop or rehearsal because they believe them to be interesting and important. The work is neither simplified nor diluted. Young people acquire knowledge and insight both directly and indirectly; often the most surprising path towards understanding is the most memorable and effective. Theatre games and exercises attempt a kind of reorientation, producing unexpected insight into the meaning of plays, and in that process of discovery revealing something about ourselves and our world.

The games and exercises below are most effective when used with a *single* problem or question in mind. If the participants are examining one property of a play, poem or story (for example, the role of the narrator, the quality of the language used by a character, or the images generated by a speech or action) their focus will be keener if they are not also trying to do something else simultaneously, such as act convincingly.

The spirit of the Young Vic's work with young people is playful, open-ended and investigative. The workshops are approached with the same curiosity and flexibility with which directors approach rehearsals, so that although the structure of a workshop is always considered in advance, it also remains open to the atmosphere and needs of that particular session. It is the responsibility of the teacher or director to move towards an overall objective by means of the workshop. The participants should feel free simply to play with words, images, ideas, actions and techniques, pursue what interests them and incorporate their own discoveries into their work.

Actress Linda Kerr Scott, who took part in the production of *Grimm Tales* and in the work with young people that accompanied it, claims that 'games are an excellent way for a group to get to know one another, have fun, become physically alert and begin to communicate with one another. The key quality of games is that they awaken a playful, childlike quality within the actor in rehearsals which feeds into the final performance. Consequently, games guard against becoming too serious or intellectual in one's approach. If an actor becomes too analytical or methodical then a performance can become joyless and heavy.'

Games, she believes, 'work best when they are seen as an opportunity for fun. The joy of games in rehearsal is also about freedom from any adverse competitive edge, as nothing is at stake. No one is going to criticise you if you miss a ball or go wrong, because nobody cares. You just have a good laugh. I find this playfulness important when I am on stage as well. The playfulness does not mean that you are not serious or dramatic, or that you are smiling all the time. What I am referring to is an internal but palpable sense of lightness and enjoyment.'

Exercises and investigations are more structured than warm-ups/games and have specific goals which are tied to the play itself. Used in conjunction, both should serve to develop quick responses and shared awareness, and help to move the group towards the ideas, issues and challenges posed by the play. No theatre game should ever be set in stone. Theatre practitioners constantly modify and add to their repertoire and adapt it to different contexts. However, it is extremely useful to have a supply of games and exercises to draw from. They can be adapted to work with young people of all ages and with professional actors, and to suit all spaces.

Body Warm-Ups

Stretching exercises work well with groups of adolescents who may initially resist more demanding warm-ups requiring greater involvement and physical commitment. Primary school students, however, may not need to stretch at all as they tend to be both flexible and energetic.

Simple stretch

- Stand in a circle. Stretch your face and fingers; make everything as wide as possible; screw up your face and clench your fists; open them out again.
- Crouch down; tighten all your muscles and screw up your face; open everything up again.
- Stand, stretch towards the ceiling and yawn, elongating your face.
- Breathe out, let the upper half of the body drop down. Shake your shoulders loose. Breathing in, roll the back slowly up; breathe out and drop down again. Repeat more quickly.
- Turn the head from side to side, loosen and shake the shoulders. Shake everything: arms, hands, legs, feet, tongue.
- Jog in a circle to the right; jog to the left; jog to the right (make the changes of direction quick and unified); jog into the centre and jog backwards to the starting point.

More stretching

- Place your feet about one and a half shoulder widths apart. Take your left arm over your head. Reach down with your right arm and hold your right ankle. Do not allow the torso to go forwards or backwards. Repeat on the left side.
- Raise your arms above your head. Lower your torso so that the top of your head is facing the wall. Keep your back straight – you should bend only at the waist. Turn from the waist and take the torso out to the right side, keeping the arms stretched out in front. Repeat on the left side.
- Reach all the way forward and down till your hands touch the floor. Move your hands as far forward as you can, then move them as far back as possible towards your feet. Move your hands round till they reach one foot. Hold on to the ankle and try to lower your head to your knees. Don't force it. Repeat on the other side. Take your hands back to the middle and slowly straighten up.
- Sit on the floor, with your legs together and stretched out in front of you (try to get the back of the knees to touch the ground). Reach forwards and hold your feet or ankles, lowering your head to your knees.

- Sit with legs straight out in front. Now bend your knees and open your legs so the soles of your feet are pressed together. Push your knees down gently towards the floor.
- Sit opposite a partner with your legs stretched out in front and your toes pointing up. The soles of your feet and your partner's feet should be pressed together. Reach forward to clasp hands with your partner. Take it in turns to pull towards each other, keeping your legs straight.
- Stand with your feet shoulder-width apart, about four feet from a wall. Lean forward and push against the wall, keeping your legs straight and your heels on the floor. You should feel the stretch in the back of your legs.

A breath and body warm-up

- Take your shoes off and stand with your feet hip-width apart. Focus on your breathing. Allow a regular, even pattern of breathing to develop, taking slow deep breaths into your abdomen and allowing your ribs to expand and contract freely. Allow your breath to fill and open up your whole body. Think of breathing into your muscles, joints, nerves, fingers, toes and face. Aim to lose all tension throughout your body.
- Try to get the soles of your feet to relax into the floor, so that as much of your foot as possible is in contact with the floor. Make sure your weight is balanced across both feet. Circle your shoulders forwards and then gently pull your shoulder blades together to open up your shoulders, back and chest.
- Inhale. As you exhale, drop your chin on to your chest. Now let your spine drop down vertebra by vertebra, your arms hanging towards the floor, until you are touching the floor with the tips of your fingers (bend your knees if you have to, but try to keep your legs straight if you can). Keep your weight balanced over the middle of both feet. Inhale when you've gone as far as you can, and as you exhale roll back up, vertebra by vertebra.
- Turn your head slowly to the right, then let your chin fall gently to your chest and raise and turn it to your left shoulder. Breathe evenly.
- Rotate both shoulders backwards and then forwards four times. Put your hands lightly on your shoulders and repeat, moving your elbows around with the movement. Stretch your arms out

to the side and repeat, so you are drawing circles in the air with your hands. Do this in both directions.

- Inhale and stretch your arms to the ceiling. Clasp your fingers together above your head. Exhale and bring your arms down so they are level with your chest (keep your hands together and your arms straight out in front). Now imagine you are trying to stop a heavy object from rolling away from you: let your back go round, bend your knees and feel the stretch in your upper and middle back. Now imagine you are paddling a canoe and bring your hands together and down to the right. Paddle once slowly, then paddle on the left hand side. Repeat four times.

- Inhale and clasp your hands behind your lower back. Exhale, pulling your hands down and away from you to open up your shoulders and chest.

- Place your feet hip-width apart, with toes facing forwards. Bend and straighten your knees eight times. Do the same with feet further apart and toes facing outwards at forty-five degrees. Try not to roll forward.

- Stand with legs straight and together and toes pointing forwards. Let your upper body hang forward, feeling the stretch in the hamstrings and calves. Try to keep your legs vertical. Breathe here for a few moments and then roll up through your spine as above.

- Now move your feet so they are hip-width apart, but with toes pointing forwards. Lift your arms over your head. Look up to your hands and reach up with your right hand towards the ceiling. Feel the stretch in your stomach. Repeat the movement with your left hand and alternate several times. Keeping both hands raised and separate above your head, look ahead and breathe in. As you exhale, bend both knees and swing the body down so your chest falls towards your knees and your arms swing down with your body and fall on either side. Then lift the body upright and bring your hands above your head as you inhale. Do this movement to the count of eight, and repeat, getting slightly faster each time and feeling your heart rate increase.

- Stand upright, loose and balanced. Bend the knees slightly. Now peel one foot off the floor until your toes are pointing downwards. Replace and repeat this with your other foot. Repeat each movement, getting faster and faster until you are running on the spot. Keep your head level, and do not pound your feet on the floor. Continue at a fast pace, breathing easily, until you come to a sudden stop and return to your neutral upright posture. Feel the energy moving through your body and your heart rate returning to normal.

- From your neutral position, move your right leg backwards, so that it is straight behind you, and bend your left leg so you are in a lunge position. Breathe easily and on every out-breath stretch your right heel to the floor behind you, so that you feel your calf muscles stretching. Ease into the stretch gradually and without bouncing. Hold this position for about thirty seconds and then release on an out-breath. Repeat the same exercise but with your left leg behind you.

- Return to your neutral position, making sure your weight is centred. Now shift the weight over to your left foot and lift your right foot up to hold it in your right hand, with the heel touching your right buttock. Find your balance and inhale. As you exhale, reach your left arm up to the ceiling. Find your balance and inhale. As you exhale, close your eyes and find your internal balance. Hold this for a few breaths and then release. Repeat the exercise with your left foot lifted and held.

Relaxing the body

- Lie on your back on the floor, with legs bent and small books or a rolled-up jacket under the head.
- Imagine the spine lengthening. Do not physically do anything to make this happen, just focus on the idea of it.
- Imagine the pelvis opening, dropping towards the floor and widening across the floor. Again, don't do it physically.
- Imagine the shoulders opening, dropping into the floor and widening across it. Again just focus on the idea.
- Imagine your back is a piece of cloth being smoothed out in all directions by a pair of hands.
- Stand feet parallel, shoulder-width apart, weight equally distributed. Imagine the spine growing longer, without locking the knees or arching the back. Then let the arms softly lift out to the sides, palms facing forwards. Keep the shoulders relaxed and the shoulder blades dropped. Think of the arms spreading wide and the spine lengthening. Stand and walk in this position with

relaxation and ease. Feel the widening and opening feeling in the back and front of the shoulders and the lengthening of the spine. Drop the arms but keep the feeling of width.

Clapping name game

An introductory or ice-breaking game for everyone. The group stands in a circle. One by one, each person speaks his or her name and claps the syllables of the name at the same time. Then the rest of the group claps the same rhythm and they work their way round the circle, repeating the name and the clapping rhythm for each person.

Gesture on name

Working your way round a circle, each person makes a gesture on his/her name – whatever his/her name *feels like* as a sound or a word – and everyone else in the circle copies this gesture.

Pat the ball

Stand in a circle and pat a ball across the circle. You must pass the ball on by hitting it with one or both hands or part of the body; you should not catch it and so stop the flow. Imagine that the ball is a story, and that by keeping it in the air you are keeping everyone's attention.

Each person must be ready to receive the ball and to pass it on without rupturing the flow of the story. The director should set a target number of passes – say forty – but should not count out loud. It's important that the players stay in the moment and remain focused and calm.

Imaginary ball

An alternative version of the above game, suitable for older participants. Throw an imaginary ball across a circle. Each person should make eye contact with the person he/she is throwing the ball to. This person should catch the ball (which may be thrown directly, or high up in the air), make eye contact with the person he/she is throwing to, and pass the ball on.

Voice warm-ups

When Dame Sybil Thorndike declared the Young Vic Theatre open in 1970, she argued for the importance of the spoken word and referred to the young people whose creative journeys would bring them into contact with the theatre: 'Even if they're protesting about something, let them protest with clarity.' Actors, like protesters, need to ensure there is a real connection between the internal response they have to the words they speak and the actual delivery of those words. The way the dialogue is written – the specific words chosen, what the words sound like, as well as the length of the sentences, the punctuation, vocabulary and so on – all these things give us insight into the psychology, emotional state and personality of the speaker. Similarly, if you look at the choice of words, the punctuation, etc., of a story or poem, you can immediately define the mood and atmosphere. These exercises help young people to trust dramatic language and the way it operates. It is as useful for an actor to feel the language physically and intuitively as it is for him/her to think about it analytically or intellectually.

It is best to break lines of verse or dialogue down into the smallest possible units, before building up to complete passages of text. Try to make the language active and give the participants a physical connection to the words. For comprehensive accounts of voice-work by professional voice coaches, see *The Right to Speak* and *The Actor and His Voice* by Patsy Rodenburg, *Voice and the Actor* by Cicely Berry, *Freeing the Natural Voice* by Kristin Linklater and *Finding your Voice* by Barbara Houseman.

Preparation

- Pretend to chew a gigantic piece of gum. Without using your hands, squeeze your face together and make it as small as possible – as if you are trying to push your whole face towards the tip of your nose.
- Now try to make your face as big as possible – like an inflated balloon.
- Now think about the shape of your mouth. Move it to the left, to the right, and up and down. Press your lips together and then stretch your mouth in a wide yawn.

- Try different exaggerated facial expressions, such as the biggest smile, frown, wink, blink, sneer, expression of disgust, surprise, delight – you can imagine.
- Make a big noise – for instance, a braying donkey or a moaning cow.

Breath and sound

- Standing with feet parallel and legs shoulder-width apart, gently bend the knees and ankles as you swing your arms back and forth. Keep the feet relaxed and the toes spread, sink into the floor, don't grip it. Continue but now allow the whole upper body to swing left and right loosely from the hips. Focus on letting go of the body and the breath.
- To warm up your vocal cords, stand easily, watching a point on the opposite wall at eye level. Breathe to that point. Then, as you exhale, make your breath into a hum. Once this is comfortable, you can open your mouth, letting your jaw drop so as to make an 'aaah' sound.
- Swing up so the arms are above the head. Let a new breath enter easily as you swing up, don't over-breathe or suck the air in. Then let the body melt into the swing and let the breath release on an 'S' sound. Don't control the breath; neither hold it back nor push it out, just imagine a steady sound and let it fall out of your body. Repeat this on 'Z', then on 'ZOO', 'ZOH', 'ZOR', 'ZAH', 'ZYE', 'ZAY', 'ZEE'. After a while, drop the arms but imagine they are still stretched wide and continue to make the sounds.
- Imagine you are holding an object such as a chair directly above your head, or actually hold a chair. This helps the body to find its balance and not collapse. It also stops the shoulders being used and the head poking forward.

  Easily but firmly say 'SH SH'. You should feel your belly move in. If you don't, work slowly, with a partner's hand on your belly to help you focus there; imagine that each 'SH' pulls your belly in. Try to keep relaxed so you don't over-tense the muscles.
- Rest, and then again with the chair, easily but with a bouncy, confident firmness say 'HOO HOO', 'HOH HOH', 'HOR HOR', 'HAH HAH', 'HIGH HIGH', 'HAY HAY', 'HEE HEE'. You can use

any consonant. Imagine your mouth/throat is in your belly and that the sounds are made there. Don't push your voice down to your belly. Imagine the sounds are coming up from there, as if the sounds pull your belly in – again, don't force it.

- Now put your attention on your lips – as if your mind is inside them and the movement they make. Say 'P-P-B-B' several times, feeling the lips bounce apart. Try to stay present with the making of every sound. Never reel the sounds off while thinking about something else as this encourages disconnected speech.
- Focus in the same way on the tip of the tongue and say 'T-T-D-D' several times.
- Now try testing your vocal range by beginning your breath on a very high note and then sliding down to a very low one. Repeat this the other way round. Breaks in the sound and the missing of some notes are common, but these can be eliminated through repeating the exercise.

Vowels and consonants

This is an exercise for older participants.

- Let your jaw drop and go through the vowels – a, e, i, o, u – as if you were speaking the alphabet. Concentrate on the shape of your mouth as you make each vowel sound as clearly and distinctly as possible. Breathe so you can imagine your stomach filling with air and then say the sounds as if the air is coming not from your lungs but from your stomach (that is, speak from your body and not just your chest or throat).
- Now repeat the exercise using certain consonants – exaggerate the movement of your mouth, tongue and lips as you speak the consonants b, d, k, m, n, p, s, y.

Throwing vowels and consonants across the room

If you have used a ball game as a simple warm-up, you can repeat the activity throwing vowels and consonants across a circle instead of a ball. Participants can throw any letter to someone in the circle, but they must speak it clearly and precisely, miming a throwing movement towards the other person with both hands as they do it. They should emphasise and exaggerate both the sound and the mouth, tongue and lip movements used in making it.

Throwing words

- Stand in a throwing stance (one foot in front of the other).
- Move your weight back, breathe in, then mime throwing something forwards and upwards with both hands, while emitting a warm, round, 'aah'.
- Throw the words, 'Hello, my name is – ', with your name being the most important thing. Really emphasise your name as you throw it forwards and up.

Tongue-twisters

Repeat 'Red lorry, yellow lorry', 'Round the rugged rock the ragged rascal ran', 'Moses supposes his toeses are roses', 'Selfish shellfish', 'Sister Suzy's sewing shirts for soldiers', 'She stood on the balcony mimicking him hiccupping and inimitably beckoning him in'.

Words and rhythm

Everyone sits in a circle. Divide the circle into three sections. The words help to anchor you to the rhythm. This exercise works well with primary school students.

- Section 1 says quietly in unison, 'Cold cup of tea, cold cup of tea' and claps once. Do this several times until a smooth rhythm is established.
- Section 2 then takes over, and says, 'Cold cup of tea, cold cup of tea' before clapping twice. Practise this rhythm with Section 2 before moving to Section 3, who repeat the line before clapping three times.
- Now run all three sections together, beginning at the same time. This sets up a round, with each section coming in on the line just after the preceding one. Each group must hold strictly to its own rhythm.

Trying to be heard

This game helps an actor to give weight to individual words and their meaning in a speech.

- One person reads a passage of text while the rest of the group stands around the room.
- He reads the passage again; this time the rest of the group stands together in a crowd and heckles and interrupts him as he is reading or speaking the lines.

You might use the following lines from *Simply Heavenly*, for example, in which a guitarist explains why he can no longer make a living as a live musician:

> GITFIDDLE: Juke boxes is the trouble now, Miss Mamie. Used to be, folks liked to hear a sure-enough live guitar player. Now, I start playing, somebody puts a nickel in the piccolo, drowns me out. No good for musicianers any more, but I got to make the rounds, try to hustle.

The actor should not shout over the heckling crowd, but should try to give the words more weight and emphasis. It doesn't matter if he can't be heard by the others; he should concentrate on getting his meaning across as convincingly as possible, in spite of the noise.

Energetic warm-up games

After stretches and name games, more active warm-ups help to break the ice, release pent-up energy and introduce cooperation and group activity. One or two energetic warm-ups in a workshop or rehearsal session will help to break down shyness and self-consciousness, by providing participants with simple roles, clear rules and shared objectives. Not all physically demanding games are appropriate for all age groups. Primary school students may not need to be energised through strenuous physical exercises, and some adolescent groups will not need the extra stimulation this provides.

Football

Even in a small space, a simple game of football is an enjoyable, high-energy warm-up.

Stuck in the mud

One person is the chaser. If she tags anyone, that person is stuck until someone else rescues him by crawling between his legs. After playing for a few minutes, appoint three people to chase the rest of the group, and then six.

Cat and mouse

One person is the cat and everyone else is a mouse. The object is for the cat to catch a mouse. A mouse can avoid capture by linking arms with another mouse. But they can only stay together for up to the count of five. Then they have to split up and the cat can chase them. When the cat catches a mouse, the mouse becomes the cat and the cat becomes a mouse and the chase begins again.

Another version of the game involves choosing one cat and one mouse. Everyone else gets into groups of three; each group stands in a line with arms linked. The mouse can save itself by hooking onto the end of a line, but as soon as this happens, the person at the far end of the line becomes the mouse and must flee from the cat. When the cat catches a mouse, they swap roles at once. This is a very active game, and can be further complicated by having two or more mice.

Iyaki

The players divide into two teams, A and B. Each team has a base in a corner of the room. The object of the game is to capture the opposing players by tapping them on the shoulder and saying 'Iyaki . . .' followed by the name of the captured player. The captured player must go to the enemy's base and wait there until a member of his/her own side touches him/her on the shoulder, calling 'Iyaki go!' This player can then rejoin the game, which continues until one side captures all the opposing players.

It

A game of fluid movement and fast reflex action. Everyone walks around the rehearsal space throughout the game. Someone is named, and designated to be 'It'. That person tries to tag another person by touching him/her on the shoulder. As soon as someone else is tagged, that person becomes 'It' and must try to tag someone else. But if the person about to be tagged calls out another person's name before being touched, then the named person becomes 'It' instead.

Only one person can be 'It' at any one time. Movement around the room should be fast, controlled (i.e. never running) and silent, except when someone is named and made 'It'.

Knee fights

A game to sharpen focus and reflexes. Sit in pairs: both cover your knees with your hands. The object of the game is to score hits on your partner by touching his/her knees while guarding your own. The first person to five 'hits' wins.

Slap hands

This game is good for concentration, coordination and close observation. Divide the group into pairs. The pairs stand at opposite ends of a room. They run towards each other and when they are face to face they stop at exactly the same moment. Then they repeat this movement, but this time they slap their hands together palm to palm when they meet. The third time, they run at each other, leap into the air and slap their palms together as before. This game is more difficult than it sounds. The two people must be in perfect unison in all their movements.

Concentration and focus games

These games help to focus the energy released by energetic warm-ups – they demand concentration and attention. They may replace more active physical warm-ups where a group is, for example, rowdy and liable to become overexcited or uncooperative.

Send a clap round the circle

This is a good game for getting started with. Everyone stands in a circle and passes a clap around the circle as if it is a ball or an object. When this game works, a rhythm is set up, with each clap being perfectly placed after the one before. It comes to seem as if the clap is, in fact, a physical object. The game requires concentration, relaxation and a desire to make something outside yourself (i.e. the rhythm that is established) work within a group. You can vary it by passing the clap as quickly as possible or by introducing a second clap that goes in the opposite direction. Alternatively, you can try playing the game where you clap to the person you are receiving a clap from and then you clap to the person you are passing a clap to – so that each person is clapping twice (see also p. 53, 'Clap and move').

Grandmother's footsteps

This well-known game requires physical control and alertness. It also introduces the idea of dramatic tension and expectation in stories and their action.

One person stands with her back to the rest of the group at one end of the room and while she is not looking the others try to creep up on her. She can turn round at any time but must count to three before turning and if she sees someone moving that person must go back to the start.

The first person to reach Grandmother and touch her back wins and takes her place.

Wink murder

This is a game of stealth which focuses the physical and mental energies of participants, and allows them to make playful theatrical gestures. It's a very good ice-breaker.

One person is secretly chosen to be the murderer. The rest move randomly about the room trying to avoid the unknown murderer.

The murderer must 'kill' the rest of the group off without being detected. He does this by catching the eye of individuals and winking at them. After being winked at the victim must 'stage' his/her death within ten seconds. Older players may die with a

Shakespearean phrase on their lips: 'A hit, a very palpable hit'. This continues until only the murderer and the last player remain. Observant players may identify the murderer and so avoid him, but should not reveal his identity to the others.

Count as a group with eyes closed

This exercise can restore calm and focus after working on a scene. Stand in a circle with your eyes open. Count round the circle, one at a time, clockwise, until you get to ten. Now try to count to ten without working round the circle, i.e. without being prompted, so someone in the group says 'one' and someone else, not necessarily the person next to him/her, will say 'two' and so on. Nobody knows who is going to speak next, and if two people say the same number at the same time, you must start again. This is surprisingly difficult to do – it requires real concentration, careful listening (i.e. for someone inhaling before he speaks) and a bit of guesswork.

Zip zap boing

This is a simplified version of a game widely used in workshops in different variations. It demands alertness and the ability to react quickly to what is happening around you.

The group stands in a circle and one person starts. He says 'Zip' while turning to the person on his right. That person also says 'Zip' while turning to her right, and so on round the circle. When you have passed 'Zip' round the circle once, begin again.

This time, when it comes to your turn, you may wish to send 'Zip' back in the opposite direction, in which case you say 'Boing' to the person who has just said 'Zip' to you. This person must now say 'Zip' to the person on her left, and so you continue, until someone else says 'Boing' and changes the direction again.

Alternatively, you might decide to pass the 'Zip' to someone who is not adjacent to you, in which case you say 'Zap' to the person you wish to send 'Zip' to and point at them across the circle. This person can now either carry on sending 'Zip' round the circle, or send it in the opposite direction by saying 'Boing', or 'Zap' it back across the circle to someone on the other side.

The game should make everyone aware that any individual can rob it of its momentum by not participating fully.

Prisoner and guardian

Place as many chairs as are needed in a square facing inwards. One person stands behind each chair with his hands behind his back (the guardian), and another sits on it (the prisoner). There should be at least two empty chairs with only a guardian behind them. The aim of the game is for the guardians to make sure they always have someone sitting in their chair.

The two guardians without prisoners can gain prisoners by winking at them surreptitiously. The winked-at person must try to get to the empty chair without being tagged by their guardian. Guardians should stand with their hands behind their backs a foot away from the chair. Prisoners should sit with their hands on their laps.

Ensemble-building games

These games require strategy, cooperation and coordination; they should give older participants an understanding of their role within a group, and encourage every member of the group to take responsibility for their choices and actions. They signal entry into the imaginative realm of the workshop, and require real commitment on the part of participants.

Empty chair

This simple game is useful for breaking the ice, concentration, teamwork and focusing a group before rehearsal.

- Everyone takes a chair and places it in the room, with equal space between each other and any wall, facing any direction, and sits down. There must be no extra chairs. One person (A) leaves his/her chair empty and walks to the other side of the room.
- A wants to sit down. To do this, he/she walks to the empty chair and sits. Everyone else wants to stop A from sitting. To do this, someone must go and sit in the empty chair, thus vacating the chair they were in. A now changes course and tries to sit in the freshly vacated chair; someone moves to get there first,

preventing A from sitting, and so on. When A has successfully sat, someone else becomes A (ideally the person responsible for letting A sit). A can only move slowly, with no speeding up whatsoever; everyone else can move as fast as they like. If you leave your seat, you must go to another – you cannot return to yours unless you have sat in another first. If you make even the slightest move with the intention of leaving your seat, you have to go. These rules must be strictly observed.

At first try, the game will be chaotic and A will probably be seated within ten seconds. As the group begins to work as a team and not to panic (for example, do not move if A is near you – let someone else do it), it is a good idea to impose silence on the game. As they improve, encourage the group to move more casually, not rushing, as if they were unaware of A's presence. This game is very good as a fun way to focus any group, and is particularly apt if the drama being explored is dealing with the concept of the outsider, status issues, etc.

Chair square: a relationships game

This game, provided by Young Vic Associate Director Rufus Norris, has various stages and can develop into more and more detailed scenarios; at the very least it is a good way to encourage commitment from a group, however timid. It involves the whole group but can focus down on to individuals, so bravery, rewarded with praise, can very quickly become infectious. The game is generally played with order participants, such as drama students or trainee directors.

The best analogy for this game is that of relationships viewed simplistically. Set up a square of chairs, facing inwards and with walking space between them. For a group of twelve to eighteen participants, the square should consist of twelve chairs, so that there are three on each side of the square. For nineteen to twenty-four, there should be four on each side, etc. The number of chairs necessary will become apparent as you set it up.

The group should be divided into three groups of equal size (A, B, C). All those in group A should sit, spread fairly evenly, on the chairs. Each A individual has a partner, B, who stands directly behind the chair occupied by A. C individuals stand behind the vacant chairs. These people are single, and must find a partner. It does not matter if there are several chairs not being sat on or stood behind but you need at least as many chairs as there are people in both groups A and C. Everyone should be facing in towards the centre of the square; those in B should be able to touch the shoulders of the A in front of them, but not put their arms around them. Each side of the square should contain at least one A/B pairing and one C.

People in Group A are bored with their partners and want to find new ones. People in Group B are possessive and want to keep their partners (the As) from leaving them. In other words, Cs are lonely, As are restless and Bs are jealous.

The game should be built up in several stages, making sure that each stage is understood and working well before adding the next. Like wink murder, members of Group C try to get the attention of an A by winking at him/her. If winked at, A should respond and move to the vacant chair in front of the winking C. C now becomes a B (a jealous partner). A's former partner B is now single and so becomes a C; he/she should start winking in order to find a new partner.

The possessive B does not want to lose his partner A, so when A tries to move to a new partner, B should try to tap his/her shoulder. If B succeeds, the departing A must return; if not, A has escaped to a new partner. (The distance between B and A should make it possible for either of these things to happen; the success of the attempt to leave or the attempt to catch depends on the guile and speed of the participants.)

If A succeeds in escaping to his/her new life, he/she should celebrate wholeheartedly with his new partner for ten to fifteen seconds before the couple settles down to their new life of boredom and temptation.

If A is unsuccessful, the jealous B should reprimand his/her partner severely for attempting to leave. Again, after ten to fifteen seconds life should return to normal; A sits again and the winking recommences.

There will inevitably be several scenarios going on at the same time. It is imperative that participants are focused on their own wants and responses and do not get distracted by other stories within the square. It will probably be necessary, perhaps several times, to insist that the improvised celebrations and reprimands are taken very seriously. This exercise comes alive only when the participants really commit to the emotional reality of being left, gaining their freedom, falling in love, growing restless, etc.

When the participants have settled into the game, the scenarios can develop into three-way domestic arguments. If A leaves B for C, then their celebration is interrupted by B crossing the square in an attempt to persuade A back and to remonstrate with C. Alternatively, if A is not successful, the winking C should cross the square to persuade B to release A (he/she would be happier with me, let him go, etc.). There should be no time restriction on this – just let the interactions develop and run a little before stopping the game and beginning again.

The final stage. Run as above, but with the understanding that once running, you will direct the group quietly to focus in on one domestic scenario of your choosing. The group to be focused on (decide when the game is running) should continue until stopped, even when twenty people are crowded round to watch their elation/distress. All you need to do is decide who to focus on, and quickly touch the other participants, pointing towards the area of focus, so there is no stop in the flow.

Balancing the floor

This is a good workshop or pre-rehearsal game. It helps to develop sensitive group work and spatial awareness, which is useful, say, for working on a stage or for defining a theatrical space within a room.

Imagine that the floor is balancing on a ball that stands underneath it at the centre of the room. The task of the group is to keep the floor level by counteracting the weight of others with your own. One person can play against one person, both of them moving around the space in response to one another, or one can play against a larger group or against a number of individuals. In other words, if a group stands on one side of the room, close to the centre, the balancing individual will need to move right to the margin of the room on the far side, to try to counteract their weight with his/her own. This also helps participants to think more creatively about space and to free them from any mundane associations that, say, a classroom might have for them.

Go!

Stand in a circle with one person in the centre holding a ball (a larger ball is good for this game). That person throws the ball to someone in the circle, who catches it and throws it back to the centre. He/she then throws it to someone else, who throws it back, and so on, until a smooth rhythm is established.

When the ball is caught by someone in the circle, someone else in the circle can call out 'Go!' and run to replace the person in the middle and catch the ball. The person in the middle moves to fill the space in the circle.

If several people say 'Go!' at once, the person who gets to the centre first stays there and the rest return to their places. This exercise demands timing and physical alertness.

Jumping game

This can be played with a large group of, say, twenty people, and is suitable for younger participants.

- Stand in four rows: A, B, C and D, all standing behind and facing the same way as Row A. Row A jumps together on the spot eight times. On the eighth time, everyone turns together to face Row B.
- Row B then jumps eight times, turning on the eighth jump to face Row C, and so on. Row D jumps eight times, turning on the eighth jump to face away from Row C.
- Row D then immediately jumps four times, turning on the fourth to face Row C again. Row C jumps four times, turning on the fourth jump to face Row B and so on. Row A turns on the fourth jump to face away from Row B, and then immediately jumps twice, turning on the second jump to face Row B, and the process begins again.
- When Row D has jumped twice and turned on the second jump, they jump once, turning back to face Row C. Row C jumps once, turning as they do so to face Row B. Row B jumps once, turning to face Row A. Row A jumps once and turns, so all players are facing the same way as when they started.

This is a good physical exercise and it aids the concentration of the group. No one person in the group is in charge, but each member has the responsibility to move accurately with the rest of the row.

Clap and move

This exercise builds on the 'Send a clap round the circle' game, and is useful in developing the ability to move together with precision; each person remaining aware of the others in the space.

- The leader stands to one side and the participants distribute themselves evenly around the room, facing in different directions.
- When the leader claps once, everyone moves forwards, making sure they are still evenly distributed around the room.
- When the leader claps again, everyone stops.

Once this starting and stopping has been perfected, the leader can add new elements. First clap: move forward; second clap: stop; third clap: turn head to the left; fourth clap: turn body to face same direction as head; fifth clap: move forwards again. And so on. If anyone in the group gets the movements wrong, you should return to the starting positions and begin again.

In the end, the movements should be simple, unified and coordinated. If this can be achieved, try the game again, only this time without clapping. The group should move forwards as one and stop moving as one. Elements like those above can also be added. Each individual should be constantly aware of the others, and, when necessary, control his/her gestures so that they accord with those of the group.

Improvisations

Improvisations form the core of a number of workshop and rehearsal methodologies. When related to specific plays and particular problems, the personal identification and imaginative liberation involved in improvising can generate keen insight into characters and their situations. But simple improvisations also serve to relax young people and encourage them to work as a group: they are useful and flexible warm-ups for more detailed work.

Feeling and action

- Working as individuals, all mime the same basic action, like brushing your hair, eating an apple, sweeping a floor, drinking.
- Do this as neutrally as possible, concentrating only on the physical movements involved in the action.
- Now mime the same actions but while feeling anger, hunger, fear, jealousy, love, etc.

Eye contact

- Divide into two groups. One half seeks and holds eye contact; the other half deliberately avoids it, and lets the eyes flick away as soon as they meet someone else's.
- Wander about the room, saying hello to one another. Some of you will make and hold eye contact; others will avoid it.
- How does this exercise makes you feel? Those who hold eye contact may well report that this gives them a feeling of power, while those who look away may both reflect and feel anxiety or discomfort.

Status cards

Status games and exercises have been comprehensively incorporated into the rehearsal processes of Keith Johnstone and Max Stafford-Clark. Their use is discussed in detail in Chapter 5, in relation to *A Raisin in the Sun*. But in their simplest form they can be used as warm-ups, introducing notions of dominance and submission and the changing power dynamics that underly many dramatic interactions.

- Split the participants into two groups. Hand out playing cards to each member of one group, removing the court cards (jack, queen, king). Don't let the other group see the cards. Ace is one, and the highest card is ten. The higher the number, the higher the status of the individual.
- The members of the group then introduce themselves to the other group in such a way as to demonstrate their status.
- The observing group has to arrange them in a line in order of their status, from lowest to highest. Consider the different

ways of using your body and voice in introducing yourself, and what this tells other people about your status.

Try varying the presentation to make your status clearer. A high status person, for example, may not necessarily swagger and speak loudly. She may be very relaxed and casual in her movements, because she has nothing to prove. It may actually be a slightly lower status person (a seven or eight, say) who feels he must make a powerful impression to establish superiority over those a little lower down the scale (say, five or six).

This exercise can be adapted for primary students. Seat the class in a semi-circle. Give five volunteers a status number from one (low) to five (high) and ask them to present themselves to the class. Do not tell anyone else what their status number is. Ask another volunteer to try to place the five according to their status.

High and low status

This exercise builds on the preceding one. Use a simple exchange between two people. For example:

A   Is this seat free?
B   I think so.
A   Do you mind if I –?
B   No, not at all.

- Ask two volunteers to act out this meeting as though A has very high status and B has very low status.
- First, consider the location (on a bus or plane, at a concert or film, in a park or a café, for example). Explore the status relationship between A and B: perhaps A is a film star and B a fan, or A is the director of a multinational company and B a junior employee on his first day at work.
- Consider how A might enter the space (perhaps casually, scanning the room, or perhaps busily, making a phone call). How might B respond (look up anxiously, speak with eyes downcast, make himself smaller to accommodate A)?

Note that the way the lines are delivered is also a strong indication of status. A low-status B might speak rapidly and emphatically, while a high-status B might speak slowly and casually, with little inflection (in order not to engage with the low-status A).

Now take another two volunteers and reverse the status, so that A is low and B is high. A might hesitate before disturbing B. B might feign indifference, or might pointedly turn his back.

Choose another pair and ask them both to play high status or very low status.

Think of the detail of your actions. How does a high-status person sit in a chair? How does a low-status person sit in a chair? He may perch on the very edge, or cross his legs tightly, or put his hands between his legs while sitting.

Raising and lowering status

- Divide the group into pairs. Each pair is getting dressed to go to a party together.
- A tries to put B down with comments or insults, while B (the low-status character) tries to raise A's status with praise and flattery.
- Now swap. Try to think of increasingly subtle ways to raise or lower one another's status. For example, B might say to A, 'I'd love to wear your shirt, but it wouldn't look any good on me.' The implication is that it does look good on A; A is therefore given higher status by B. Alternatively, A might say to B, 'Those shoes would look beautiful on someone with small feet.' A is suggesting that B has big feet, and that the shoes look bad. B's status goes down in relation to A.

Status relationships

- Use the cards again to assign status. But this time, each person takes a job title before choosing a card (i.e. cleaner, policeman, referee, pilot, chef, CEO, waiter, etc). Status can be 'read' by an onlooker not only in the behaviour of an individual, but also in the behaviour and attitudes of others towards that individual.
- In pairs, greet one another according to your high or low status. Thus you may have a low-status policeman (whose card is, say, a two) meeting a high status cleaner (whose card is a nine). Try to think of a scenario in which this status relationship could occur: e.g. the policeman may have been caught stealing from

an office by the cleaner. Explain the scenario to the audience before presenting each greeting.

The point is that anyone's status can be reversed, either by intention or by the situation in which the character finds herself. Defining status relationships and status shifts helps us to understand the dynamic nature of dramatic characterisation.

These warm-ups and games can be used before, during and after a workshop/rehearsal session, whenever the director feels there is a need to refocus, relax or invigorate a working group. Though not all professional directors use games in their work, preferring to move from physical warm-up to direct investigation of the play in question, most teachers and practitioners see games as an indispensable tool in their work with children and young people. Games bring participants by the most direct and familiar route into the sphere of physical ritual, orchestrated movement, ensemble work and performance. They can dissolve inhibition and self-consciousness; each is defined by its intrinsic action, and each has a single unambiguous purpose. Tailor the exercises to the group you are working with. Different groups require different levels of explanation and justification. For example, offering more detailed explanations for the intended aims or outcomes of an exercise may help older students become more focused and make sense of the overall structure of a workshop or rehearsal session. Younger participants tend to benefit most from performing the exercise without discussing it in advance – in this case it is often better to attempt something before you define it. If it is successful, the results can be more readily incorporated into subsequent work.

In a sense, every game is a miniature drama, and the players, without realising it, are at once its actors and its audience; discovering their physical potential and their interconnectedness and sharpening their senses in a relaxed and playful way.

Chapter 3

ACTIVE STORYTELLING – GRIMM TALES

The stage is the setting, the atmosphere of the stories is the cement and the audience's imagination provides the rest.

Grimm Tales (1994)

The fairy tales gathered by the Brothers Grimm and published in 1812 are well known to many of us in various versions. Most of our knowledge of fairy or folk tales comes from the Grimm anthology or from a French anthology published by Perrault in the 1690s. In the three hundred years since then, the stories have been adapted, stretched and compressed into many shapes, most notably in Walt Disney's animations. The original tales, however, are leaner, darker and more violent, and when Tim Supple produced *Grimm Tales* as the Young Vic's Christmas show in 1994, he returned with poet and adapter Carol Ann Duffy to the nineteenth-century German originals.

His aim was to create a show which would appeal to adults and children alike, and which would emphasise both the Young Vic's unique space and the pure theatricality of the event. The result was an experimental and innovatively staged show (designed by Melly Still) supported by eclectic live music (composed by Adrian Lee), with an ensemble of performers trained in physical as well as classical theatre. The production was an unprecedented hit, and later toured internationally.

Grimm Tales and the subsequent *More Grimm Tales* (1997) developed out of Melly Still's enthusiasm for the visual potential of the stories: 'The priority for me was to make the stories vivid and really, really alive; to use textures and materials that were effectively alive.' Carol Ann Duffy adapted a selection of the original Grimm tales including *Hansel and Gretel*, *The Golden Goose*, *Ashputtel*, *Iron Hans*, *Little Red-Cap*, *The Hare and the Hedgehog* and *Snow White*. Duffy did not dramatise the tales; she kept the third-person narrative voice in each, and it was up to the company, with the help of their audiences, to find the best way of incorporating the narration into the action.

Marina Warner, whose cultural history of folk tales, *The Beast and the Blonde*, informed Duffy's adaptation, felt that this was 'an inspired approach to the problem of adaptation, because it preserves the memory of story-telling and respects the formal unrealitites of the genre. Fairy-tale heroes and villains hardly ever question their own behaviour . . . the characters act as a chorus to one another's drama, without any pretence at an inner voice or subjective reflection.' Supple's intention was to let the stories, quite literally, speak for themselves; to animate the auditorium with the riveting simplicity of their language and gestures. 'The relationship with the audience was one of the main concerns from very early on,' according to Melly Still. 'In the round you really have to keep a connection with the three dimensions all around you.'

Duffy worked from existing English versions of the original Grimm stories. She broke the sentence structure of the stories down into shorter units, and emphasised the strong and simple images in each. She stripped away the nineteenth-century formality of the language and where possible put it in the mouths of the characters in the stories so that they absorbed the narrative and propelled it forward. This process of turning third-person storytelling into first-person dialogue was further developed during rehearsals, and as a result the stories became more immediate and vivid.

For example, the Routledge edition of *Grimm Tales* (1948) provides the following account of the Wolf's actions in *Little Red-Cap*:

> The wolf thought to himself: 'What a tender young creature! What a nice plump mouthful – she will be better to eat than the old woman. I must act craftily, so as to catch both.' So he walked for a short time by the side of Little Red-Cap, and then he said: 'See, Little Red-Cap, how pretty the flowers are about here – why do you not look round? I believe, too, that you do not hear how sweetly the little birds are singing; you walk gravely along as if you were going to school, while everything else out here in the wood is merry.' (p. 140)

Duffy's version (Faber, 1994) uses plain, direct prose, dividing the narrative up between the principal characters, and dramatic action takes the place of description. Every word and gesture now moves the story forward:

> WOLF: How young and sweet and tender she is. I could eat her. She'll make a plumper mouthful for my jaws than the old woman. If I am wily, though, I can have the pair of them!

> *The Wolf walks beside Red-Cap for a while.*

> WOLF: Look, Little Red-Cap. Open your eyes and see! There are beautiful flowers all around us. And there's wonderful birdsong that you don't even listen to. You just plod straight ahead as though you were going to school – and yet the woods are such fun! (p. 4)

The immediacy of the story carries the audience on a journey and needs little more than the words themselves to be gripping. 'All we have done,' Supple pointed out, 'is to adapt the original voices of the stories to the modern ear and split their telling between narrator, character, musician and chorus.' Supple found that the wolf is 'far more powerful when he stands still and does nothing in his first encounter with Red-Cap than he is when he tries to behave in a way that is sinister and "wolf-like".'

Following Supple's desire that the work with young people be investigative and experimental rather than strictly educational, he and Emmas initiated a line of research work in which professional practitioners went into schools and supported the young people in the creation of their own dramatised versions of individual stories. The children were then invited into the rehearsal room at a very early stage of rehearsals, before any decisions had been made on how the stories should be presented. Supple asked the children to present their versions to the actors, and the actors to reciprocate, presenting their work to date. Then the two groups improvised versions of the stories together. These sessions gave Supple and his cast a great deal of insight not only into the latent power of the stories but also into how they could be best presented. Those elements of the stories emphasised by the young performers became the lynchpins in the professional company's interpretations, and the young people were invited to attend the final performance and see the results of their collaboration.

Age-old stories have vivid descriptive words on their surface, but they also have an inner world which draws the listener deeper into the story and is as striking and real as the ideas and events on the surface. Their language, colours, characters, journeys, objects, repetitions and contrasts, their births and deaths, their rituals and ceremonies, the passing of time, the geography of their land-scapes, their lies and evasions, their episodes, their joys and their horrors must all be identified and understood by the actors/tellers if they are to be transmitted compellingly to an audience. Any investigation of how to tell strong stories needs to be accompanied by an exploration of their hidden structures and codes.

What makes a story enthral an audience? Storytelling is central to much live performance for young people and lies at the heart of theatre. These exercises, which were used in the teaching and participation work associated with Tim Supple's productions of the *Grimm Tales*, are intended to introduce and develop the craft of storytelling, and can be adapted for use with any narrative poem or strong and simple story. Some of the exercises that follow are more involving and time-consuming than others. If an exercise is not working for a particular group, end it, refocus the group with a game, and try another one. The overall aim of these exercises is to demonstrate that any story can be invigorated and developed through the process of telling it, and that a handful of simple tools and approaches can give young people of all ages the confidence and skill to become storytellers.

Telling stories with words

In introducing young people to the *Grimm Tales* it is important to emphasise the power of words in the stories. These tales form part of an oral tradition which was handed down and adapted over centuries. Even when the tales were written down they retained a strong sense of the spoken word. The principle of orality informs the *Grimm Tales* on stage: 'If narration feels like dialogue and dialogue like narration, the script will live.'

What's the time, Mr Wolf?

This is a familiar variation on grandmother's footsteps. 'What's the time, Mr Wolf?' is, in effect, a very simple story, with a narrative which progresses to a climax and a resolution. If children can recognise the structure of this story, they have begun to understand the dynamics of storytelling.

- One player is Mr Wolf, and he stalks the room with the rest of the group following him. At intervals they ask him, 'What's the time, Mr Wolf?' and each time he turns and answers, 'One o'clock', 'Two o'clock' etc. until he suddenly turns and cries, 'Supper time!', at which point everyone flees to the safety of a wall, while Mr Wolf tries to grab someone to eat.

Telling a story in a circle

Here are some examples of opening lines of well-known stories:

Far out at sea the water is as blue as the bluest corn flower, and as clear as the clearest crystal.' (*The Mermaid*, Hans Christian Anderson)

Far away where the swallows take refuge in winter, lived a king who had eleven sons and one daughter Elise.' (*The Wild Geese*, Hans Christian Anderson)

There was once a poor tailor, who had a son called Aladdin, a careless, idle boy who would do nothing but play all day long in the streets with idle boys like himself.' (*Aladdin and the Wonderful Lamp*)

Now try this exercise:

- Sit in a circle and build a story together using either a conventional opening phrase like 'Once upon a time', or a more particular phrase like 'Across the mountains and over the river, there lived a fox with silver eyes'.
- The next person now adds a word, phrase or sentence to your opening phrase and the story is passed round the circle.
- Sometimes this is done holding an object, which is then handed from person to person as the story progresses. When it's your turn, you don't have to come up with an event, you can

simply say, 'And then . . .' The object is to keep the story flowing. It belongs to all of you; you are all responsible for its twists and turns, for its combination of the familiar and the strange; the real and the magical. For younger participants use a single word each.

Stories develop most successfully when a routine is set up and then suddenly interrupted, as when the Grandmother suddenly turns around in the game of grandmother's footsteps. For example, someone might say 'The fox woke with the shining dawn . . .' and someone else might interrupt this familiar routine by adding '. . . and heard in the distance the baying of hounds and the drumming of hoofs'. This interruption opens up new possibilities and gives the story momentum. Children love telling and hearing stories; exercises like this encourage them to think about the structure of the stories they tell, and remind them that they can play an active role in holding an audience's attention.

- Keep going with the story until it has a clear shape (beginning and middle), at which point you should bring it to an end, e.g. 'And with that, the fox melted into the cool black night.' Finish the story before it returns to the first person again.

Using an object to tell a story

Find a variety of old objects – shoes, coins, stones, a chipped mug – and again in a circle create a story. Tell a story about something that happened long ago or in a distant place; this may give you a greater sense of freedom in imagining the events that take place. The first person picks up the object and begins the story, for example, 'Years ago, somewhere hot and sunny, a farmer on his way to market dropped a coin by the road.' Pass the object to the next person who adds his or her contribution: 'A piglet snuffled up the coin and ran with it all the way to the great green forest.'

The story might continue until the coin finds its way back to the farmer, or into the hands of a hungry child. It might be buried for ever, melted in a furnace to become a tooth filling; it might adorn the ear of a gypsy or fall to the bottom of the sea. Alternatively, the object may simply start the story off, then disappear. It doesn't matter, as long as the story grows and moves forward, gathering detail, but remembering its origins.

Tell me about the time when . . .

Prompt the person next to you with the words, 'Tell me about the time when . . .' Invent a situation to follow: '. . . you had to escape when your house caught fire.' Your neighbour then tells you this story in a few sentences. Try to focus on strong, clear actions. What did you see/hear/touch/taste? What did you feel? What did you do? As you go round the group, try to come up with increasingly unusual situations: 'Tell me about the time when the snake swallowed your aunt in Luton.'

The story of Little Red-Cap

The following, more detailed storytelling exercises explore the use of words, images and character, principally in relation to the story of Little Red-Cap:

> RED-CAP: There was once a delicious little girl who was loved by everyone who saw her.
> GRANDMOTHER: But most of all by her grandmother, who was always wondering what treat to give the sweet child next.
> RED-CAP: Once she sent her a little red cap which suited her so well that she wouldn't wear anything else and she was known from then on as Little Red-Cap.
> MOTHER: One day her mother said, 'Little Red-Cap, here are some cakes and a bottle of best wine. Take them to Grandmother. She's been poorly and is still a bit weak and these will do her good. Now, hurry up before it gets too hot. And mind how you go, like a good little girl. And don't go wandering off the path or you'll fall over and break the wine-bottle and then there will be none left for Grandmother. And when you go into her room, make sure you say "Good Morning" nicely, instead of peeping into every corner first!'
> RED-CAP: 'Don't worry, I'll do everything just as you say.' Her grandmother lived out in the wood, a half-an-hour's walk from the village, and as soon as Little Red-Cap stepped into the wood . . .
> WOLF: A wolf saw her.
> RED-CAP: Because she didn't know what a wicked animal it

was, she wasn't afraid of it.

WOLF: 'Good morning, Little Red-Cap.'

RED-CAP: 'Thank you, Wolf.'

WOLF: 'And where might you be going so early?'

RED-CAP: 'To my grandmother's house.'

WOLF: 'And what's that you're carrying under your apron?'

RED-CAP: 'Cakes and wine. We were baking yesterday – and my poor grandmother has been ill, so these will strengthen her.'

WOLF: 'Where does Grandmother live, Little Red-Cap?'

RED-CAP: 'She lives a quarter-of-an-hour's walk from here, under the three big oak trees. Her house has hazel hedges near it. I'm sure you know it.'

WOLF: 'How young and sweet and tender she is. I could eat her. She'll make a plumper mouthful for my jaws than the old woman. If I am wily, though, I can have the pair of them!'

The Wolf walks beside Red-Cap for a while.

WOLF: 'Look, Little Red-Cap. Open your eyes and see! There are beautiful flowers all around us. And there's wonderful birdsong that you don't even listen to. You just plod straight ahead as though you were going to school – and yet the woods are such fun!'

RED-CAP: So Little Red-Cap looked around her; and when she saw the sunbeams seeming to wink at her among the trees, and when she saw the tempting flowers leading away from the straight path, she thought, 'Grandmother will be very pleased if I pick her a bunch of lovely fresh flowers. And it's still early, so I've got plenty of time.' So she ran from the path, among the trees, picking her flowers, and she kept seeing prettier and prettier flowers which led her deeper and deeper into the wood.

WOLF: But the wolf ran fast and straight to the grandmother's house . . . And knocked at the door.

GRANDMOTHER: 'Who's there?'

WOLF: 'Only Little Red-Cap bringing you cake and wine. Open the door.'

GRANDMOTHER: 'Lift the latch. I'm too feeble to get up.'

WOLF: So the wolf lifted the latch and the door flew open and without even a word it leapt on the old woman's bed and gobbled her up. Then it pulled her clothes and her night-cap over its wolfy fur, crawled into her bed and closed the curtains.

RED-CAP: All this time, Little Red-Cap had been trotting about among the flowers and when she'd picked as many as her arms could hold, she remembered her grandmother and hurried off to her house. She was surprised to see that the door was open and as soon as she stepped inside she felt very strange. 'Oh dear, I always look forward to seeing Grandmother, so why do I feel so nervous today?'

'Good Morning?'

But there is no reply. She walks over to the bed and draws back the curtains. Grandmother lies there wearing her night-cap.

RED-CAP: 'Oh, Grandmother, what big ears you have.'

WOLF: 'The better to hear you with, my sweet.'

RED-CAP: 'Oh, Grandmother, what big eyes you have.'

WOLF: 'The better to see you with, my love.'

RED-CAP: 'Oh, Grandmother, what big hands you have.'

WOLF: 'The better to touch you with.'

RED-CAP: 'But Grandmother, what a terrible big mouth you have.'

WOLF: 'The better to eat you.'

The Wolf gobbles up Red-Cap. Then he drags himself into the bed, falls asleep and starts to snore loudly.

HUNTSMAN: The huntsman was just passing the house and thought, 'How loudly the old woman is snoring. I'd better see if something is wrong.'

He goes into the house and when he reaches the bed he sees the Wolf spread out on it.

HUNTSMAN: 'So you've come here, you old sinner. I've wanted to catch you for a long, long time.'

He was about to shoot when it flashed through his mind that the wolf might have swallowed the grandmother whole and that she might still be saved. So he got a good pair of scissors and began to snip the belly of the sleeping wolf. After two snips, he saw the bright red colour of the little red cap. Two snips,

three snips, four snips more, and out jumped Little Red-Cap!
RED-CAP: 'Oh, how frightened I've been! It's so dark inside the wolf!'

Then out comes Grandmother, hardly breathing but still alive.

RED-CAP: Little Red-Cap rushed outside and quickly fetched some big stones and they filled the wolf's belly with them.

When the Wolf wakes up, it tries to run away, but the stones in its stomach are too heavy and it drops down dead.

RED-CAP: When the wolf was dead, all three were delighted.
HUNTSMAN: The huntsman skinned the wolf and went home with its pelt.
GRANDMOTHER: The grandmother ate the cake and drank the wine and soon began to feel much better.
RED-CAP: And Little Red-Cap promised herself, 'Never so long as I live will I wander off the path into the woods when my mother has warned me not to.'

(*More Grimm Tales*, pp. 3–7)

Telling a story in gobbledegook

Stand and tell the story of Little Red Cap, but speak in a made-up language throughout. Try to make the important events in the story sound as exciting as possible in the way you deliver them, through the use of tone, facial expressions, movements and gestures. Even without knowing the story, your audience should be able to recognise its moments of tension, calm, terror and humour and the tone of its resolution. Each word has a meaning, even if only the storyteller knows what it is. Try having two narrators feeding back and forth.

Changing direction with punctuation marks

A 'storyteller' reads out *Little Red-Cap* sentence by sentence. Everyone else walks silently across the room. At every full stop the reader calls out 'Go!', and everyone runs a few steps before the speaker continues.

This helps the listeners connect with the rhythm of the whole story, and it clearly marks every shift in thought or perspective (literally, its turning points). It gives participants a dynamic sense of the shape of the story.

Your own story

Using two or more of the main characters of *Little Red-Cap* (the mother, the grandmother, the wolf, the huntsman, Red-Cap) tell a different version of the story to the class. Try to think of an unusual way to begin your story. You might mention the time, the place or the weather:

'The rain battered the tin roof as Grandmother lay huddled in bed . . .'

'One morning Red-Cap skipped down to the river . . .'

'Just before dawn when the first birds were stirring . . .'

It need not be a long story, but you should try to tell us something about the nature of the characters you have chosen. Is the Grandmother kind and mild or fierce and demanding? Is the Wolf suave and cruel, or playful and skittish? Is Red-Cap sensible and responsible, or curious and reckless? What happens to the characters in your story?

Telling stories with images

The following exercises were widely used in rehearsals for *Grimm Tales* and their object is to try to find ways of making familiar tales come alive in new and surprising ways. Sometimes a literal illustration of an image or event is less powerful than something more simple and unexpected. In Supple's production, for example, the cold snow falling at the beginning of *Snow White* was represented by a mysterious figure dragging a white sheet around the Queen. Blood was 'created' with a red ribbon unfurling from a wound. Use your imagination, and the available materials, to breathe new life into old tales by creating bold and striking images for them.

Snapshots

- Get into groups of four and without any preparation form yourselves into a snapshot of scenes suggested by the teacher/ director, such as a forest, a boat, a happy house, an evil castle. Think about the noises you might hear in each place.
- When you have made your frozen picture, hold it still. If you have trouble doing this, remember how you froze every time grandmother turned around in 'Grandmother's footsteps.' Use your whole body, including your facial expression, to make the snapshot. Try things out without discussing them with the others in the group.
- Now make snapshots related to the objects and images of *Little Red-Cap* (a wood, a path, a tree, a grove of flowers, a woman in bed, a wolf in bed, a wolf's pelt).

Illustrating a story

- Tell a story – what you did on the weekend, for example – while others act it out. This requires fast action and spontaneity. 'Actors' will have to become parents or friends or animals or strangers as they are introduced to the story. The group might work together to represent a storm, for example, or traffic, or a crowd in a street. The unrehearsed nature of the exercise is part of its fun. Whenever the leader claps, freeze the image.
- Now try the same thing with *Little Red-Cap*, focusing on the sequence in which the wolf gobbles the Grandmother and then answers Red-Cap's questions before eating her. Some of you will need to become a bed; others curtains, pillows, a front-door; whatever the story requires at the moment it is needed. There is no right or wrong way of carrying out this exercise; just try to use your body inventively and suggestively.

Transformations

There are numerous transformations in the *Grimm Tales*: the prince transforms himself into a dove and a lion in *The Lady and the Lion*; Rumpelstiltskin spins straw into gold. Even Ashputtel's shift from grimy servant to beautiful princess is a transformation, as is the Wolf's disguising himself as the grandmother.

- Sit in a circle. Think of an object (a rabbit, a hot potato, a wasp) and then mime using or holding the object.
- Now pass it to the next person who must also mime using or holding it. Pass it right round the circle. Now transform the object into something else (a pen, a flea, a palmful of mercury), and pass it round again, and so on.

Newspaper animation

This exercise transforms an inanimate object into an animate one, and is beautiful to watch.

- Sit in front of a single sheet from a broadsheet newspaper. Look at the newspaper. Concentrate on it. Imagine the newspaper is not a newspaper but is a living thing. Watch it. Imagine it is breathing. Pinch up the centre or lift up the edges of the paper to make it breathe. Move it slowly up and down as it breathes in and out.
- Focus on the paper. It is a living creature. Start to find a shape for it. Let its character emerge as it breathes in and out. You might crumple the paper into a more solid shape or fold it, twist it, or let it float as you look for the shape and structure of its body.
- Think of its body having weight and mass, and being pulled to earth by gravity. How does it stand or move on the floor? Make it move. Let it explore the space around you.
- Bring it towards another paper-creature. How do the two creatures greet one another? Is your creature shy or bold? Does it move lightly or heavily? Does it have legs or does it slide on its belly? What is its name?
- Now imagine it is Red-Cap's grandmother. Make any alterations you need to transform your creature into an old, frail woman. Lay her down gently in her bed.

More transformations

Look at these moments of transformation from *Grimm Tales*. The first is from *Ashputtel*, and describes the death of Ashputtel's mother:

"My darling girl, always try to be good, like you are now, and say your prayers. Then God will look after you, and I will look down at you from Heaven and protect you."

When she'd said these words, she closed her loving eyes and died. The young girl went out every day to cry beside her mother's grave. When winter came, the snow put down a white shroud on the grave, and when the sun took it off again in the spring, the girl's father re-married.

Here the transformation is caused by time. The story jumps suddenly ahead in time to a new season (winter to spring) and introduces a new stepmother for Ashputtel.

The second transformation takes place in *The Golden Goose*. The woodcutter's son Dummling has been given the magic goose as a reward for sharing his food with a stranger. He stays at an inn where the innkeeper's daughters try to steal its golden feathers but find themselves stuck fast to the goose:

As soon as Dummling had gone to sleep, she grabbed the goose by its wing. But her fingers and hand stuck to the goose like glue.

Soon afterwards, the second sister came along with exactly the same bright idea of plucking out a golden feather all for herself. But no sooner had she touched her older sister than she was stuck to her.

- Create frozen pictures to describe these moments of trans-formation. You can be an animal or an object as well as a person. Try to show in your face and actions how you feel.
- Try out some other instant changes (for example, from a frog to a prince and back again; from a baby to an old woman) and some more gradual ones (Little Red-Cap and her Grandmother being pulled from the belly of the wolf).

Transforming objects

The aim of this exercise is to stimulate the participants' natural creativity and resourcefulness by encouraging them to use simple objects to represent other things.

- Pass round a tea towel and see how many things the group can make from it or what ideas they can generate with it. It might, for example, become a turban or a matador's cape. It might be laid on the ground to represent a swimming pool or a deep hole. It might be a beach towel or a trapdoor. How could you use a tea towel to suggest some of the objects or events in *Little Red-Cap*? It might become Little Red-Cap's hood, for example, or her apron. It might wrap the wine and cake. It might be a pathway, a wolf's tail, a bunch of flowers, a door, a grandmother's nightcap, a curtain, etc.
- Try this with other objects: a pen (which could become a snake, a fish-hook, a rocket, a nail, a bridge), a shoe, a chair. Try to find an action which will help the audience to understand what the object has become; e.g. if the chair becomes a horse, you could lift up its hoofs, hold its head still, or jump back as it delivers a heap of manure.

Spells

Magic and enchantment often feature in children's stories; with magic anything is possible and the familiar world can suddenly become unfamiliar and often dangerous. There are many magical moments in the Grimm stories: the appearance of the dresses in *Ashputtel* ('the white bird threw down a golden and silver dress and a pair of slippers embroidered in silk and silver'); the boy's hair turning gold when dipped in the magic well in *Iron Hans*; the 'little grey man' causing the woodcutter's sons to injure themselves in *The Golden Goose*. There are no spells in *Little Red-Cap*, but Red-Cap's transformation into a beautiful girl when she wears her hat, her encounter with the Wolf and her restoration from the Wolf's belly have a magical quality to them.

What are some other examples of magic spells and enchantment in stories?

- Create your own spell that transforms something into something else (a person to a lizard; a shoe to a bird, etc). Devise a spell and say it out loud while someone else demonstrates the transformation.

Character in stories

Even in a very simple story you can add plenty of physical detail to the performance of your character and so give the story colour, originality and vitality.

Character description

- As a group, read the text of *Little Red-Cap*, pausing to make a gesture for each word or action that describes Red-Cap; for example 'loved by everyone', 'tender', 'surprised', 'felt very strange', 'nervous', 'frightened', 'delighted'. Don't try to act out or simply illustrate; say each word aloud and concentrate on what it suggests, what atmosphere it creates.
- Now do the same for the Wolf: 'wicked', 'wily', 'leapt', 'gobbled', 'crawled', 'gobbles', 'sinner'.
- Do the same for the Grandmother: 'always wondering what treat to give', 'poorly', 'a bit weak', 'hardly breathing', 'much better'.

Improvisation with cards

Improvisation is one of the core skills of an actor, though some training and rehearsal methods place greater emphasis on it than others. It is a very good way of helping children develop the skills they will use in performance, and it taps into their natural creativity and tendency towards complex role-play. If they have never improvised before, children may at first be shy or uncertain about their ideas. The main purpose is to encourage them to work as a team, to be open to everyone's ideas and to work with them. Some of these exercises are challenging and can be useful source material for secondary-age students as well as primary. It is helpful to provide them with basic structures to work with. An improvisation needs:

- A beginning (the situation)
- A middle (the complication or interruption)
- An end (the solution)

Participants need to know who they are, where they are and what is happening.

- Work in pairs or groups. Use cards to indicate character, location and action. Give each person a character card, and then give the whole group one location and one action card. The group should discuss the scene for a few minutes before acting it out. You can bring together characters from different stories. The aim is to have fun with the unlikely situations that the cards create. Grimm cards could include:

  Character – Little Red-Cap, the Wolf, Grandmother, Mother, Huntsman

  Location – pathway, wood, deep in the wood, Grandmother's house, Grandmother's garden;

  Action – Red-Cap's mother gives her a basket of cakes and wine; Red-Cap wanders along the path; Red-Cap meets the Wolf; the Wolf convinces Red-Cap to pick flowers deep in the forest; the Wolf gobbles Grandmother; Red-Cap hurries to Grandmother's house; Red-Cap is nervous as she enters Grandmother's house; Red-Cap questions the Wolf; the Wolf eats Red-Cap; the Huntsman hears snoring; the Huntsman snips open the belly of the sleeping Wolf; Red-Cap and Grandmother emerge from the Wolf's belly; Red-Cap, Grandmother and the Huntsman fill the Wolf's belly with stones; the Wolf dies; everyone celebrates; Grandmother eats the cake and drinks the wine.

- If your character isn't directly involved in the action described, try to imagine and demonstrate what he/she might be doing at this point in the story. While Red-Cap is being eaten by the wolf, her mother might be making soup, or drinking tea in a wicker chair.

- As the game continues, you can add other categories such as emotions or character traits to build up a more detailed picture. Or you might choose your own character and then be given a location and action to work with.

Points of view and audiences

- Tell the story of Little Red Cap from the points of view of the different characters in the story. Imagine the characters are telling the story to their friends, in private. Would they tell it differently? Would Red-Cap try to make herself seem brave? Or might she admit that she was very frightened? How might her mother describe the events of the day to her friends at work? Is she angry with Red-Cap for talking to the Wolf? Imagine the huntsman is with his mates at the pub. What sort of language would he use to talk about his adventure with the Wolf?

Each volunteer should try to put him/herself in the shoes of the character he/she is speaking for, and think also of the listeners (school friends, work colleagues, mates in the pub). We tell stories in different ways to different people. To make the story come alive, we have to climb inside the characters, just as the Wolf climbs into the clothing of Red-Cap's grandmother. When characters speak directly to one another, a story may become more immediate and vivid. But narrators who stand outside the story are free to move around in time and space and follow any character they please. Which kind of story-telling do you find most immediate and interesting? Many fairy and folk tales combine third-person narration and direct speech to make them seem at once strange and magical and very much alive.

Staging the world of the story

You can add another dimension to your story by creating a strong sense of its location and atmosphere. Fairy and folk tales often have magical or other-worldly settings. Using the simplest of objects and the most expressive tool of all – your body – you can generate an unforgettable sense of place and context, adding movement, sound, light, colour and physical detail to the words of the story.

Imagining yourself in a space

- Stand individually or in groups of two or three. Spread out around the room, and think of where you are and what it feels like. Is it hot or cold, stuffy or airy in the room? Can you see others standing around you? Are you relaxed, itchy, sleepy?
- Now imagine you are standing on a narrow ledge on the summit of a very high mountain. How do you stand? If anyone is beside you, do you hang on to that person? How do you breathe? What do you see? Are you exhilarated or terrified?

- Now imagine you are in a lift which has broken down. What does it feel like? Are you able to move around the space? Do you panic? Do you stay very still?
- Now imagine you're alone in a vast empty desert. What does it feel like to be in this gigantic space? Is it hot or cold? Day or night? Are you thirsty? Are there rattlesnakes?
- Finally, imagine your bed is Grandmother's bed in *Little Red-Cap*. Imagine the size and width of the bed. Does it have thin blankets or a fluffy duvet? Are the mattress and the pillow hard or soft? Are there flowers in the room? What else can you see in Grandmother's room?

Actions for places

- One person leaves the room. The rest of the group thinks of a location from the *Grimm Tales*. Each person must think of an action appropriate for the chosen location. Don't discuss your ideas with anyone else – perform the action silently. Be as simple and precise as possible in your movements.
- The volunteer returns and must guess where you are. Then the volunteer tries to identify what each of you is doing in that location. Are some actions more suggestive and characteristic than others? Pinpoint those actions – they may not be the most obvious ones.

Creating an environment

Look at how Carol Ann Duffy begins the story of Hansel and Gretel:

FATHER: It was no more than once-upon-a-time when a poor woodcutter lived in a small house at the edge of a huge, dark forest. Now, the woodcutter lived with his wife and his two young children – a boy called Hansel and a little girl called Gretel. It was hard enough for him to feed them all at the best of times – but these were the worst of times; times of famine and hunger and starvation; and the woodcutter was lucky if he could get his hands on even a simple loaf of bread. Night after hungry night, he lay in his bed next to his thin wife, and he worried so much that he tossed and he turned and he sighed and he mumbled and moaned and he just couldn't sleep at all.

"Wife, wife, wife. What are we going to do? How can we feed our two poor children when we've hardly enough for ourselves? Wife, wife, wife, what can be done?"

And as he fretted and sweated in the darkness, back came the bony voice of his wife; a voice as fierce as famine.

MOTHER: "Listen to me, husband. Tomorrow at first light we'll take the children into the forest, right into the cold, black heart of it. We'll make a fire for them there and give them each one last morsel of bread. Then we'll pretend to go off to our work and we'll leave them there all by themselves. They'll never be able to find their way back home on their own. We'll be rid of them for good and only have to worry about feeding ourselves."

Look at the words used to create the atmosphere at the opening of the story: 'poor', 'small', 'huge', 'dark', 'little', 'famine', 'hunger', 'starvation', 'bony', 'fierce', 'cold', 'black'. The story immediately establishes a strong sense of mood and place – the setting for Hansel and Gretel's frightening adventure in the witch's house.

- In small groups, take a typical fairy-story location such as the wood in *Little Red-Cap*, a castle, the witch's house in *Hansel and Gretel,* and try to create a physical image of that environment. Don't present moments from the story but concentrate on showing the location and trying to express the feeling of the place.

  You might do this by representing trees, animals, birds, a woodcutter, etc., and by making atmospheric or specific noises. Try to express the mood of the place in the way you move your body or the position you stand in (is the wood sunny and cheerful or dark and frightening? Are there statues in the castle? Are there rats and scuttling things? Is the wind blowing? Do doors creak, or is it deathly quiet?).

- When you have created the environment, bring someone from another group into it. What effect does it have on this visitor? Is he frightened, careless, angry, lonely, confused? What does he do when he enters the scene? How does he move (cautiously, confidently, aggressively)? The way we feel about places affects everything from our facial expression to the way we move and speak. How does he say, 'Hello? Is anybody there?'

Marking out a journey

- Tell the story of *Hansel and Gretel* or *Little Red-Cap* in your own words. As you do this, others should mark out the different places that are encountered in it; e.g. arrange around the room whatever objects are at hand to represent the pathway, the forest, the Grandmother's house. The storyteller should lead the listener to them as the story progresses. The aim is to create each environment as convincingly and atmospherically as possible before moving on to the next.
- As we come to each new environment, describe it to the group so they get a vivid sense of it. What does it feel like to be in each of these places? The woods beyond the path are sunny and full of flowers. What is it like in the deep wood, where the sunlight hardly penetrates, and where things with no names rustle among the leaves? When she arrives at her grandmother's house, Little Red-Cap feels nervous and strange. Describe the atmosphere when she enters the house. Is it silent? Does she hear a clock ticking? Is someone breathing? Is there an unusual smell in the house? Try to engage all of our senses.
- As a group, walk around in each of the story's environments, and try to imagine what each feels like to Little Red-Cap.

Using sounds to create atmosphere

- Tell the story of Little Red-Cap with sound effects. The rest of the class divides into three groups (or 'orchestras') and one person will be a conductor.
- Each group finds a sound they will use to accompany the story (an atmospheric whistling like the wind in trees, or creaking doors, or an effect made by clapping, or stamping, or making sounds with whatever is in the room – chairs, radiators, etc.). During the telling, the conductor points at the group when he wants their sound effect – he can instruct them to make the sound louder or softer, and he can bring in more than one sound at a time.
- How does using sound change your response to the story? What effect does changing the volume have? Sometimes a

very low sound under the telling of part of a story might increase the suspense, especially if it culminates in a sudden eruption of loud noise. Horror films use music very effectively in this way.

When Tim Supple's company improvised the Grimm stories, using props and sound effects, 'these improvisations started as quite extravagant affairs, with a profusion of billowing walls of silk and scattered flowers and sweeping movements across the space'. But when the company went into schools as part of the work-shop/rehearsal process, they were forced to abandon complex props and gadgets. As a result, the improvisations 'became simpler and clearer, and the heavy-handed symbolism that they were sometimes embellished with fell away'. The method of story-telling generated immediacy, simplicity and focus. The actors followed the principles defined by Brook in his account of 'Rough' theatre, which grows out of 'trial and error, search, elaboration, rejection and chance'. The influence of Theatre de Complicite was also apparent in the minimalism and inventiveness of the work; the company used simple, adaptable props, mime, acrobatics, gesture, song and puppetry. The stripped-down aesthetic imposed by working in classrooms was carried back to the auditorium, so that nothing was wasted, nothing was simply brandished for effect. As set designer Ian MacNeil has pointed out, 'God makes trees and he makes them better than we can so there is no point in shoving a real tree on stage, and theatre is an artificial environment and you have to find a way to acknowledge that.'

When the children themselves created their own dramatised versions of the stories or parts of the stories, actor Dan Milne saw that 'the way they brought them to life often told you a lot about what was important to them about the character and how they responded to it'.

The responses of children also offered insight into what characters frightened, intrigued or amused them; what form of narration best suited each story (i.e. whether a narrator should be employed or whether one or more of the characters should deliver the narrative to make it more immediate); how the stories should be paced, expanded, pitched and structured. Dan Milne recalls that the young people 'would start to show us just in the way that they listened or in the way that they talked about something afterwards – what they said they remembered, liked or didn't like, or what they wanted to investigate further. We'd say to each other afterwards, "Well, they all switched off during the third spinning of the straw," or whatever. So that would get us thinking about how to represent that moment better.'

These workshop/rehearsal sessions were based on creative exchanges and simple presentations of actions and images. Composer Adrian Lee improvised live with musical instruments from around the world and Melly Still used the sessions to inform and inspire her own design for the production. Head teacher Ros Lines sat in on the sessions and immediately saw the value of bringing the children into direct contact with professional actors: 'One moment they were just ordinary people in street clothes talking with us – and then suddenly they were involved in telling this story, suddenly they had transformed into these characters. It struck all of us, seeing the way they transformed themselves like that. I remember on the way back to school all the children were really quiet, really quiet because they felt satisfied, as if they had had a good meal.'

'What I was hoping to get out of the work with young people during the rehearsals of *Grimm Tales*,' said Supple, 'was to make the actors more brave and to make the work that we did more simple and more responsive to its audience.' Using their bodies, their imaginations and the available materials, the actors led the children to recognise the transformative power of the imagination. Melly Still felt 'the Grimm experience with young people was very playful; the idea of using a small amount of objects that were very real but could also be used to create special things that were beyond their own life is very true to theatre – so that you have a stick and it can be a snake or a wand or a sword . . . You have a bucket and you can sit on it or you can play on it like a drum, or it can become a kind of precious golden object.

'We would look at a moment where, for instance, Hansel and Gretel had to cross a river on a duck and we wouldn't have a duck or a river – so the children would make one up. There was a girl who had a cloth wrapped around her head which we used as water and someone curled up under it to be a stone and then they created a boat, using someone's leg as an oar. And I remember another moment where a character was fighting with a lion, and one girl took off her hairgrip and put it in her mouth to create these long, jagged teeth and then she used this massive comb as the claws.'

The simplest solutions always proved to be the most striking. For example, when the actors looked for a way to dramatise the plucking out of the eyes of Ashputtel's cruel sisters, they experimented with a number of gory devices, as the scene seemed to dictate:

ELDER: As the bridal procession was entering the church, the eldest sister was on the right
YOUNGER: and the younger was on the left; and the two doves flew at each of them and pecked out one of her eyes.
ELDER: And as they were all coming out of the church, the elder sister was on the left
YOUNGER: and the younger on the right
ELDER: and the doves swooped again and pecked out their other eyes.

Eventually, however, the company settled on ping-pong balls and red elastic bands to represent the tearing out of the sisters' eyes. The effect was theatrical and direct, and the children were thrilled. In the production, Linda Kerr Scott donned gloves with giant fingernails as the Wicked Witch in *Ashputtel*; these poked up through the floor as she died screaming. Kerr Scott put a simple white glove on her chin to become a goat in *The Magic Table, the Gold Donkey and the Cudgel in the Sack*. And the eating of Red-Cap's grandmother by the Wolf involved nothing more than the Grandmother crouching down between the Wolf's legs and being wrapped in his shaggy fur. Melly Still watched him from the audience: 'He was wearing that grey underwear, those long johns, and those big boots. I remember that my three-year-old daughter's heart just started pumping really quickly at that moment – because it was so devastating.'

'What marks it out as a landmark event,' critic Irving Wardle commented, 'is its treatment of the audience as equals in a shared act of imagination. What happens on the stage is a starting point for you to complete in your head . . . A loop of string narrows around the children, light thickens, and you see them straying into the depth of the forest. A duck takes them over the river: enter an actor in a bowler hat, pulling a hand-cart.' The production incorporated many elements first identified and developed during the workshops and schools' visits: 'A few domestic objects – buckets, a knife, a blanket, a plate, a jug, an axe, create both the house and the forest and appear in the witch's house' (Melly Still, on *Hansel and Gretel*). The set for the production combined earth and wood and created a simple pathway for the play's numerous journeys. It became a space where 'rare, strange and magical events can take place'.

The result was 'the best demonstration all year of the living power of theatre, the children squealed with delight and so did I' (*Observer*). Marina Warner was struck by the enthusiasm and engagement of the children in the audience: 'When the actors hurled food (imaginary) from the magic table where they were feasting, the children caught it and ate it, and sometimes gamely threw it back.' Poet Laureate Ted Hughes praised Tim Supple for bringing 'a new kind of stage imagination' to his production of *Grimm Tales*. The stories, he felt, were 'astonishing pieces of theatrical invention – demonic, delicate, with a great range of effects'. In essence, Supple and his team had simply acknowledged that an old kind of imagination – that of the traditional story-teller – could be as potent in its simplicity as any highly technical modern approach. He recognised that the first and primary audience for good stories, well told, is children, and that their imaginations can feed the process of theatrical invention.

Chapter 4

POETRY AND LANGUAGE – DOCTOR FAUSTUS

You find iambic pentameter on the lips of people the whole time.
And I love listening on trains to people speaking unconsciously in a
meter that's natural to English speech.

Tony Harrison

Christopher Marlowe's 1588 tale of a scholar seduced into selling his soul to the devil in return for twenty-four years of power and fame is described by critic Paul Taylor as a 'highly-charged, broken-backed and compellingly weird Elizabethan play'. Its author died at twenty-nine, stabbed in the eye in a Deptford brawl in 1593. Rumour and speculation surround Marlowe's short, eventful life. He was variously described as an atheist, an anti-Catholic spy, a homosexual, a subversive and a blasphemer.

The play is based on the real-life story of Doctor Johann Faust, a calendar-maker in Heidelberg in the early sixteenth century, who claimed magical powers and called himself 'the prince of necromancers'. His exploits were recorded in a German 'biography' known as the *Faustbuch* in 1587. The story survived in puppet and pantomime versions, and was rediscovered in Goethe's *Faust* in the nineteenth century, and in Thomas Mann's twentieth-century novel, *Dr Faustus*.

Marlowe's Faustus is a renowned scholar and theologian, who, bored by his studies, and urged on by his peers, uses necromancy to summon spirits who will 'fetch me what I please'. His arrogant act unleashes Lucifer's agent Mephistophilis, who convinces Faustus to sign away his eternal soul in exchange for a period of power and pleasure. When he tries to repent, Mephistophilis distracts him with promises of wealth and diverts him with a pageant of Seven Deadly Sins.

Puffed up by his power and his growing reputation as a magician, Faustus scales Mount Olympus in a chariot drawn by dragons; he confounds the corrupt justice of the Pope, dines with

Emperor Charles V, plays cruel tricks on a simple horse-courser and makes ripe grapes appear in the dead of winter to satisfy a pregnant noblewoman's cravings. At the urging of a group of scholars, he summons Helen of Troy from the dead. But too soon the hour of his appointed end draws near and Faustus realises with horror the enormity of his fate. Accompanied by Lucifer, Beelzebub and a gloating Mephistophilis, and by the prayers of the helpless scholars, he is dragged to the 'vast perpetual torture house' of hell.

The Young Vic's 2002 production of the play, directed by David Lan, sought to illuminate the complex and contradictory character of Marlowe's anti-hero Faustus, harnessing the energy of his bold, magnificent language to vigorous dramatic action and stark, suggestive staging. The 'irresistibly modern' production combined energy and theatricality, irony, knockabout comedy and a sense of physical (and moral) precariousness. Alongside the Main Stage production, assistant director Titania Krimpas rehearsed and presented *The Fall* in the Young Vic Studio, a young people's hour-long version of the original, which focused on the downfall of Faustus and the physical representation of good and evil. Krimpas's adaptation stripped the play to its essential and most striking action while retaining its muscular dialogue and poetry to create a large-cast ensemble piece with driving momentum. Many of the same questions were explored in both rehearsal processes and the director was encouraged to develop ideas and probe issues of dramatisation encountered in the main house rehearsal. The work with young people took place in the context of a professional production, assisted by professional designers and technicians, and it was a fertile training ground for both the participants and the director. Both companies sought simple solutions to the questions raised by the play (such as: How can angels and devils be depicted on stage? How do actors find their way into the language of the play, in order to unpick the complexities of its characterisation? How can the different forms of evil be dramatised?).

Doctor Faustus has all the urgency, curiosity and ambition of a young man's play. It satirises authority, through the pretensions of academics and the Catholic Church, and places Faustus at the centre of his own world. The play gathers new meaning for each age and each new generation. For some Faustus is the ultimate consumer, driven by greed and a hunger for fame to a point of no return, where he looks into the abyss and finally realises the terrible consequences of his actions and discovers the literal reality of hell. Lan stressed the play's timelessness, and its continuing relevance, by combining elements of Elizabethan costume with modern dress in a simple, unadorned set. And he set up an ironic play of ideas about the price of fame by casting international star Jude Law as Faustus.

Though *Doctor Faustus* is a complex and challenging play, its Elizabethan language is unexpectedly direct and accessible. Its exploration of good and evil and the price of fame and greed are as relevant to contemporary audiences as they were to Marlowe's audience, and Faustus' relationship with Mephistophilis provides rich material for the dramatic exploration of notions of friendship, betrayal, seduction, manipulation and suffering. Investigation of the play in workshops and rehearsals sought to open up the implications of Marlowe's dramatic language by anchoring it to the play's world and finding concrete images to embody its abstract ideas.

The context of the play

David Lan describes *Doctor Faustus* as 'a play about people trying to work out what it is to be a human being'. The sixteenth century inherited from the medieval world a coherent system of beliefs in which the universe, the earth and man were indissolubly linked. Everything in the universe was thought to hold an established place or degree, from the four physical elements to divine creatures such as angels. Man's place in this natural order was lowly; full of sin, he was expected to suffer life on earth and remain subordinate to God's will. But new ideas had begun to take hold during the fifteenth and sixteenth centuries. The Reformation, along with the spread of humanism which accompanied the Renaissance rediscovery of influential classical texts, fostered a spirit of enquiry which placed man at the centre of his world and emphasised the value of his experience in this life, rather than the next one.

Marlowe's scorn for Catholicism is reflected in his representation of the Pope as a scheming and acquisitive powermonger (Lan emphasised the mockery of Rome by having a Pope Joan figure clamber gracelessly atop a rickety throne of tables and chairs). On the Continent, Protestant reformer Martin Luther advocated a personal relationship with God, unmediated by the rituals of the Roman Church. Like the scholars, rulers and servants around him, Faustus tries to understand and master his world on his own terms, not those of the Church. Unlike them, though, he (mis)uses the tools of science and magic to bypass theology and find short cuts to ultimate knowledge.

Faustus' attitude to scientific discovery is revolutionary and exciting in its curiosity and its resistance to blind faith. Traditional cosmology placed the earth at the centre of the universe, surrounded by a series of crystalline spheres in which the sun, stars and planets were fixed. Faustus, responding to the discoveries of Galileo and Copernicus, has the temerity to question this divine order, and demands to know of Mephistophilis, 'Are there many spheres above the Moon? / Are all celestial bodies but one globe / As is the substance of this centric earth?'

In his understanding of natural philosophy, by contrast, Faustus' views are more traditional, though his hunger for further knowledge is insatiable. He has inherited a belief that the universe itself is alive and peopled with spirits. Magicians were thought able to tap the influence of the stars and divert it to other purposes, employing the hidden properties of material phenomena for their own use. They were considered scholars, though their means were dangerous and might bring them into contact with the devil. A number of stories were recorded throughout the sixteenth and seventeenth centuries of individuals who sold their souls to the devil and met with terrible ends. Doctors' casebooks record patients being troubled by visits from the devil – often in the form of a black dog, an owl, a bear, a fiend, and sometimes in the shape of a well-dressed and charming man.

A Good Angel pleads with Faustus to 'lay that damned book aside / And gaze not on it lest it tempt thy soul / And heap God's heavy wrath upon thy head. / Read, read the scriptures. That is blasphemy.' But its evil counterpart tempts him with the opposing view, encouraging him to 'Go forward . . . in that famous art / Wherein all nature's treasury is contained.' Faustus stands at the core of a dilemma for scientists of his generation: whether to risk God's wrath by investigating His creation too minutely, or to use advances in science and technology to pursue the humanist hunger for knowledge and self-advancement.

The tension between good and evil in *Doctor Faustus* points to the play's origins in the early modern morality play. Morality plays are a transitional form between medieval mystery plays, drawn exclusively from the Bible, and more modern secular drama. They were popular in the fifteenth and sixteenth centuries, and then died away. In the morality play, a central character represents humanity and begins in a state of innocence, before encountering figures of temptation in the form of vices or the devil. The Everyman figure inevitably falls but is redeemed by God's grace. Despite their serious message, the plays often used earthy humour and bawdy scenes. Marlowe's Good and Evil Angels, like his Seven Deadly Sins, are drawn directly from the morality tale, as is the clowning comedy of the scenes between the servants Robin and Wagner. Lan found the play much funnier than he had expected: 'It has much more wit built into it not only in what people say but also in the structure of the play in terms of what scenes follow each other.'

In Faustus and Mephistophilis, however, Marlowe presents complex psychological portraits of convincingly contradictory characters. Faustus is not an innocent Everyman to begin with, but a talented intellectual swollen with ambition and desire, while Mephistophilis is not merely a figure of temptation, but a tortured and bitter anti-hero. Marlowe's interest in the psychology of his characters and in the tragic figure of the over-reacher looks towards his contemporary Shakespeare, who was born in the same year (the poet Tennyson saw Marlowe as the 'morning star' to Shakespeare's 'dazzling sun'). The relationship between Faustus and Mephistophilis – like the issues of temptation, ambition, rebelliousness, desire and sin which it fleshes out – has a compelling contemporary edge, which provides rich material for investigative work on the play and its staging. The play's robust and forceful language, far from obscuring its meanings, is a tool with which to open up and inhabit Faustus' strange and compelling world.

The rehearsal work for the young people's production of *Doctor Faustus* builds on the language work associated with *Grimm Tales* and incorporates precise movement and detailed explorations of character and context to build up a convincing sense of the world of the play. These exercises and explorations could be adapted to any classical play which might at first seem remote, archaic, or difficult to access. The key is to give real substance to the ideas behind the language – to build confidence in interpreting and speaking it. By concentrating on individual thoughts – breaking down passages of poetry or prose into their component parts and finding images for each – it is possible to lay claim to the underlying and recognisable emotions and intentions behind them. As Barbara Houseman points out, the way into Shakespeare and his contemporaries is through a recognition that the plays are really concerned with basic human emotions, 'love, hate, doubt, ambition, pride, greed, etc.'.

Much of *Doctor Faustus* is written in unrhymed iambic pentameter verse. Aristotle noted that this metre (with five stressed syllables in each line) resembled the rhythm of natural human speech while being suited to the nobility of tragedy. Marlowe proved this to be as true of early modern English as it was of ancient Greek. Marlowe adapts the form (moving from verse to prose) to suit the character or the context; when he uses rhyme he does so selectively, for emphasis or contrast. An understanding of how language *works* in classical drama offers a direct pathway to characterisation and meaning in performance. Actor Dorian Healy claims that gaining verbal command over a play is like 'breaking the combination to a safe'. And despite the elegance and weightiness of the verse, David Lan also found a 'very unusual conversational tone' in the play, which draws the audience into its profound questioning of the limits of human knowledge. His adaptation combined elements of the two existing versions of the play (published in 1604 and 1616), and in places cut or compressed the text to accentuate the strength and plainness of the language and the simplicity and power of the action.

In Lan's production the actors spent most of the first week of rehearsals reading the text of the play, stopping to clarify or discuss ideas in an attempt to pin down meaning and suggestions. Lan considers that there is a 'hidden play' within every play, and that it is the responsibility of the director, through the actors, to uncover and present that meaning. In the young people's production, the strategy throughout was to work with self-contained passages of text and identify crucial ideas and images which could be used to inform the rest of the work.

Voice, language and text exercises

The following exercises are based on the idea that dramatic language in general, and classical language in particular, can be lifted off the page through a few simple techniques, and used as a tool for exploring character, imagery and ideas in the play. The aim is to make the language active and give the actors a physical connection to the words. Some of the work which follows draws on the influential voice and text exercises of Barbara Houseman. Houseman, who worked at the Young Vic with Tim Supple and was senior voice coach at the Royal Shakespeare Company, points out that if actors speak classical language aloud 'word by word, phrase by phrase or line by line – while moving across the space or making big physical gestures, the text begins to seep into them and feel less strange and incomprehensible.' These exercises are more suited to secondary-age students but can be adapted for sessions with primary school participants. They apply to all dramatic texts – not just to Renaissance drama – and to any workshop or rehearsal where the aim is to unlock the language and absorb it into the dramatic action.

Delivering words

- Stand with legs relaxed, looking at a point on the wall. With each out-breath, intone the numbers one to ten (like singing on a single note).
- Speak the following line, like the numbers above, in a single breath and on a single note:
  'Tis magic, magic that hath ravished me. (I.1)
- Read the same line of text without sound but moving your mouth as precisely as possible. Now read the line aloud again. Are the words clearer and more distinct? Notice the feeling of the words in your mouth. Are they harsh or soft? Do they run quickly or slowly?

Marking words

Consider Faustus' words at the beginning of the play as he abandons his books of law, medicine, philosophy and divinity in favour of the study of magic:

> These metaphysics of magicians
> And necromantic books are heavenly.
> Lines, circles, scenes, letters and characters,
> Ay, these are those that Faustus most desires.
> O, what a world of profit and delight,
> Of power, of honour, of omnipotence
> Is promised to the studious artisan?
> All things that move between the quiet poles
> Shall be at my command. Emperors and kings
> Are but obeyed in their several provinces
> Nor can they raise the wind or rend the clouds
> But his dominion that exceeds in this
> Stretcheth as far as doth the mind of man.
> A sound magician is a mighty god.
> Here tire my brains to get a deity. (I.1)

- Read each sentence aloud from full stop to full stop. Note that some finish at the end of a line, and others halfway through a line; some are short and heavily stressed; others are longer and more complex. This is the architecture of the speech.
- Now get inside the sentences as though the passage is a room (Faustus' mind) full of individual objects. Find the nouns in each sentence, and hit, stamp or click your fingers on each one. Make a list:

metaphysics	delight	provinces
magicians	power	wind
book	honour	clouds
lines	omnipotence	dominion
circles	artisan	mind
scenes	things	man
letters	poles	magician
characters	command	god
world	emperors	brains
profit	kings	deity

These words represent the *matter* of the speech, and give an immediate insight into Faustus' character. Some refer to material things; others are abstract ideas, but they all have equal substance in Faustus' mind. His attention at the play's opening is on the practice of magic (the tools of his endeavour) and the power it grants the user (the fruits); his imagination ascends via kings to the skies and the heavens themselves. His ambition is immediately manifest.

- Now make a movement for the verbs or 'doing words', to get a sense of the actions implied in the speech: make a big gesture, than a small one, then whisper.

desires	rend
promised	exceeds
move	stretcheth
obeyed	tire
raise	get

All these words imply yearning and effort, and they indicate clearly the strength of Faustus' intention. This is how Faustus moves about in the 'room' of his imagination. Decide between you which of the words in the speech are the most important. Which tell us the most about Faustus at this point in the play? While someone reads the speech aloud, find actions for each of its verbs and try to express Faustus' striving.

- One person reads the passage aloud. The listeners repeat in a whisper any word which strikes them as interesting, strange or confusing.
- Now stand about the room and speak the lines together, shouting the most important words and taking a giant stride forward or throwing your arms wide as you say them (e.g. 'Magicians! Books! Heavenly! Lines! Circles! Desires! Profit! Delight! Power!' etc.).

Thought as movement

David Lan sees the words in a play as 'a consequence of an impulse'. In his production of *Dr Faustus* he worked with choreographer Kate Flatt, exploring the 'physical language' of the play to help him find the movement that expresses the impulse which in turn generates the word. The movements explored may or may not be incorporated into the final performance, but they help to give a sense of urgency and immediacy to the actor's delivery of the words. This exercise introduces the idea of the interrelatedness of thought and movement.

- Stand apart around the room. Walk forward, reading Faustus' following speech aloud (the punctuation of the speech is based on David Lan's edited version for production). With every full stop, stand still and change direction before walking forward again on the new thought. Each of the changes of direction corresponds to a shift of thought or mood in the speaker:

> Now, Faustus, must thou needs be damned
> And canst thou not be saved?
> What boots it then to think of God or heaven?
> Away with such vain fancies and despair.
> Despair in God and trust in Beelzebub.
> Now go not backward, no, Faustus. Be resolute.
> Why waver'st thou? O, something soundeth in mine ear.
> 'Abjure this magic. Turn to God again.'
> Ay, and Faustus will turn to God again.
> To God? He loves thee not. (II.1)

Faustus is struggling here with the realisation that he cannot ask for God's mercy. His indecision and uncertainty are reflected in the number of shifts of direction in his thinking (there are thirteen), which will be reflected in your movement around the room.

This exercise reveals attitudes and emotions which may at first be hidden behind the language. Look, for example, at Faustus' last words:

> It strikes! It strikes! Now, body, turn to air
> Or Lucifer will bear thee quick to hell.
> O soul, be changed into small water drops,
> And fall into the ocean, ne'er be found.
>
> *Thunder and enter devils.*

> My God, my God! Look not so fierce on me!
> Adders and serpents, let me breathe awhile!
> Ugly hell gape not! Come not, Lucifer!
> I'll burn my books! Ah, Mephistophilis! (V.2)

Faustus changes direction, or signals new thoughts, eleven times in this short, agonised passage.

- Repeat the exercise with this passage. When his mental agitation is expressed physically, Faustus' distress immediately becomes clear.

Speaking the metre

> It *strikes*!// It *strikes*!// Now, *bo*// dy, *turn*// to *air*
> Or *Lu*// ci*fer*// will *bear*// thee *quick*// to *hell*. (V.2)

Marlowe's use of iambic pentameter – an unaccented syllable ('It') followed by an accented syllable ('*strikes*') to make up five stresses or beats in each line – provides a clear and predictable rhythm for each line of verse which helps to break down the meaning of longer sentences and to focus on their strongest, most emphatic ideas and images. When speaking the verse, the accent falls naturally on the highlighted or significant syllables. The rhythm of a line of verse can be used as a valuable acting guide – the intentionally stressed words or parts of words are those which are most important in the speech.

- Read the passage above, clicking on unstressed and clapping on stressed syllables. The whole words which are emphasised are 'strikes!' 'strikes!' 'turn', 'air', 'bear', 'quick', 'hell'.

Faustus drives home the horror of the moment by stressing the chiming of the clock, his vain desire to become nothing, and his fear of being carried into hell. More verbs than nouns are emphasised in these lines; *active* words dominate, and so create a sense of movement, panic and change.

When first encountering a speech in blank or rhymed verse, it is helpful to break it down in this way, using the rhythm as a guide to the speaker's state of mind. When you become familiar with the workings of regular metre such as iambic pentameter, you will also become aware of interruptions to or distortions of the rhythm for the specific purpose of emphasising an important word or words. For example, look at the lines which follow Faustus' plea above:

> _Add_ers// and _serp_//ents, _let_// me _breathe_// a_while_!
> _Ug_ly/ _hell_ gape/ _not_!

- Read the lines aloud, clapping the rhythm. Note here that the emphasis falls, quite deliberately, on the first, not the customary second syllable of each line. Speak the stressed syllables emphatically but without shouting, until the images behind them seem vivid and tangible.

In these lines, Faustus forces us to focus on the words 'adders', 'serpents', 'ugly' and 'hell'. His mind is now full of the horror that awaits him, and his language reflects his feelings in its form.

In another example of unusual emphasis, Mephistophilis' description of the fallen angels repeatedly stresses the word 'Lucifer'. This repetition is unusual, and the threatening implication is clear:

> Unhap/py spi/rits that fell/ with _Lu/cifer_,
> Conspired/ against/ our God/ with _Lu/cifer_
> And are/ forev/er damned/ with _Lu/cifer_.

- Speak these lines aloud with five beats to each, but shout the word 'Lucifer'. Keep speaking them over and over, until the room is filled with the devil's name.

What is the effect of the repetition of Lucifer's name? It is similar to a religious chant or prayer, but Marlowe is describing hell, which is the inverse of heaven. The effect is ironic, insistent, and threatening. Lucifer's presence is growing as Faustus moves closer to his fall. Language and action constantly reinforce one another in classical drama.

Language and intention

Characters in plays _use_ words as tools to bring about their desires. Just like storytellers, they use words to achieve an outcome, to manipulate, inspire, woo, impress, reprimand, placate and frighten the listener(s). The language they wield can be turned into action as a way of making clear the speaker's intention. For further work on intention, see pp. 134–36 ('What you do to get what you want' and 'An improvisation on intention'), pp. 155–56 ('Intention to communicate'), and p. 167 ('Diary of a rehearsal').

- Think how you might try to convince someone to do some-thing – to give you something that belongs to her, for example. Try improvising a short scene, in pairs, in which A has something you want but refuses to give it to you. What strategy do you use to convince her to give it to you? Do you use a different tone of voice when trying to manipulate someone? Is there any particular gesture or facial expression you might employ to get your way? Try to convince your partner to give you the object. Then swap roles. As a group, identify the range of devices (verbal and physical) you have used.
- Consider a passage from later in the play, as Faustus approaches damnation:

> FAUSTUS: Is't not too late?
> EVIL ANGEL: Too late.
> GOOD ANGEL: Never too late if Faustus can repent.
> EVIL ANGEL: If thou repent, devils will tear thee in pieces.
> GOOD ANGEL: Repent and they will never raze thy skin.
> FAUSTUS: Ah, Christ my saviour,
> Seek to save distressed Faustus' soul. (II.3)

What strategies do the Angels use to try to convince Faustus? How do the Good and Evil Angels differ in their style of speech? In the imagery they use? In their attitude to Faustus? The Good Angel tries to coax Faustus to repentance, while the Evil Angel bluntly threatens him with the consequences of abandoning his course. How can coaxing and threatening be dramatised through the actions and expressions of the Angels?

- Act out the passage above, using your whole body to try to sway Faustus in one direction or the other.

Possessing the words

This exercise steers you towards confident ownership of the words of a speech.

- Read aloud the corrupt Pope's speech about power:

> Is not all power on earth bestowed on us?
> And therefore, though we could we cannot err.
> Behold this silver belt whereto is fixed
> Seven golden seals, fast sealed with seven seals
> In token of our seven-fold power from heaven
> To bind or loose, lock fast, condemn or judge,
> Resign or seal or whatsoe'er pleaseth us.
> Then he and thou and all the world shall stoop
> Or be assured that our most dreadful curse
> Will light as heavy as the pains of hell. (III.1)

- Intone the lines without allowing the voice to drop at the end of each line.
- Speak the words silently, and consider what feelings you have in response.
- Note the first and last words in each line. First words are often minor words which drive you forward to the main, stressed words. Final words are usually emphasised and contain important images and ideas ('us', 'fixed', 'heaven', 'judge', curse', 'hell').
- Beat out the rhythm as you speak the lines, noting which words are emphasised by the metre (for example, ideas and images associated with power and punishment).
- Find all the nouns in the passage, and find images for each of them.
- Find all the verbs and whisper the ones you think are most important.
- Find each of the three new thoughts/sentences in the passage. Practise saying each sentence without trailing off or losing the intention to communicate the thought.
- Try delivering the speech from a position of power and authority (e.g. standing on a chair or table). Does this help you with your delivery?

By the end of the exercise, all the words should have a powerful, personal meaning, and at this point you will really own the speech and be able to deliver it confidently and clearly.

Through language to character

Rehearsals are in some ways defined by the questions that need to be answered and the problems that need to be solved in order to deliver a clear and coherent interpretation to an audience. Once the mechanics of the language are understood, you can begin to incorporate it into an exploration of character and situation. Improvisation was central to David Lan's approach to the play, and formed a significant part of the work with young people in schools and on stage. Improvisation allows actors to discover their characters for themselves, and provides them with a range of approaches to developing character which can be used at different times and under different circumstances, and which help them to flesh out characters and to see the world from the character's perspective.

Director Titania Krimpas approached her shorter version of the play through its imagery, using stage 'pictures' as a way of breaking down the language into manageable units. Images are both external pictures and internal ideas. Encouraging young actors to develop personal responses by devising mental images of the characters and action helps them to take possession of the words they speak. (This approach is further developed in Chapter 7.) The company started by looking for 'tag lines' or touchstones within the play, which expressed in the simplest and most emphatic terms the reality of each character's situation. For example, Mephistophilis' line, 'Why this is hell, nor am I out of it', sums up his private torment and underlines his separation from the world. Likewise, his explanation for Lucifer's temptation of men is simply, 'Misery loves company.' This small phrase speaks volumes about Lucifer's nature.

Rehearsals of the young people's production took place twice a week over twelve weeks (and included a half-term week of daily rehearsal). They incorporated or adapted exercises used by the professional company. When a younger company attends professional rehearsals of the same play, they are often reassured to find that the problems they encounter in relation to language, characterisation and staging are also faced by their professional counterparts.

Character gesture

An introductory exercise.

- Give each participant a principal character from the cast list (Faustus, Mephistophilis, Lucifer, Wagner, Robin, Ralph, Good and Evil Angels, the Pope, the Horse-Courser).
- As you tell the story of the play, each person makes a 'characteristic' gesture for his/her character whenever the character is mentioned. The gestures might change as the story develops. Faustus' opening gesture, as in Lan's production, might be to throw away his books of divinity like a spoilt child. By the play's end it might be to try to ward off the devils as he feels the heat of hell on his face. Mephistophilis might arrange his bitter features into an impassive mask as he prepares to meet Faustus. Later, he might appear in triumphant majesty, towering and gloating. Each time the character is mentioned, the actor will redefine the gesture according to the circumstances.

Faustus

The central challenge in both productions was to find a means of access to the psychological drama of Faustus' fall. Jude Law was drawn to the 'huge questions' that Faustus' experience raises for both actor and director. 'I just saw a really exciting journey for an actor and exciting themes – rebelling against the institution, embracing the darker side of humankind, the balance that in life without bad there's no good.' Actor Richard McCabe describes Faustus' 'deep journey' as one of 'learning too late what it means to have a soul'.

In the opening scene, Faustus fretfully and petulantly discards his books ('Philosophy is odious and obscure. / Both law and physic are for petty wits. / Divinity is basest of the three, / Unpleasant, harsh, contemptible and vile. / 'Tis magic, magic that hath ravished me.') As his power grows, so does his pride, and he ignores the signs of his impending doom.

- Present a series of five tableaux or frozen pictures which show Faustus' journey through the play. They might include Faustus among the scholars, Faustus conjures Mephistophilis, Faustus signs away his soul, Faustus interrogates Mephistophilis about the universe, Faustus watches the pageant of the Seven Deadly Sins, Faustus torments the Pope, Faustus cheats the Horse-Courser, Faustus summons Helen of Troy, Faustus stands between the Good and Evil Angels, Faustus is dragged down to Hell.

David Lan looked for ways to represent the abstract idea of Faustus' pride on stage. His Faustus joins in during the Pageant of the Seven Deadly Sins, playing the role of Pride, and wearing a mask of his own face. When he summons Helen of Troy, it is not the legendary beauty whose face has launched a thousand ships that he sees, but his own visage in a mirror. Both images make the point clearly and wordlessly that Faustus' pride and ambition have blinded him to any knowledge or belief beyond himself. They also imply that Faustus' magical powers are merely illusory; he is, in a sense, in a room full of mirrors, conjuring nothing but himself over and over again.

Throughout the play, Faustus' urgent and restless action is contrasted with Mephistophilis' stillness, self-control and patience. Lan saw Faustus' journey as one of 'negative therapy'. The more his nature is revealed by Mephistophilis, the less he is able to determine his fate. His journey through the play is one of gradual loss of self.

Tug of war

Divide into two teams of equal size. On one side are those who support Faustus' desire to practice necromancy and deal with the devil, and on the other are those who oppose it. Choose a Faustus to stand between them on a line drawn on the floor.

Each of the teams takes hold of a length of rope. Faustus holds on to the rope at its mid-point and must not let go. Members of the teams try to entice Faustus to their side (or warn him off approaching the other side), as they pull on the rope and try to draw him across the line into one or other realm. There will be a lot of shouting and tugging. This game vividly demonstrates the opposing forces in Faustus' mind, and his inability to control the forces he has summoned.

Mephistophilis

In their rehearsal, the young people's company tried to find a way to represent Faustus' journey towards evil. They wanted to emphasise that though Faustus falls of his own free will, he is actively tempted by Mephistophilis. Krimpas decided to use women to play this fallen angel, emphasising the idea of seduction and temptation. But she wanted to suggest destructive power too. She drew on the image of the many-limbed Hindu goddess Kali, the destroyer. To develop a shared understanding of the image, she showed the cast pictures of Kali and played South Asian music and encouraged them to respond physically to it, moving together, beginning with hands and heads, and followed by the rest of the body. Finally, the three Kali actors chose their own movements and improvised ways of combining them as though they were part of a single, many-limbed body.

In David Lan's interpretation, Mephistophilis arrived on stage as a devil in a fierce red mask and was ordered by Faustus to reappear in a less threatening guise. He returned, apparently chastened, in a Franciscan friar's habit, looking innocuous, remaining still and quiet while Faustus moved about restlessly and impetuously. Richard McCabe, who played Mephistophilis in Lan's production, describes him as 'highly manipulative. On the surface he is very obedient and full of humility – he even seems a little feeble. But what he is doing is appealing to the overweening pride in Faustus.' McCabe played Mephistophilis as an amalgam of devils, but essentially as the 'thinking man's devil', relaxed, articulate, erudite on the surface; tormented, selfish and suffering within.

- Two actors, side by side, represent the two faces of Mephistophilis, as a) tempter and b) destroyer of Faustus. Make a cup of tea for Faustus. How does the 'civilised' and alluring Mephistophilis behave towards his guest? How does the unmasked devilish Mephistophilis perform the same action? (He might, for example, pour the scalding water directly onto Faustus' hand, or force him to drink cup after cup after cup until he is sick.) His actions should both express and produce torment.

The devil you know

How does Mephistophilis' behaviour towards Faustus change in the course of the play? In his first appearance, he claims to grieve at the loss of heaven, and begs Faustus to 'leave these frivolous demands, / Which strike a terror to my fainting soul' (I.3). Mephistophilis implies that Faustus is attempting something dangerous, and pretends to be frightened by the possibilities.

Next, Mephistophilis seduces Faustus into signing away his soul, playing down his power and wheedling, 'Tell me, Faustus, shall I have thy soul? / Then I will be thy slave and wait on thee' (II.1).

When the time comes for Faustus to offer up his soul, Mephistophilis drops the mask of friendship altogether and condemns the regretful scholar as a 'traitor', ordering him to 'Revolt or I'll in piecemeal tear thy flesh' (V.1).

- Now Mephistophilis' true self is revealed. Try to deliver this line with chilling authority.
- In pairs, choose one of these lines and present it to the group after a two-minute rehearsal. One of you plays Faustus and one plays Mephistophilis.
- Try to show Mephistophilis as either false friend or fiend. Imagine that Faustus has high status in the first encounter, even higher status in the second, and very low status in the third. Faustus' very low status makes Mephistophilis seem bigger than he is in the final lines. The actor playing Mephistophilis should stand tall, head held high, shoulders back. Throw your arms wide; express your power.

Lucifer

Traditionally, and in Milton's *Paradise Lost*, Lucifer is portrayed as a magnificent being – the King of Hell – once a bearer of light, whose beauty has now been lost for ever. He takes revenge on God by seducing God's creation – mankind – away from heaven. Lucifer is sometimes represented as a black goat – particularly in medieval and Renaissance images. In Lan's production, Lucifer

KINGSTON LEARNING RESOURCES CENTRE COLLEGE

was imagined as a huge fallen angel – a counterpart to Faustus, who also came too close to God. Mephistophilis describes him as 'Arch-regent and commander of all spirits'. He says Lucifer became prince of devils 'by aspiring pride and insolence, / For which God threw him from the face of heaven'.

- As a group, speak Lucifer's final lines to Faustus, when he appears from hell to claim the scholar's soul:

> Thus from infernal Dis do we ascend
> To view the subjects of our monarchy,
> Those souls which sin seals the black sons of hell
> 'Mong which as chief, Faustus, we come to thee
> Bringing with us lasting damnation
> To wait upon thy soul. The time is come
> Which makes it forfeit. (V.2)

- Find gestures to accompany Lucifer's speech. He is the most powerful fallen angel. How does he stand? How can you make your body seem bigger, stronger, more threatening? Emphasise the important words in the speech – use the five-beat metre to help you identify them ('infernal', 'Dis', 'ascend', 'subjects', 'monarchy', 'souls', 'sin', 'hell', 'chief', 'Faustus', 'damnation', 'soul', 'time', 'forfeit'). Speak the words clearly, loudly, forcefully; make them sound as hard as possible; stress the 's' sounds so that you are hissing the lines like a snake. Put as much power, hatred, vehemence and certainty as you can into the lines.

An improvised debate

Playing cards can be used in rehearsal to prescribe the actors' choices and so help them focus their imaginations on specific points or subjects. The subject under discussion here is whether or not Faustus should sell his soul to the devil for twenty-four years of power and glory.

- Give everyone a card (removing jacks, queens and kings from the pack). Red means you think Faustus should sell his soul; black means you are opposed to the idea. The higher the

Tom Wright directs young actors

Workshops on stage with young people

Stage configuration for *Monkey*

Jude Law as Dr Faustus

Lennie James in *A Raisin in the Sun*

Ruby Turner and Clive Rowe as Miss Marnie and Melon in *Simply Heavenly*

Michael Nardone in *Peribanez*

The set for *Peribanez*, designed by Ian MacNeil

number on the card, the more passionately you feel about saving or destroying Faustus' soul. For example, a ten of spades means you desperately want to stop Faustus from signing the pact with the devil, and you will do anything to protect him from harm. A two of hearts means you think he might as well sell his soul, but you don't care much either way.

- Go round the group. Each person should try to demonstrate what card he/she holds simply by the way he/she tries to persuade Faustus for or against the pact. The group should try to guess which card the person holds.

Temptation improvisation

- Use playing cards to set up an improvisation on temptation. Place an object in the centre of the room. Everyone takes a card, which determines how greatly they are tempted to possess the object. Imagine that it is something potentially dangerous (drugs, a gun, a nuclear weapon, a key to a safe, etc.).
- If your card is an ace or a 2, you might walk past the object and barely give it a second glance. If it is a 3 or a 4 you might slow down, turn towards it, look wistfully at it and consider it before moving on. A 5 or 6 would stop you in your tracks. You might pick the object up carefully, as though you were going to take it with you, and only relinquish it after holding it for a while. And so on, to 10, at which point nothing will stop you from possessing the object. One at a time, walk past the object and demonstrate the degree of temptation. Then tell the group your card number, who you are and what the object is. If you chose an ace, try to convince the holder of the highest card not to take the object.

Tableaux of heaven and hell

In his final moments on earth, hell is revealed to Faustus by an Evil Angel. His description is graphic, and recalls the paintings of Hieronymous Bosch:

> Now Faustus, let thine eyes with horror stare
> Into that vast perpetual torture-house.
> There are the furies, tossing damned souls

On burning forks. There bodies boil in lead.
There are live quarters broiling on the coals
That ne'er can die. This ever-burning chair
Is for o'er tortured souls to rest them in.
These that are fed with sops of flaming fire
Were gluttons and loved only delicates
And laughed to see the poor starve at their gates.
But yet all these are nothing. Thou shalt see
Ten thousand tortures that more horrid be. (V.2)

- Ask small groups to make tableaux or frozen pictures of heaven and hell. Examples of these might be 'a lazy day in heaven', 'my idea of hell', 'fallen angels'. You are looking for strong images and postures which convey a sense of paradise or torment.

In David Lan's production, at the moment when we expect Faustus to fall into hell, Mephistophilis simply hands him the book of knowledge for which he has sold his soul. The plain gesture makes clear what a little thing Faustus has got in exchange for such a vast and inexpressible loss. There is no attempt to find actions for the words; the point is that nothing can accurately represent hell, and that its real horrors are inside Faustus' mind. In the same way, Mephistophilis has his own private vision of hell, which he cannot share with anyone:

Hell hath no limits nor is circumscribed
In one self place but where we are is hell
And where hell is there must we ever be. (II.1)

- Sit or stand anywhere about the room as though you are someone whose mind is 'in hell'. How does this manifest itself? You may shriek and tear your hair, or you may experience this hell as a kind of depression, and become very quiet and hunched over. You might simply sit in a corner facing the wall. You are in constant pain – it will never end. Try to find repetitive gestures that signal your unending misery. You might speak the same words over and over, scratch yourself, rock back and forth, try to tear your skin off, weep. Find your own private hell and, just for a while, go inside it.

- Now treat yourself to a brief sojourn in a personal heaven. Enjoy the moment of perfect peace.

The language of movement

Just as words are effectively gestures in theatre, so the movement of actors can be as eloquent and expressive as the spoken word. Every movement on stage, even stillness, communicates a thought, feeling or intention. On the first day of rehearsals, choreographer Kate Flatt worked with David Lan's entire company, exploring the movement of angels, and these explorations were later incorporated into the work with young people. Flatt asked, 'How do we make sense of supernatural beings in the time we live in now, and also how do we avoid cliched behaviour of supernatural beings?' . . . 'In the absence of real wings, how might an angel move?'

Flatt uses images as the starting point for movement work with actors: 'the actor works so strongly through the imagination, rather than "I'm using this set of muscles or that kind of impetus for my body." ' She encourages actors to transform themselves by imagining their bodies changing shape, structure and mass: 'It's to do with using gravity in different ways, but through the image rather than, "Put your weight here or do this", which is I think very hard for actors to do.' In the end, actors learn physical movement in the same way as text. It has to be learned, repeated, adjusted, understood and communicated. Movement can help to shape a role and emphasise the language: 'Sometimes I have explored ideas with actors physically which has helped them to find something else in the texture of the piece – I stimulate actors to connect the imagination to their bodies.'

There are also elements of slapstick and clowning in *Doctor Faustus* which provide opportunities for playful physical work. Some of the minor characters, like the Seven Deadly Sins, the Pope and the Horse-Courser, reveal as much about themselves by the way they move as by their language.

Angels

In the Bible, angels are commonly God's messengers. The evil or fallen angels oppose God's will and assist Satan. They are sometimes considered to have been good angels who have fallen into sin (some by lusting after women) and have been cast out of heaven.

- Divide into Good Angels and Evil Angels. Lie down. In rehearsal Kate Flatt instructed the Good Angels to 'think of your bones being full of light, being weightless. Try rolling across the floor with your bones full of light.'
- Explore the space as a Good Angel. How might Good Angels move? How might they walk 'without disturbing the air'? Do these angels have wings? If so, what does it feel like to have wings? How heavy are they? How do you stand when your wings are folded on your back? When they are spread out? How do you begin to move? How do you come to rest? What does it mean to move with grace, with power? Move about the space, rolling, standing or sitting on chairs or on the floor. A Good Angel might, for example, not sit directly but hover above a chair.
- The Evil Angels, meanwhile, imagine their bones 'having lava inside them, molten lava to give a sort of weighted, heavy sense of movement'. Explore the space as an Evil Angel. Are these angels still powerful and graceful? David Lan sees the Evil Angels not as romantic rebels but as 'cramped, creepy copycats of high command up in heaven'. This implies stiff or cringing motion, as though the heat of hell presses down on them. In Lan's production, the actor who played the clown Robin doubled as the Evil Angel. How do you see these angels? They are not merely rebellious; they are in a state of perpetual punishment. Try to express this in their movement.

Conflict

- Divide into groups of three. Consider the angels' response to Faustus' question, 'Contrition, prayer, repentance. What of them?'

GOOD ANGEL: O, they are means to bring thee unto heaven.
EVIL ANGEL: Rather illusions, fruits of lunacy
That make men foolish that do trust them most.

GOOD ANGEL: Sweet Faustus, think of heaven and heavenly things.
EVIL ANGEL: No, Faustus, think of honour and of wealth. (II.1)

- Set up an improvisation, in groups of three, which grows out of this passage. One person in each group is a modern-day Faustus who is about to do something dangerous or damaging (kill someone, steal money from a pension fund, burn down a house, etc.). The Good Angel tries to dissuade him, while the Evil Angel tries to tempt him into committing the crime.
- Your Faustus stands on the boundary between salvation and damnation. Start with the lines above, and then add your own words and continue the scene. What do the angels say to try to convince Faustus? Whose arguments are strongest?
- Try the scene again; this time imagine that the act itself is not illegal, but its consequences might be terrible. Say Faustus is a scientist who has discovered a potentially deadly bacterium which could, if properly used, cure cancer and if misused wipe out the human race. Should he destroy it or preserve it and hope it won't fall into the wrong hands? How would you advise him? Time is running out.
- Now try the exercise without words, using only movements and gestures. How does the Good Angel try to get and keep Faustus' attention? What is his/her expression? Does the Good Angel touch Faustus? What does the Evil Angel do to persuade Faustus to act now and ignore the consequences? Try to find precise gestures for each attempt to persuade Faustus, and to show an increasing pressure to win the battle for his soul as time ticks by.

Moving in a group

On the first day of rehearsal of the main stage play, David Lan showed the actors images of the Seven Deadly Sins from the paintings of Hieronymous Bosch, and asked them to present a pageant of the sins. This provided the company with a playful group ritual which could be repeated through the rehearsal process as a warm-up. The sins were explored as much through movement as through character, as they are essentially medieval types rather than fully-fleshed individuals. The aim was to collaborate physically in representing each of the sins.

FAUSTUS: What are thou, the first?

PRIDE: I am Pride. I disdain to have any parents . . . Fie, what a smell is here? I'll not speak another word except the ground were perfumed and covered with cloth of arras.

FAUSTUS: Thou are a proud knave indeed. What art thou, the second?

COVETOUSNESS: I am Covetousness, begotten of an old Churl in an old leather bag and, might I have my wish, I would desire that this house and all the people in it were turned to gold that I might lock you up in my good chest. O, my sweet gold!

FAUSTUS: What art thou, the third?

ENVY: I am Envy, begotten of a chimney-sweeper and an oyster-wife. I cannot read and therefore wish all books burned. I am lean with seeing others eat. O that there would come a famine over all the world that all might die and I live alone, then thou should'st see how fat I'd be. But must thou sit and I stand? Come down, with a vengeance.

FAUSTUS: Out, envious wretch! But what art thou, the fourth?

WRATH: I am Wrath. I had neither father nor mother. I leapt out of a lion's mouth when I was scarce half an hour old and ever since I have run up and down the world with this case of rapiers wounding myself, when I had nobody to fight withal. I was born in hell! And look to it, for some of you shall be my father!

FAUSTUS: What art thou, the fifth?

GLUTTONY: Who, I, sir? I am Gluttony. My parents are all dead and the devil a penny they have left me but a bare pension, and that buys me thirty meals a day and ten bevers, a small trifle to suffice nature. O, I come of royal parentage! My father was a gammon of bacon, my mother a hogshead of Claret wine. My godfathers were these: Peter Pickled-herring and Martin Martlemas-beef. But my godmother, oh, she was a jolly gentle-woman, and well beloved in every town and city. Her name was Mistress Margery March-beer. Now, Faustus, thou hast heard my progeny, wilt thou bid me to supper?

FAUSTUS: No, I'll see thee hanged. Thou wilt eat up all my victuals.

GLUTTONY: Then the devil choke thee.

FAUSTUS: Choke thyself, glutton! What art thou, the sixth?

SLOTH: Heigh-ho! I am Sloth. I was begotten on a sunny bank where I have lain ever since. You have done me a great injury to bring me from thence. Let me be carried thither again by Gluttony and Lechery. Heigh-ho! I'll not speak another word for a king's ransom.

FAUSTUS: And what are you, Mistress Minx, the seventh and last?

LECHERY: Who, I, sir? I am one that loves an inch of raw mutton better than an ell of fried stock-fish and the first letter of my name begins with lechery.

LUCIFER: Away, to hell. Away! On, piper! (II.3)

• Explore the Seven Deadly Sins as a group, using your bodies and whatever materials are available (such as chairs, cloth, table, mirror).

In the young people's version, the participants created tableaux of each sin, with one actor at the centre representing the vice in question. Wrath raged and fumed while others tried vainly to hold him back and cool his temper. Gluttony was represented by the whole group, each playing a part of his enormous, insatiable body. Lechery reacted lasciviously to the seductive gestures of the others.

• When you have represented each of the sins, try to imagine a fitting punishment for one or more of them. Gluttony, for example, might be forced to sit at an empty place, while everyone around him gorges themselves. Covetousness might be tied up just out of reach of something he craves.

Staging *Doctor Faustus*

These exercises extend the participants' involvement to the point of an envisaged production. The words the characters speak might seem the be-all-and-end-all of the play on the page. But in performance they are lifted, supported and delivered not only by the actors but also by the other 'languages' of theatre: sound, light, costume and set design. How would you create an overall 'vision' for *Doctor Faustus* in performance and communicate your ideas to an audience through material means? The emphasis here is on encouraging a personal imaginative response to the play, and harnessing this to the practice of theatre-making and the combination of creative roles that it involves. In the absence of complex equipment, young people need little more than paper, pencils, simple tools, their bodies and their minds to begin the process of staging a play.

The stage

Sketch out the stage area for your 'production.' Where will the audience be sitting? How large is the stage? Where are the entrances/exits? You might mark out the dimensions of the stage with chalk or tape.

The set

In staging a play the director and designer need to make clear decisions about what the audience sees on the stage and how each element looks. For example, if a script specifies that a character sits on a chair, a designer needs to know what sort of chair it is. Is it an old antique, or a glossy, modern chair?

- In groups, design a set for a scene from *Doctor Faustus* which is set in Faustus' study. Use large sheets of paper or notebooks to jot down ideas as you work through the following stages. First of all, think very clearly about when and where the scene is set. Is it contemporary or historical? What sort of room is it? What might the study tell us about Faustus?
- Now write a list of exactly what is on stage, starting with what is essential (any furniture the cast might need to use, and any objects discussed or used in the scene). This list should include any props that the actors use (such as reading glasses, a glass of water or wine, a candle). The group might then choose to add further objects as *dressing* to the set. Dressing objects might tell the audience a little more about where the play is set (for example, the kind of objects in the room can tell us whether Faustus is rich or poor, and what his individual tastes are: does he collect art, for example? Does he have rich carpets or

curtains in the room, or is his mind on higher things?).

- Finally, ask the groups to think about the *atmosphere* of the play they are staging. How do they want their set to make the audience feel? Scared? Safe? Is the design familiar or strange? Bright or subdued? What materials would they use to convey the atmosphere (fabric, wood, metal, stone)? Ask each group what *colours* might best create that atmosphere. How else might they get the effect they want? For example, how might the stage *space* affect the audience? Is the acting area wide and open or closed and claustrophobic? Will the audience sit in front of the stage, or around the stage, close to the action and watching it from every angle? How might this decision affect the audience's experience of the play?

- Working from their notes, each group will now research visual material that will help them put together a picture of where and when the play is set. They could use magazines, photocopies from books or images from the internet, swatches of fabric, sketches, photographs and postcards. This material can either be a direct representation of an element of the set (a picture of a chair) or something more general and suggestive (a photograph that makes them feel the same way that the play does). Ask them to think carefully about colours and textures.

- Each group should assemble all their visual research on a piece of cardboard or paper. This can be shown and discussed as part of the final presentation.

A designer would then go on to use these research materials to design a set. He/she would create a set model (a very small version of the set in three dimensions), which would include the shapes, colours and textures of the design. This would be used to discuss his/her ideas with the director and changes might be suggested. Sometimes designers go through several set models before settling on a design. From the model box, the designer will then produce a set of plans for the set builders and stage management team to work from.

In the main stage production, the set consisted of a narrow, diagonal wooden platform – a kind of gangplank – which bisected the auditorium and lent a sense of precariousness and unease to the action. A few chairs stood about. A circle above the stage represented heaven, and coals below, the pit of hell. The actors teetered on a spit, balanced between salvation and damnation. One by one, Faustus discarded the props of his scholarly life beneath the runway in a graphic image of his undoing.

In the young people's production, an even simpler design was used. A medieval circle was painted on the floor – a beautiful image representing both the earth and the heavens, and the conjuring circles used by magicians and necromancers. Images of a dark sky were painted on the walls. Two ladders referred to Faustus' library, and his books were scattered about the space. A red cloth was unfurled to represent the Vatican. The planets were signified by pieces of fruit held in the hands of the characters. What images/ideas do you see as fundamental to *Doctor Faustus*?

Lighting

How would you light the final moments of *Doctor Faustus*, as the clock strikes twelve and Faustus approaches damnation?

Lighting helps to define the world of the play and also gives definition to the movement of the actors. It can create a general mood, and at the same time can emphasise individual characters and their actions and feelings. You can use light to emphasise:
  – Character
  – Action
  – The set
The elements of lighting which you should consider are:
  – Brightness (to create atmosphere and a sense of place and time)
  – Angle (the creation of shadows and shapes for dramatic effect)
  – Colour (to create mood)
  – Movement (to emphasise action or suggest change, as when light fades up or down or sweeps across the stage)

• In small groups using whatever lights are available, decide and demonstrate how you would light the final image of Faustus surrounded by the devils. You should have at least three sources of light, for example, torch, candle, lamp, paper lantern. First of all, consider what is happening at this moment: Faustus is desperately begging for salvation as the devils close in on him and prepare to drag him to hell. You will need to light:

– Faustus
– The set
– Mephistophilis, Lucifer, Beelzebub

What would the main source of light be in this scene? How might you suggest hell just with lights and no scenery? Would you harshly illuminate Faustus to emphasise his isolation? Or would you light the devils with fierce light and instead show Faustus disappearing into darkness? What principal colour would you use?

- You might choose to use candles or lanterns to give the scene a ghostly atmosphere or to make an ironic link between Faustus' damnation and a religious ceremony. Or you might imagine the scene in utter darkness except for a single candle held by Faustus. Think what you want the audience to see and understand at this climactic point in the play.
- You can light a character or object from
  – Above
  – Below
  – In front
  – Behind
  – The side
  – Above and in front
  but it is only where you begin to combine these lighting angles that the stage picture begins to gain depth and interest.
- Try holding a torch or lamp above, below, in front of, behind and to either side of a volunteer's face, to see the different effects this produces. Where you position your lights will have a great impact on what the audience sees and understands. Be as imaginative as you can in your lighting design. It will help to tell the story of the play and create a powerful sense of atmosphere.

David Lan's production was characterised by harsh, industrial lighting. Hell was suggested by pulsing, glowing coals and embers below the stage. In the Studio production a candelabra with burning candles hung from centre stage above the painted circle. This made the walls seem to disappear into blackness; only the painted circle was lit. This was a cheap, simple and atmospheric effect.

Sound

What sound effects would you use for this scene? You can use sound and music to emphasise:
- Character
- Action
- Atmosphere
- Entrances and exits

Sound effects can greatly enhance the impact and mood of a scene, though they should not be overused, or they will overwhelm the actors.

- Choose sounds to accompany:
  - The vision of hell
  - The entrance of Lucifer, Beelzebub and Mephistophilis
  - The clock striking twelve
  - Faustus' death

Your sound effects could be pre-recorded, or you might choose to use live music or other effects. Marlowe refers to the sound of thunder and the clock striking in his stage directions, but you might not use these sounds literally. You could, for example, use the sound of a heartbeat instead of a clock. This would emphasise not only the passing of time but also Faustus' own growing fear. It depends whether you want to suggest that all of this is happening in Faustus' mind, or whether it is taking place literally, in front of us. Sound, like lighting, can guide us to the play's meaning in performance.

The young people's production used pre-recorded classical and contemporary music to show that Faustus straddles both ancient and modern ways of thinking, and that his story belongs to all times. The company also chose signature sounds for some characters. Lucifer, for example, was accompanied by the sound of flies buzzing. The sound of wings flapping heralded Faustus' fall, along with the chiming of clocks. In Lan's production, 'spooky, subsonic soundscapes' underscored the action, while a clock ticked ominously from the moment Faustus signed away his soul.

Costumes

- Choose one of the following and design and draw a simple costume for your character:
    - Mephistophilis
    - Lucifer
    - Horse-Courser
    - Helen of Troy
    - Gluttony
- Choose the fabric for the costume. You might imagine Mephistophilis in a slippery dark cloak of satin, for example, to emphasise his seductive, manipulative nature. In Lan's production he donned a flame-red tuxedo, to emphasise his pride and flamboyance. How could you use costume to characterise Gluttony? The Horse-Courser is an ordinary, if impetuous man, who is tricked by Faustus into riding a devilish horse into a river, where it disappears. What sort of costume would you design for Faustus' foolish victim?

In the young people's production, costumes were made up of contemporary black clothing with symbolic additions (crimson cardinals' hats, scholars' gowns, books, spectacles, etc.). Lucifer's costume had echoes of a Mafia boss. The Evil Angel had branches as wings and wore a steel vest and leather jacket. In the main house, the characters wore combinations of Elizabethan costume and contemporary clothing: they donned Elizabethan capes, jeans and shaman's beads in a 'jumble' of outfits which lifted the play free of a specific time frame. Lucifer pulled a stocking over his head to distort his features.

In their different ways, both productions of *Doctor Faustus* were unadorned, visceral and immediate; using the simplest theatrical devices, both revealed the compelling questions at the heart of the play. Participants and young audiences were encouraged to respond critically not only to the ideas of the play but also to the production choices made by both companies. One teacher reported that her students were 'overwhelmed – not only by Jude Law's excellent central performance but by the production and the play – discussions afterwards centred on both the skills of the actors/director and the themes that came across. One Year 11 could not sleep for excitement.' Others 'loved the Seven Deadly Sins. They really were interested in the ideas, and spent twenty minutes of our drama lesson today arguing about interpretation and performances.' A critic added, 'There can be no better endorsement than that the average age of the audience on a Friday night is half that you would find on Shaftesbury Avenue.' Michael Billington pointed out that the play presents a 'volatile scenario' through which we each find our own personal meaning. Through the potency of its language and images, Faustus' fall, and the questions it raises about curiosity, temptation, power and sin, continues to reverberate across the ages.

Chapter 5

CHARACTER AND STATUS – A RAISIN IN THE SUN

A theatre experience which lives in the present must be close to the pulse of the time.

Peter Brook

David Lan's production of Lorraine Hansberry's 'uplifting, heart-breaking and scarily prescient' 1959 play opened the Young Vic's season of Young American writers in 2001 (the play was a co-production with Salisbury Playhouse, where it premiered). Although this classic African-American play about a poor family poised between self-advancement and despair in Southside Chicago is well known in America, it had been largely forgotten in England and had not been produced in London for fifteen years. Lan was convinced that its insights into struggle and survival remained relevant, and that Hansberry's neglected classic still presents great opportunities for complex characterisation and great challenges for actors and for those who dig down to its roots in search of its ideas about family and identity.

The title of the play comes from a poem by black playwright and poet Langston Hughes: 'What happens to a dream deferred? / Does it dry up like a raisin in the sun?' The play is about an extended African-American family living and dreaming in a cockroach-infested apartment in 1950s Southside Chicago. Lena Younger (Mama) is the matriarch; recently widowed, she is struggling to hold the family together under the pressure of poverty and conflicting ambitions. When Lena receives a substantial payment from her husband's insurance policy, her son Walter, a chauffeur, sees his chance to better himself, and wants to invest the cash in a liquor store with his friends Willy and Bobo. But his younger sister Beneatha is training to become a doctor, and needs the money to support her education. His wife Ruth discovers she is pregnant with their second child (their son Travis is a restless adolescent schoolboy) but considers aborting the baby rather than bringing it into a life of poverty in the overcrowded apartment. Walter spirals into alcohol-fuelled depression, and Mama relents, giving him some of the money for himself and some for him to bank for Beneatha's education. The rest she uses as a down payment on a new house in an all-white residential neighbour-hood. Beneatha, who has been in a half-hearted relationship with wealthy George Murchison, rejects him when she realises he wants her to suppress her intellect and ambition, and she turns instead to fellow student Joseph Asagai, who fuels Beneatha's interest in her African heritage and instils a new pride in her cultural identity.

A quietly spoken man arrives; a member of the 'Welcoming Committee' from the new white neighbourhood. He advises the family not to move in and offers to buy back their house. Enraged, Walter throws him out. Walter's liquor-store investment (which included Beneatha's share of the inheritance) disappears along with his friend Willy. All the family's hopes seem on the point of collapse. Walter decides to accept the buy-back offer on the house, but Lena condemns him for his lack of pride. When the white man, Lindner, returns, Walter finally finds the strength to reject the proposal and claim the family's right to make a future for themselves, unbowed by bigotry, in their new home.

A Raisin in the Sun is one of the great plays of black American experience. The *New York Times* claimed that it 'changed American theater forever'. Bonnie Greer describes it as the wellspring to which all black writers consciously or unconsciously return: 'It is the foundation.' Beneatha's struggle alone prefigures, in one gesture, the rise of the civil rights movement, feminism and pan-Africanism. Aged twenty-nine when *A Raisin in the Sun* opened, Hansberry was the first black playwright to win the New York Critics' Circle Award, and the play was adapted for film, with Sidney Poitier in the lead. Hansberry died of cancer at the age of thirty-four. *A Raisin in the Sun* contains rich seams of social history and questions of identity which suited it ideally both to production at the Young Vic and to the young people's workshops which grew out of the production.

The work of this chapter focuses on the play's characters and the problems and dilemmas they face. Improvisation and text exercises are used to probe the play's historical and social context, exploring status in society and other detailed ways of defining and staging character. Assistant director Afia Nkrumah and the TPR team wanted to investigate how dramatic character grows out of and reflects back on the social world of the play, and to consider the different choices that an actor might make in order to demonstrate this: 'We experimented with scenes – seeing how a scene changes when different characters have different status. Also how a character's understanding of their own status can change during a scene depending on what they discover and the way the other characters react to them.'

Status

Exploring character through status gives young people a clear insight into the dynamic nature of relationships in drama (see introductory status exercises on p. 54–57). Harold Pinter claims that life is a 'series of negotiations for advantage' in which everything comes into play. In their interactions, characters are never merely talking to one another – they are negotiating, manipulating, resisting and seducing one another. They do this with words and with actions, using the full range of their expressive capabilities. It is fascinating to look at the status 'transactions' that take place within a play and to use them to chart a character's progress through his/her public and private worlds.

Insults

This warm-up is used to generate a sense of the tension and potential for conflict that exists in the pressure cooker of the Younger household. Insults ricochet around the apartment throughout the play as weapons aimed at undermining the status of a perceived opponent. They are examples of a rich vernacular, drawn from life, particular to the Younger family and their private squabbles. The frequency with which insults are used demonstrates not only the tension in the crowded household, but also the creativity and resourcefulness of the characters, who have little more than the clothes they stand up in and the words they speak to define and defend them: 'crazy good-for-nothing clowns', 'you all some evil people', 'slubborn', 'good-for-nothing loud mouth', 'horrible-looking chick', 'you're a nut', 'backward race of people', 'flip', 'Prometheus', 'Monsieur le petit bourgeois noir', 'toothless rate'.

- Stand in two groups, one on each side of the room, facing one another. Choose one of the above insults. One member of the group on the left takes a step forward and shouts the insult at the other group. Everyone in the second group repeats the insult in an outraged tone ('Slubborn?!') Then one member of this group steps forward to deliver another, different, insult to the first group, and so on. Eventually both groups will be standing face to face. You can then deliver insults at random.

  Note how your body language changes when you are deliberately insulting someone. You might try to make yourself taller, open your eyes wide, stab your finger at the person opposite. What does it feel like to be insulted?
- Unwind by shaking hands and apologising profusely to all the people in the opposing group.

Establishing status

We are constantly trying to raise (or sometimes strategically lower) our status, or to raise or lower that of another. It is hard to change our public status, but our private status can change moment by moment, depending on who has the upper hand in an encounter. Status is something we *do*, and we may play a higher status than we actually have. Through their experiments in rehearsal, the actors in *A Raisin in the Sun* discovered that even the smallest shifts in status can alter the meaning of an entire scene.

- Improvise a short and simple scene in which A, a high-status character (say the fat-cat chairman of a company, or a doctor), enters a room and delivers bad news to B, a low-status character (a casual employee, a patient). B then leaves the room.

  A enters.
  A: I'm afraid it's the end of the road for you.
  B: Is it?
  B leaves.

As the high-status character, concentrate on your entrance – how do you establish your status by the way you enter your office? Where do you sit in relation to the other person? How do you 'inhabit' the space? What body language, tone of voice, gesture will accompany your line? What do you do when you have delivered it, and while B is leaving the room?

Is B standing or sitting when A enters? Would you establish your low status by leaping up from your chair as A arrives? What do you do while A delivers the bad news? Do you look A in the eye as you say, 'Is it?' How do you leave the room? Do you shake A's hand, brush the seat clean after you have stood up, close the door quietly on your way out?

- Try the scene again, but reverse the status, so that the employee or patient now has high status and the chairman or doctor has very low status. Notice how very different this interaction is from the preceding one, although the stage directions, characters and dialogue are the same.

Private status/public status

Keith Johnstone claims that 'a great play is a virtuoso display of status transactions'. The difference between private status (within the family, for instance) and public status (in the context of 1950s America, which still had race laws in the South – including segregation on buses and in some schools) is one of the main causes of tension in *A Raisin in the Sun*. A character might have high status within the family (Mama) but low status in public life. For some characters, particularly Walter and Beneatha, their low public status is a source of constant frustration and anger. Although there were fewer race laws in Chicago, where the play is set, than in the South where lynchings were still taking place, nonetheless many unwritten prejudices still governed that society. These affected the relationships between black and white Americans, and also between men and women. In the following scene, Beneatha uncovers the true feelings of her boyfriend George towards her:

BENEATHA: I'm *trying* to talk to you.
GEORGE: We always talk.
BENEATHA: Yes – and I love to talk.

GEORGE: *(exasperated; rising)* I know and I don't mind it sometimes . . . I want you to cut it out, see – The moody stuff, I mean, I don't like it. You're a nice girl . . . all over. That's all you need, honey, forget the atmosphere. Guys aren't going to go for the atmosphere – they're going to go for what they see. Be glad for that. Drop the Garbo routine. It doesn't go with you. As for myself, I want a nice *(groping)* simple *(thoughtfully)* sophisticated girl . . . not a poet – O.K.?

She rebuffs him again and he starts to leave.

BENEATHA: Why are you angry?
GEORGE: Because this is stupid! I don't go out with you to discuss the nature of 'quiet desperation' or to hear all about your thoughts – because the world will go on thinking what it thinks regardless –
BENEATHA: Then why read books? Why go to school?
GEORGE: *(with artificial patience, counting on his fingers)* It's simple. You read books – to learn facts – to get grades – to pass the course – to get a degree. That's all – it has nothing to do with thoughts.

A long pause.

BENEATHA: I see. (*A longer pause as she looks at him.*) Good night, George. (II.2)

Status is reflected not simply in words, but in actions too. When Beneatha tries to engage him in debate in this scene, George stands up to assert himself; he counts his thoughts off on his fingers as though talking to a child. He tries continually to establish his superiority over Beneatha. What is interesting about the encounter is that there is a conflict of different kinds of status going on. Within the black community, George is an important man who comes from a wealthy family; as such, he believes he has a higher status than Beneatha, which makes him patronising and dismissive. Yet Beneatha is George's superior intellectually, and it is his denial of her intellectual worth that finally convinces Beneatha that the relationship is over. She values her intelligence and imagination more than George's 'love'. In rejecting George,

Beneatha's status rises; she wishes him good night, ending the encounter, and so has the last word.

- In pairs, create frozen pictures or snapshots to illustrate:
  a) George's sense of his status in relation to Beneatha
  b) Beneatha's sense of her status in relation to George
  You will soon see that, even though they may express it differently, both characters consider their status to be higher than that of the other. But George's sense of his worth is largely derived from his public position (his wealth, his gender) while Beneatha's comes entirely from her private sense of identity (she is educated and strives to improve herself all the time).

Eye contact

- Sit facing a partner and read the lines between George and Beneatha aloud. Don't move any part of your body except your head. Think about where the characters make eye contact, and where one of them deliberately avoids it by looking away or engaging in another activity.

In this passage, the stage directions imply that it is Beneatha who seeks to make eye contact with George, while he tries to avoid it by rising from his seat, counting on his fingers, turning to leave the room. Beneatha's direct questioning of George suggests that she is searching his face and his mind for clues to her dissatisfaction with him. When she finally decides to reject him, she does it by looking at him for some time.

Holding eye contact can be a sign of power – it can reflect a higher status even when the dialogue itself or the social situation does not demonstrate it. Beneatha proves herself to be more powerful – more steady – than George in the course of this scene.

Now consider Walter's speech to Lindner at the end of the play. This speech is the climax of the play; it is the moment at which Walter recognises he has failed his family by pursuing his own selfish objectives and putting his personal pride before the honour of the family. Having initially accepted Lindner's offer to buy back the Youngers' house, Walter now rejects it, recognising it as racist and oppressive. Even as he breaks down in tears, Walter's status rises as he asserts the family's pride, their birthright, their human right to determine their own future. Lindner's status falls as Walter's rises, and the action of the scene drives this home moment by moment:

> WALTER (*starting to cry and facing the man eye to eye*): What I am telling you is that we called you over here to tell you that we are very proud and that this is – this is my son, who makes the sixth generation of our family in this country, and that we have all thought about your offer and we have decided to move into our house because my father – my father – he earned it . . . That's all we got to say. (*He looks the man absolutely in the eyes.*) We don't want your money. (*He turns and walks away from the man.*) (III)

- In pairs, play this encounter between Walter and Lindner, remembering that it is Walter who initiates eye contact, Walter who maintains it with great intensity, and Walter who breaks it when he has made his point. You can improvise Walter's speech – the important thing is to emphasise the accompanying actions. Walter is physically in control throughout, just through the assurance of his gaze, and his status has never been higher. How does it feel to be on the receiving end of this kind of determination and certainty? How does Lindner respond? What can he do once Walter has dismissed him? It is difficult to make a dignified exit when someone has turned his back on you.
- Swap roles and play the scene again.

Status and movement

Status transactions are not confined to tussles in dialogue or to eye contact. A character can signal his or her status by the way he/she enters or leaves the stage, as well as through countless gestural signals. Understanding your (changing) status as a character can help to define your physical behaviour and vice versa. 'In order to enter a room,' according to Keith Johnstone, 'all you need to know is what status you are playing.'

- In pairs, read aloud the scene above between George and Beneatha (on pp. 121–22), but concentrate in particular on the movements and gestures of the characters, including eye contact. At first, George and Beneatha are sitting side by side on a sofa, but George rises, 'exasperated', and then goes to leave. Note that Beneatha does not move from her seated position throughout the exchange, not even when she bids George goodnight and he is forced to go. She establishes her status through her stillness and self-control, while George's actions are agitated and uncertain. You can improvise the dialogue, but your actions should make clear the very different energies of the characters and the fact that, for all his bravado, George is unable to take control of the situation.

Raising and lowering status

In a confined space such as the Youngers' apartment, constant status transactions take place as individuals negotiate or battle to get what they want. Walter and Beneatha quarrel frequently and try to undermine one another's status. Consider the status transactions between brother and sister in the following passage (stage directions have been removed):

WALTER: You a horrible looking chick at this hour.
BENEATHA: Good morning, everybody.
WALTER: How is school coming?
BENEATHA: Lovely. Lovely. And you know, biology is the greatest. I dissected something that looked just like you yesterday.
WALTER: I just wondered if you've made up your mind and everything.
BENEATHA: And what did I answer yesterday morning – and the day before that?
RUTH: Don't be so nasty, Bennie.
BENEATHA: And the day before that and the day before that!
WALTER: I'm interested in you. Something wrong with that? Ain't many girls who decide . . .
WALTER AND BENEATHA: . . . 'to be a doctor.' (I.1)

This exercise offers a vivid demonstration of how status transactions work.

- In groups of three, stand or sit at a table and read this scene out loud.
- Read it again, this time each holding a booklet of sticky Post-it notes or paper markers. Every time you think you have scored a point by lowering the status of your 'opponent', reach over and stick a note on him/her. For example, you might think Walter 'tags' Beneatha when he tells her she looks horrible. She tags him back with her comment about dissected corpses. You may consider that she tags him again by insisting repeatedly she has already answered his question about medical school (she treats him like a child). Ruth steps in and tags Beneatha by pointing out her cruelty. Beneatha effectively tags Ruth back by ignoring her. Walter makes a final attempt at tagging Beneatha, when he suggests becoming a doctor is a strange choice for a woman. By finishing his sentence with him, Beneatha demonstrates his chauvinistic attitude and so gets a final tag in.

Played in this way, it becomes clear that status transactions and small struggles for dominance take place continually throughout the play.

Which character would have the most Post-it notes stuck to his or her body at the end of the play? It is very likely to be Walter, who, according to critic Kate Kellaway, 'paces like a turkey cock and puffs himself up with rhetoric', making himself an easy target for the other characters. Characters are never at rest; their dialogue always signals an intention or desire, and a scene will come to life on stage when these intentions become visible.

Character and conflict

We can move beyond broader analyses of status to a probing exploration of character in action. *A Raisin in the Sun* is characterised by psychological realism – its action and setting, as defined by its author, are naturalistic, and the audience looks in on the Younger family conflicts as if we have simply removed the fourth wall from their apartment. Lorraine Hansberry's detailed stage directions are typical of much naturalistic drama of the nineteenth and early twentieth centuries. The directors of these plays often sought to reproduce exactly the physical environments described in the text. Not all directors and designers adhere closely to stage directions – some choose to ignore them altogether in order to make their own decisions about set design, costumes, lighting, sound and movement. But Hansberry provides minute and convincing detail in her descriptions of the Youngers' physical environment, and they offer insight into the lives and minds of her characters. Hansberry intended the Youngers to be real and recognisable to her audiences. On stage, we see versions of ourselves, flawed human beings caught up in universal dilemmas and in familiar forms of conflict. It may be helpful, then, to draw on Hansberry's stage directions, as well as on our own lives and experiences, when trying to flesh out the characters and interpret their choices and motivations.

Domestic setting

Because everything that happens in *A Raisin in the Sun* takes place in one small room on Chicago's Southside, it's important to have a strong sense of this physical environment. The characters cannot escape from it (except to go out to work or school), and it affects all of their interactions:

> Its furnishings are typical and undistinguished and their primary feature now is that they have clearly had to accommodate the living of too many people for too many years – and they are tired . . . Now the once loved pattern of the couch upholstery has to fight to show itself from under acres of crocheted doilies and couch covers which have themselves finally come to be more important than the upholstery. And here and there a table or a chair has been moved to disguise the worn places in the carpet; but the carpet has fought back by showing its weariness, with depressing uniformity, elsewhere on its surface . . . Everything has been polished, washed, sat on, used, scrubbed too often . . . A section of this room . . . slopes backward to provide a small kitchen area where the family prepares the meals that are eaten in the living-room proper, which must also serve as dining-room. (I.1)

The pressure in the play is generated, in part, by the fact that the members of the Younger family live on top of one another and cannot make space for their dreams. The design of the set, the materials and objects used, and their relation to one another, can provide important and suggestive information about the characters. Hansberry intended that the set for the play should reflect both the poverty and the pride of the Younger family.

- Design a simple set for the play. You don't have to follow Hansberry's description, but you should try to express the feeling and atmosphere of the place in your design (see notes on set design on p. 111). What sort of furniture would you have in your set? How would you suggest the poverty of the Younger family? You might want a naturalistic set, following Lorraine Hansberry's own detailed stage directions, or you might add some symbolic detail to suggest the claustrophobia in the apartment (a pressure cooker, for example, or a whistling kettle on the point of boiling over). Even the simplest object can become a resonant symbol in the theatre. It's up to you to decide whether you want to create the impression of a real apartment or to aim for a more poetic, symbolic use of materials, furniture and props. The most important thing is to think about the *setting* of the action in space and time; try to lift the play off the page when you read it, and imagine it in three dimensions.

Although *A Raisin in the Sun* is a naturalistic play which is usually performed with a cluttered, realistic set, in the Young Vic production the creative team adapted the design to suit the demands of playing on a thrust stage with the audience on three sides. When the audience sits all around the stage, sight lines can be obstructed by pieces of furniture, so the designer and director looked for ways to *suggest* poverty and claustrophobia rather than to illustrate them.

Designer Francis O'Connor included some expressive elements in an otherwise spare and minimalist set. She wanted every object on the stage to have a resonance, and felt that nothing should be superfluous, so that the subtle and complex relationships between the characters could be exposed. The action took place in the living room and kitchen, and the stage furniture consisted of two tables, some chairs and a small bed which stood against a bare tenement wall. Out of this bed all the members of the family emerged one by one. The wall represented the outside of the Younger house, and during set changes black and white footage of family members looking out onto the street was projected onto it.

This set thus combined two perspectives at once – the audience saw the family from outside and from inside the house, as though we were both passers by and flies on the wall. Distance and intimacy were generated at the same time. The set suggested that the Youngers are trapped and isolated by their poverty, but that they are also part of our world and our society. Some critics objected to the symbolic nature of the set and felt the design should have been more literal and realistic. What do you think? Francis O'Connor feels that 'design is the best playground in the world for a visual artist because the scale of stuff is so big. You don't just get to work with physical stuff like scenery, props and costumes, but moving people as well.'

Domestic life

The lives and interactions of the Younger family are inevitably, and profoundly, affected by their proximity to one another, and by the tension generated by their differing habits, desires and ambitions. So the physical representation of their encounters and the ways in which they use the space are very important.

This exercise is an extension of a simple warm-up (p. 54, 'Feeling and action'). Here it is developed as an exploration of the relationship between feeling and action on stage.

- Find the references to domestic routines in the play. They include:

    An alarm clock sounds from within the bedroom at right. Ruth enters from that room and closes the door behind her. As she passes her sleeping son she reaches down and shakes him a little. At the window she raises the shade . . . She fills a pot with water and puts it on to boil. (I.1)

    The child [Travis] . . . drags himself out of bed and almost blindly takes his towels and 'todays clothes' from drawers and a closet and goes out to the bathroom. (I.1)

    Ruth starts to scramble eggs. (I.1)

[Walter] rises and finds a cigarette in her handbag on the table and crosses to the little window and looks out, smoking and deeply enjoying this first one. (I.1)

The boy [Travis] obeys stiffly and crosses the room, almost mechanically, to the bed and more or less carefully folds the covering. He carries the bedding into his mother's room and returns with his books and cap. (I.1)

[Ruth] rises and gets the ironing board and sets it up and attacks a huge pile of rough-dried clothes, sprinkling them in preparation for the ironing and then rolling them into tight fat balls. (I.1)

Beneatha goes out to the bathroom and bangs on the door. (I.1)

[Mama] crosses through the room, goes to the window, opens it, and brings in a feeble little plant growing doggedly in a small pot on the window sill. She feels the dirt and puts it back out. (I.1)

House cleaning is in progress at the Youngers . . . Mama is giving the kitchen walls a washing down. Beneatha . . . is spraying insecticide into the cracks in the walls. As they work, the radio is on . . . Travis, the sole idle one, is leaning on his arms, looking out of the window. (I.2)

Walter . . . finds a beer in the refrigerator, wanders over to George, sipping and wiping his lips with the back of his hand and straddling a chair backwards. (2.1)

- Choose one of the actions above and mime it. Try to do this entirely neutrally – show no emotion at all. Concentrate only on the physical movements involved. Repeat the action again and again until it is mechanical; imagine you have done it countless times before and do it without thinking. Exaggerate the action, so that it involves your entire body and becomes a kind of dance.
- Now mime the same action but while feeling anger. Try it again while feeling (and showing) exhaustion; now jealousy; now sorrow. Note how the physical expression of the action changes with each emotion.

Even the simplest domestic rituals may be rich with suggestion and infused with feeling. They contain important factual information about the relationships between the characters. Walter takes no part in the housework. He demonstrates his masculinity in straddling the chair. Ruth does the lion's share of work in the house. The actions contain crucial symbolic and emotional information too: 'How you hang on [Mama's] care for her little plant pot!' cried a critic on seeing Lan's production. The struggling plant symbolises the survival of the entire family; it is at the centre of Mama's attention, and is the last thing she removes as she departs for ever from the apartment.

What you want and obstacles to what you want

As Aristotle points out in his *Poetics*, we come to know a character by his actions, and his 'moral qualities are reflected in those actions'. Characters generally have a main or overall objective or want in a play. Their desire to achieve this goal gives them consistency as characters, and it drives them to *act* to achieve it. But a character may also have smaller or more immediate objectives in any scene. Identifying and naming these smaller objectives can be extremely helpful as a way of defining your character's actions.

Tension in drama is generated when a character encounters *obstacles* to getting what he/she wants, moment by moment. In the Younger household, the characters are continually placing obstacles in one another's way.

Consider the following scene between Walter and Ruth. Walter is trying to secure Ruth's support in his bid to invest Mama's money in the liquor store:

WALTER: This ain't no fly-by-night proposition, baby. I mean we figure it out, me and Willy and Bobo.
RUTH (*with a frown*): Bobo?
WALTER: Yeah. You see, this little liquor store we got in mind cost seventy-five thousand and we figured the initial investment on the place be 'bout thirty thousand, see. That be ten thousand each. Course, there's a couple of hundred you got to pay so's you don't spend your life just waiting for them clowns to let your licence get approved –

RUTH: You mean graft?

WALTER (*frowning impatiently*): Don't call it that. See there, that just goes to show you what women understand about the world. Baby, don't *nothing* happen for you in this world 'less you pay *somebody* off!

RUTH: Walter, leave me alone! (*She raises her head and stares at him vigorously – then says, more quietly*) Eat your eggs, they gonna be cold.

WALTER (*straightening up from her and looking off*): That's it. There you are. Man say to his woman: I got me a dream. His woman say: Eat your eggs. (*Sadly, but gaining in power.*) Man say: I got to take hold of this here world, baby! And a woman will say: Eat your eggs and go to work. (*Passionately now.*) Man say: I got to change my life, I'm choking to death, baby! And his woman say (*in utter anguish as he brings his fists down on his thighs*): Your eggs is getting cold!

RUTH (*softly*): Walter, that ain't none of our money. (I.1)

Lennie James, who played Walter in the Young Vic production, sees Walter as the equivalent of Jimmy Porter in John Osborne's *Look Back in Anger*. He is a man who has 'reached an age where, if he doesn't become the man he wants to be pretty soon, it's all going to run away from him'.

- Work on this scene in pairs. First, discuss the needs and desires of the characters. What does Walter want in this scene? His objective in *this* scene is to gain Ruth's support for his plan to use Mama's money ('All you have to do is just sit down with her when you drinking your coffee one morning . . . And the next thing you know, she be listening good.')

  But Ruth puts an *obstacle* in Walter's way. What does she want in this scene? She immediately dismisses the project. If he is to get her support he has to prove she is wrong to dismiss it. Ruth's action *changes* Walter's objective in the scene above: he must *first* demonstrate how her attitude is holding him and the family back. Then he must win her support for the plan, and then he must secure the money, and only *then* can he can raise his family's status in society.

Helping an actor to understand his/her character's objective at every stage of the play is one way to ensure that the character's journey is coherent and convincing for an audience.

Dramatic tension is sparked by the clash between characters' objectives and the obstacles they encounter in trying to achieve them. This friction creates energy and 'heat' on stage. Again, there are obstacles to *overall* objectives (Walter's social status is affected not only by his lack of ready money but also by the racist attitudes he encounters in society) and to *immediate* objectives within a scene (his desire for the money is thwarted by Ruth's wariness of Walter's scheming friends, her refusal to consider the paying of bribes, her opposition to the entire venture).

- Describe the obstacles to each character's main and immediate objectives. What does Mama want overall? She wants to buy a larger house for her family and so help to secure their future and their pride. What are the obstacles to this objective (for example, the racism represented by Lindner; Walter's selfishness and naivety)? What is Beneatha's overall objective? What is her immediate objective in the scene with George?

  Sometimes actors give each scene a title which expresses the immediate objective of their character. This acts as a kind of compass, to keep the performance on course towards the overall objective. What title would you give to the scene above? It might be 'Walter tries to shame Ruth into supporting his investment scheme'.
- In pairs, rehearse the scene above for ten minutes. Focus on the characters' wants and obstacles to those wants. Expressing the character's intentions here is more important than remembering the actual words or giving a polished performance.

  Try to concentrate in particular on Ruth's *opposition* to Walter's plan, and how this makes it difficult for him to get what he wants. Ruth's objective is to shut the discussion down as quickly as possible. How does she do this? Don't try to put too much detail into Walter's actions; the emphasis should be on how Ruth places obstacles before him. The director might choose one or two of the clearer interpretations and present them to the class.

Physical resistance

This is a good way of demonstrating the kinds of tension that exist between characters when one sees the other as an obstacle to getting what he/she wants. It helps to make dramatic language active, and to give characters a strong and sure sense of what they want and what it feels like to be opposed.

- In pairs, play Ruth and Walter in the scene above. Stand facing one another with your hands raised and placed palm to palm. As you speak your lines, push against one another whenever one of you is trying to dominate or place pressure on the other. When Walter says, 'This ain't no fly-by-night proposition, baby,' he puts a little pressure on Ruth, and when she says, 'Bobo?' suspiciously, she pushes back. But she pushes back harder as she cries out, 'Walter, leave me alone!' and he backs off slightly before coming back much harder than before, with 'Man say: I got to change my life, I'm choking to death, baby!'
- Sometimes a character will get his way, defeat resistance, and push the other character right off balance. In the scene above, though, Ruth has a trick up her sleeve. At one point, she responds to Walter not by pushing back but by *turning her back* ('Eat your eggs, they gonna be cold').
- Try it out; Walter pushes hard against Ruth and she suddenly steps back and refuses to engage with him. What happens to Walter? In the play this happens psychologically rather than physically, but the effect is the same.

What you do to get what you want

When people want something, they usually develop a strategy. They might write it down, or it might be less conscious and more instinctive. When a character's objectives have been clarified, actors can consider the different strategies their character uses in trying to gain those objectives – or in trying to overcome the obstacles to those objectives. Once a character has a strategy – even if it is never revealed to the other characters – the playing of that character will be more coherent and convincing.

Walter's strategy is a clumsy one; his desire for the money is so great that it affects every word and every gesture he makes, and his family soon sees through his blatant attempts to manipulate them. Ruth, whose wish is for the family to stay together and live honestly and with dignity, is less openly strategic in her behaviour. But she is determined to protect the family's chance for a better future, and so must stay one step ahead of Walter, even if it means considering terminating her pregnancy. This is an intensely private stratagem, which Mama picks up on but which Walter misses until it is pointed out to him.

Look at the scene above and consider what Walter does, or tries to do, to get what he wants in the scene. Is the strategy apparent in the words he uses? In his movements and gestures? In the way he interacts with Ruth? Note that Walter begins by trying to *enlist* Ruth's support, and when he does not get it, he changes his strategy and tries to *shame* her instead.

- Play out the scene, this time focusing on Walter's *wants*.
- Now repeat the exercise. This time the actor playing Walter stands a short distance away from a chair, on which an object of great value to him is lying. In Walter's case, it might be a bundle of banknotes. Another character, representing the obstacles to Walter's dreams (Ruth, the family, society) stands behind him and holds him back physically. As he speaks his lines, he should strain towards the object on the chair – his words should be projected towards it. He should strain with all his might towards the object, but not succeed in reaching it.
- Now play the scene again, without the holder or the object. Remember the sensation of straining towards the banknotes. They may be invisible to Ruth, but they give life and purpose to Walter.

Each of Walter's wants in the scene produces an *action*. When he tries *to enlist* and *to shame* Ruth, he may not carry out a physical action (like throwing things or hitting Ruth), but his behaviour is expressive of a mental or emotional action. He wants something; he must *do* something to get it. These two actions involve *pulling* Ruth towards him (emotionally) and then *pushing* her away again. Dramatic dialogue is always active – it implies movement (especially attraction and repulsion) even when that movement cannot be seen, or is only seen in minute gestures, moments of contact and rejection, hesitations, impatient interruptions, etc.

Try to make the dialogue work in the same way that the body does, to express the *movement* of your character's thoughts.

An improvisation on intention

- Improvising the dialogue, play the scene between Walter and Ruth. This time, start with the premise that Walter wants to move Ruth from one end of the room to the other. He should use his words, expressions and gestures to push, pull, crowd, cajole, entice and bully her, but he must not force her bodily to cross the space.

  Ruth may argue, turn back or try to ignore Walter but she must *listen* and *respond* to him at all times. The aim of the exercise is to find physical expression for the character's intention in the scene.

- Play the scene again, this time without actually crossing the room. Remember what it was like to use your whole body to try to get what you wanted.

Waking up in character

This is an evocative and involving rehearsal exercise, which works best in a rehearsal, when young actors have made a commitment to a role. It can be adapted for the exploration of character in any play or story. Because of its essentially private, contemplative nature, it is also a good way of bringing a rehearsal session to an end.

- Lie down and imagine all the tension in your body is a liquid which can be drained away through your feet and hands into the floor. Imagine the tension flowing along your arms to your fingers, and from your head to your neck and shoulders and down into your back and hips and pelvis, along the thighs to the shins, ankles and feet, and then out of the feet and onto the floor, where it drains away to nothing.

- When this process is complete, you will 'wake up' as a character of your choice, and in this way 'enter' the space and explore it as though it is your home. You may speak to other characters also waking up in the space, but you do not need to. If you have any elements of costume to hand, put these on as you wake.

Move slowly (you are still tired), and think of how your character sees his/her world and the objects and people in it. Are you dreamy, irritable, hung-over, hopeful? Do you shuffle or stumble? What is the first thing you do when you enter the room (Walter lights a cigarette; Ruth puts on an apron, runs her hands through her hair and begins to make breakfast; Beneatha makes a beeline for the bathroom, etc.)?

Bring together all the elements of your character you have uncovered in the preceding exercises. Remember what you want and how badly you want it. If you are Mama and you want a new house, for example, you might reflect this by gazing out the window at the world beyond the apartment.

Your character is many things at once, and they are all connected: she is her words and silences, her actions and evasions, her domestic rituals, her shouting, smiling, crying. She is what others say about her and she is what she *does* in her interactions with other characters.

A Raisin in the Sun gave new meaning to the experience of live theatre for many of those who took part in the work generated by the production: 'I like this drama because it's got something to do with my grandmum and my life' (Sheila, Year 10). By exploring the dreams and hopes of the Younger family and using games and exercises to bring their dilemmas to life, the work gave young people access to the play's universal relevance: 'It made me think of my heritage, my self and who I really am' (Mary, Year 10). David Lan acknowledged the profound impact the play had on those who saw it and the excitement created in the moment of connection between a drama written almost half a century ago in another country, and a young and diverse contemporary British audience: 'The audience we had for *A Raisin in the Sun* was a dream. And I have absolutely no doubt that the fact that we got that audience affected the quality of the production. You get feedback during the performance. It's rare and precious.' He insists, 'The play hasn't dated at all. Partly because it's a fine piece of art, partly because this core theme of family touches all of us. It also deals with a subject – racism – which is still highly topical. Like all great plays it's a play about the great emotions of life.'

Hansberry's play proved itself to be a masterpiece, which gave strong, authentic, original and unsentimental voice to the problems and possibilities encountered by African-Americans in the exploration of their post-war identities. It was big enough in stature and complex enough in its ideas to inspire and reward investigation at every level. Martin Luther King claimed Hansberry would 'remain an inspiration to generations yet unborn', and indeed young people, particularly those from African and Caribbean backgrounds, 'could greatly identify with the characters' (Pat, Year 10). It is at once funny and profoundly moving. Teacher Maurey Lancaster pointed out that 'for some girls, it was their first experience of live theatre. They loved it, were traumatised, some wept, all thoroughly enjoyed it. One boy paid and went and saw it with his family a second time.'

Kananu Kirimi, who played Beneatha, had a similar response on her first encounter with the play: 'If Lorraine Hansberry can write something that will affect me, so many years after she died, and have that kind of an impact on someone who's just reading it for an audition, then it shows what power you can have to change things, and to inspire.' Actress Novella Nelson (Lena) had sat in the audience of the original production: 'I saw those people up on the stage and thought, "My God – that's my family up there." In the fifteen years following the original production, six hundred African-American theatre companies were founded in America. *A Raisin in the Sun* continues to inspire young people to act to shape their destinies. One critic pointed out that the play's message – that all human beings need their place in the sun – still 'sings out loud and clear if the reaction by Southwark's young British blacks – and whites for that matter – is anything to go by. They stamped, they cheered; above all, they recognised the Younger family's bickering, suffering and painfully rising above the blight of racial discrimination . . . as if it were their own.'

Lennie James described the impact of the play on its audiences: 'During the run of *Raisin* we had what you would call the typical theatregoers but also many more young people and basically more black folks . . . I was party to many post-show discussions. They spoke of its power and its timelessness. They wondered at Lorraine being so young when she wrote the play – and yet knowing so much and getting so much right. Writers who came to see it were inspired, and people who had never been to the theatre before said they would come again. I cannot overstate the effect this play and David's production had on some of the people I talked to –

regardless of age, gender, race or cultural background, the play, which was written over forty years ago, spoke to them. It was pure theatre – it did all the things theatre, at its best, should do and I was proud to be a part of it.'

Chapter 6

LARGER THAN LIFE – SIMPLY HEAVENLY

Langston Hughes, novelist, playwright, poet, essayist and column-ist, was known as the 'Poet Laureate of Harlem'. His musical *Simply Heavenly*, with music by David Martin, was produced in 1957 and transferred to Broadway and later to London. When it was produced at the Young Vic in 2003, directed by Josette Bushell-Mingo, it had not been seen in Britain for forty-five years. The main house production was accompanied by a parallel young people's production of the play in the Studio, directed by Kate Wild.

The hero of *Simply Heavenly* is Jess B. Semple, or 'Simple', a character Hughes created in 1943 in a weekly newspaper column for the *Chicago Defender*. Jess is a simple man, an 'ordinary, hard-working, lower-income bracket' Harlemite, who 'tries hard to succeed, but the chips seldom fall just right'. In his weekly reports, in which he sometimes sparred with his educated friend Boyd, Simple considered the lot of African-Americans in an unequal society, and commented on the disparity between his dreams and his circumstances. But Simple's frustration and disillusionment with his situation is balanced by an enthusiasm for life and a capacity to survive its hard knocks. Hughes described the Simple pieces as 'just myself talking to me, or else me talking to myself'. He collected his Simple stories in several volumes and adapted one of these, *Simple Takes a Wife,* as the musical *Simply Heavenly*.

The play tells the story of Jess's attempts to woo and keep his girlfriend Joyce, whose moral compass steers her away from Jess's rowdy friends and his vivacious lifestyle. Much of the play takes place in Paddy's Bar, where Hughes' characters gather to escape their small rooms and overcrowded apartments and to gossip, woo one another, argue, sing and dance the nights away. Jess's good intentions (he plans to divorce his first wife and marry Joyce) are continually threatened by his friendship with Zarita, 'a lively bar-stool girl wearing life like a loose garment', who tempts him to replace propriety with pleasure, and who lures him early in the play into a reckless car journey which lands Jess in hospital and convinces Joyce that he is flirting too literally with danger. The central figures in the bar are Miss Mamie, a larger-than-life domestic worker, who is hopelessly pursued by Melon, a watermelon seller, laconic bartender Hopkins, dockworker Bodiddly and his irrepressible family, and guitar player Gitfiddle, whose career is declining, along with the blues he plays, under the growing influence of jukeboxes, TV and radio. His plaintive songs are a powerful reminder of the passing of a way of life, and of the history of the Negro slaves, out of whose work songs the blues originally grew.

Jess veers between the bar and Joyce's quiet apartment, where he tries (mostly unsuccessfully) to prove himself responsible enough for her. His grand plan threatens to collapse when Joyce visits him unexpectedly one night to find the denizens of the bar, led by Zarita, carousing drunkenly around his bed. The couple's estrangement leaves Jess forlorn and regretful, and ends when Jess at last demonstrates that he has learned his lesson and become 'the me I ought to be'. His divorce comes through, and Christmas bells turn to wedding bells in a final, celebratory scene.

Simply Heavenly's energy and vitality spring from the streets of Harlem, and, in particular, from gospel music and from the blues, jazz and soul that had filled its bars during the Harlem Renaissance of the 1920s. When it opened on Broadway, critics praised the spirit and directness of the play; Jess Semple's experiences illustrate 'the humor, the quarrels, the intrigues, the crises and the native shrewdness that makes life possible from day to day.' The Young Vic's production, choreographed by Paul J. Medford, sought to recreate the atmosphere of 1940s and 50s Harlem. The production was a hit, and its audience included many young black people from Lambeth and Southwark, some of whom had never been to the theatre before.

The action of *Simply Heavenly* alternates between three main locations or spaces. The most significant of these is Paddy's Bar, which is the public space in the play. Joyce and Simple's apartments make up the other locations. Beyond these spaces (public and private) there is the larger environment of the play itself – 1950s Harlem, with its jazz and blues bars, its street-life, its poverty and its dynamic self-made characters; and beyond that the divided society of mid-century America, with its strict moral standards and its racist laws which would later become the focus of ground-breaking civil rights campaigns led by, among others, Martin Luther King.

How can a company create in performance an engaging, convincing and theatrical sense of a play's contrasting spaces, and of the pressures and conflicts that exist in the world beyond?

In her work with young people, assistant director Rae McKen explored the issue of race and the broad moral and social ideas that inform the action of *Simply Heavenly*. The exercises that follow explore the context of the play and its effect on character and action, and link Langston Hughes' representation of 1940s/50s Harlem to the particular conventions of the musical play. As *Simply Heavenly* is a large-cast ensemble piece, the exercises are also used to build up a shared and unified approach to the characters and the play as a whole.

The world of the (musical) play

The choices you make in rehearsal or workshops about how characters behave and interact will to some extent be defined and determined by your understanding of the wider world they inhabit. In a musical play the action, characterisation and atmosphere tend to be exaggerated. The world of the play is often painted in broad brush strokes; certain elements are emphasised over others (social inequality, for example, or virtue and vice); the expectations of the audience are lifted slightly to allow them to make the transition, along with the actors, from more naturalistic performance styles to heightened, stylised moments of solo or ensemble singing and dancing. In musical theatre, the characters may represent certain values or attitudes from wider society. Performers in musical theatre have to 'reach up' to their roles, and sometimes commit themselves to larger, more demonstrative gestures than those in plays characterised by naturalism or psychological realism (such as *A Raisin in the Sun*).

Society map

- On a large sheet of paper, map out the concepts that define the larger world of the play (1940s/50s America). They might include the Church, the law, race, men and women, money, culture. For each heading or concept, try to think of words or images that relate to it. Try to build up a picture of the world beyond the bar and the bedrooms of the characters.

Start with the information given in the play itself. There are no white characters in the play, but the off-stage action points clearly to a society cleft by racism: a white cop kicks Gitfiddle down the stairs from the street; whites put Semple out of work; at the end of the play a draft card arrives for Arcie's son Abraham Lincoln; as a black soldier, he will be segregated from white soldiers, and this fact leads Semple to dream of a future where black and white soldiers can fight side by side for their country. In the year the play was first produced, an Arkansas governor sent in state troops to deny black children admission to Little Rock High School. Hughes' America is tainted by racism, and its impact is felt by many of the characters in the play.

Morality

This improvisation considers the moral framework of 1950s American society.

- Choose a group: church or bar.

    The church group improvises around one of Joyce's typical Sunday mornings, which might involve attending a morning service, drinking tea with other churchgoers, sewing, etc., probably in the company of women.

    The other group, which is mixed-sex, improvises around a typical evening in Paddy's Bar, with music, dancing, drinking, gossiping, arguing, flirting, fighting.

- One character from each group is then sent with a message to deliver to the other. What does it feel like for a churchgoer like Joyce to enter a rowdy bar? And how does it feel to burst in, uninvited, on a quiet sewing circle? Are the churchgoers all meek and mild? Joyce too has a determined and passionate streak in her; she's not all sugar and spice and clean white bedlinen. When a play sets up seemingly contrasting environments it is tempting to play their inhabitants as polar opposites. But characters and their conflicts become more interesting when they are more complex and contradictory and less like simple stereotypes. What if Joyce has a passionate streak in her and stands up to berate the drunken messenger for throwing his life away? Try it. Let Joyce reveal her hidden strength.

Discrimination

Some of the characters in *Simply Heavenly* – particularly Simple – comment angrily or despondently on the racial prejudice which affected every aspect of the lives of black Americans in the 1950s. The *Simply Heavenly* workshops took place among ethnically diverse groups of young people in Lambeth and Southwark, and Rae McKen set up simple improvisations to explore notions of discrimination and exclusion. Most of us have experienced some form of discrimination in our lives – racism is a more extreme and (often) institutionalised version of discrimination. This exercise does not attempt to lay bare the experience of racism, but focuses instead on discrimination *in action*, as part of the process of defining the world of the play.

- Split the class into two groups or 'types' according to an arbitrary form of discrimination, such as those who have birthdays in the first half of the year (Group A) and those who have birthdays in the second half (Group B).

  Imagine that those in Group A are discriminated against, and will not be served in a café. Instead, they have to stand in a queue by a window at the side, where they will be given the scrapings from other people's plates. Some of the Group A people work as waiters and kitchen hands in the café. The B group is made up of more senior café employees and the 'acceptable' customers.

  It is morning in the café – rush hour – and hungry people are on their way to work. What happens when an A customer insists on entering the café and ordering coffee and toast at a table?

- Start the improvisation with the rest of Group A standing outside the café. How do the B customers react when an unwelcome A person enters their space? Someone might order the newcomer out. Another might fetch the manager. Someone else might speak up for the A customer, but be shouted down by the crowd. What does the manager do? What do other A people do (the employees inside and the rest outside)? Let the improvisation develop naturally; don't stop to discuss things before they happen. If one participant comes up with a particularly interesting or challenging line or gesture you can freeze the improvisation to discuss it – it may push everyone's work in a new direction.

• What if Group A joins forces and refuses to let anyone in or out of the café until the A customer has been served? What if the A employees refuse to keep working until all the As outside in the street are allowed into the café? What if some of the B customers walk out in protest at the management's policy? What if group A decides to set up its own café, out on the street, where everyone will be welcome?

Identity and the world

Look at the comments made by characters in the play about their position in 1950s American society:

MAMIE: Hopkins, them white folks over in Long Island done like to worked me to death. (I.3)

SIMPLE: You know, no matter what a man does, sick or well, something is always liable to happen – especially if he's colored. (I.4)

SIMPLE: I just spent my last nickel for a paper – and there ain't no news in it about colored folks. Unless we commit murder, robbery or rape, or are being chased by a mob, do we get on the front page, or hardly on the back. (I.5)

SIMPLE: This great big old white ocean – and me a colored swimmer. (I.7)

SIMPLE: Boyd, I been caught in some kind of riffle [turbulent water] ever since I been black. (II.5)

MELON: Colored generals never command white troops. (II.9)

SIMPLE: I know some of them Dixiecrats [southerners/racists] would rather die than left face [turn on command] for a colored man. (II.9)

Mamie's status as a domestic worker among the wealthy white community of Long Island is low, but she is a proud woman, content to be herself among her people. Simple, however, carries inside himself an abiding awareness of discrimination and of the limited opportunities that exist for him in a divided society. His good humour is frequently punctured by an awareness of the forces in the wider world which press down on him.

Now look at the scene in which the writer Boyd exhorts Simple to assert his true identity:

> BOYD: You're not the first man in the world to have problems. You've got to learn how to swim, Jess, in this great big ocean called the world.
> SIMPLE: This great big old white ocean – and me a colored swimmer.
> BOYD: Aw, stop feeling sorry for yourself just because you're colored. You can't use race as an excuse forever. All men have problems. And even if you are colored, you've got to swim beyond color, and get to that island that is you – the human you, the man you. (I.7)

- Use this exchange as the starting point for an improvisation set in the bar. In groups, each choose a character from the play (Mamie, Jess, Boyd, Simple, Melon, Zarita, Bodiddly) and one by one answer two questions put to you by a volunteer: 1) What's wrong with your society?; 2) What do you like about your society?

  Before answering the questions as your character, list as a group the different kinds of prejudice that exist in the society in which the play is set (you might identify prejudice around women, class, disability, religion, race).

  In your answers to the questions, try to express what you know about your character's attitudes. If your character is likely to be passionate and animated in his/her answers, don't hold back. If he/she doesn't have strong views either way, make this clear in your tone as well as your replies.

Character in the world of the play

Having begun to define the concepts and qualities that make up the larger world of the characters, you can move towards a more precise, moment-by-moment exploration of their actions and attitudes. First, you need to place the characters in the physical environments they actually inhabit in the play. These create the context for their actions and will specifically influence and affect their behaviour and our understanding of them.

What can the physical environment of a play tell us about its characters? Characters in plays exist in time and space – they may both influence and be influenced by their environments. It can help to imagine your character in a particular space and to consider what kind of interaction with that space he/she might have.

Paddy's Bar is the main location of the play. Hughes doesn't provide a detailed description of this space, though he tells us the bar is 'like a neighborhood club' frequented by 'hard-working lower-income-bracket Harlemites.' He tells us there is a 'battered old piano in the corner' and that characters tend to sit at their 'usual' tables. There is a long bar. On Saturday night, 'the joint is jumping' and the characters dance between the tables.

When he is not drinking in the bar, Simple is either in his own small apartment, or visiting Joyce in her bedsit. Joyce's apartment provides important detail about her life and her character. It indicates her economic position, and its order and cleanliness suggest her sense of propriety. Joyce is poor but proud – unlike Simple, she lives within her means and according to her Christian values.

Rob Howell's set for the Young Vic production married domestic and public scenes 'in a single scenic picture. Between the Harlem bar counter and its silvery, mirror-like back wall is a raised area where there regularly appear, at opposite ends, single beds for the long-term romancers'. In a single image, the contrasting environments, with their different moral and social values, were made visible to the audience, and so we could see, quite literally, how Simple is torn between them. The bar thrust out into the audience, incorporating the observers into the action and involving them in the energetic ensemble scenes.

The characters in musical theatre move fluidly from private encounters to moments of overt self-display, or transform their individuality effortlessly into the single voice of a chorus. But while their behaviour may be heightened and their characters defined with broad brush strokes, they sing, dance, flirt, fight and forgive according to their nature, which remains consistent, no matter how exaggerated their actions.

Word for a character

With the characters located in the wider world and the specific environments of the play, you can begin to examine their individual traits, and then consider their interaction.

- The group sits in a circle. Each person chooses a character from the play and thinks of a word that helps to define their character. A word for Joyce might be 'pure' or 'determined'; for Jess it might be 'confused' or 'playful'.

Character sheets

Director Kate Wild used character sheets in her production with young people.

- Fill in details about a chosen character on a sheet of paper (name, age, marital status) and answer such questions as: 'Where were you born (Harlem, the South)? Where do you live (house, boarding house, apartment)? What are you wearing now? (Draw a diagram of your outfit.) What is your favourite possession? What is your favourite colour? Your favourite food? What is your best quality? What is your worst fault? Your greatest fear? What do you dream of? Each actor should keep a copy of his/her character sheet, and add to it as rehearsals/ workshops progress and opinions are revised.

Hot-seating

This exercise fleshes out the one above. It can give an actor confidence in his/her representation of a character. It is used here not just as a rehearsal technique, but as a means of encouraging young participants to speak with authority, by licensing their interpretation of their character.

- Sit in a semicircle, with one character on a chair – the hot seat – facing the rest of the group. Each participant will take turns to sit there as his/her character. He/she will be asked questions by the director and members of the group. The questions can be banal or very challenging; the only guiding principle is that the exercise is purely for the actor in the seat, not everyone else. This means that questions should only be asked that will help that actor's understanding of the character, and help him/her to explore that understanding.

The actor should remain in character throughout. He/she should answer in the first person and respond as that character would. If a question bores the character, and if the character would be likely to say so, then say so. Use facts from the play in your answer. If the question is offensive and would in reality prompt a walkout or a fight, so be it. Similarly, questions that pedantically pursue factual information the actor does not have must be avoided. The person in the hot seat should try to imagine his/her chosen character's life in as much detail as possible; but the starting point should be the information contained within the play. Is your character educated? Is he married? Does he drink in bars? Does he play a musical instrument? Does he have a violent temper? What does he love most in life? Does he have brothers or sisters? What does he do for fun? What does he like to drink? How does he dress? If you don't know the answer, say 'pass'. Someone else in the group should make a note of those things that need further exploration or development.

You might be asked specific questions about your motivation in particular scenes. Someone might ask of Jess Semple, for example, why did you go driving with Zarita when you knew it would upset Joyce? What do you hope for in your life with Joyce? Why did your first marriage fail? Will you keep on seeing Zarita after you've married Joyce?

Looking in the mirror

This is a private visualisation exercise which can be used to relax and focus actors while encouraging them to take responsibility for the definition of their character. A version of it was used by Kate Wild in rehearsal. 'I got them all to lie down and shut their eyes (a darkened room or closed eyes goes a long way to getting rid of self-consciousness – they know no one is watching them!)'

- Imagine you are your character, lying awake in bed at dawn. Imagine your bed, the feel of the sheets and pillow. Imagine the room around the bed, and the house beyond, and the street coming to life outside. Now, still lying down with your eyes closed, imagine you are getting out of bed and going to stand before a mirror. What do you see in the mirror? Who are you, all alone at this time, without your 'public face' on?

'I asked them questions about who the person in the mirror is. What is the look in their eyes (anger, sadness, hope, etc.)? This exercise gives them quiet, reflective time and space to think about their character and flesh out lots of detail.'

Walking around the room in character

This exercise follows on from the one above. The aim is to 'inhabit' your character's body. 'This terrifies even experienced actors,' according to Wild, 'and it is really important to give them starting points. So I get them to try extremes: e.g. walk very tall, proud and happy . . . then walk slumped, humble and unhappy. Then find somewhere between the two that fits their character.' This exercise can help actors to find convincing detail in their representations. They will remember the exaggerations at either end of the scale, and know that their character has the capacity, in moments of exuberance or despair, to reach those extremes.

- Choose a character and walk around the room as that character. Imagine your character is feeling proud and happy. How does Mamie walk when she is in this mood? How does Joyce walk? What about Simple? Lead with one part of your body.
- Now imagine your character is dejected and depressed.
- Consider any character tics or eccentricities.
- Now try to walk around the room in character on a 'normal' day, when you are neither buoyant nor miserable, just yourself. You might have a slight tendency towards one or other mood, depending on how you see your character and how the playwright describes him/her.

- Having found this 'true' movement and expression for your character, try to express different moods for that character: sassy/uptight; old/young; vigorous/tired, etc.
- If costumes are available, put them on. How does your character wear his jacket, or her hat? Would he be likely to leave his laces undone? Does Joyce do up all the buttons on her dress or jacket? Imagine your character is getting undressed at the end of the day. How does he treat his clothes? Does he fold them neatly or drop them on the floor? Simple might, unless he is thinking of Joyce, and his responsibilities as her future husband, at the time.

Kate Wild claims, 'I think the most important thing these exercises did was to make their characterisation their responsibility. It got them interested, involved.' This is, in effect, a physical version of hot-seating.

Where have you come from?

This exercise is used specifically to help actors with their entrances into scenes, by giving them a physical starting point for the scene and helping them to enter in character, rather than having to 'find' the character in the course of the scene. It is based on the idea that off-stage action may influence on-stage action, and that realistically drawn characters are assumed to continue their lives between scenes. This doesn't apply to all plays, of course, but in *Simply Heavenly*, as in *A Raisin in the Sun*, the playwright makes a number of references to the offstage lives of the characters.

Langston Hughes' characters have jobs and families beyond the bar. They drive cars, have accidents, clean the houses of wealthy white people, work on the docks, play music. These other unseen lives and activities, these encounters with policemen and passers-by, all influence the way the characters enter Paddy's Bar or the private rooms in the play.

Look at Jess's arrival at the bar after his car accident with Zarita:

MAMIE: Look who's coming there!
PIANIST: Hy, Jess!
MELON: Jess Semple!
HOPKINS (*Lifting a bottle of beer*): It's on the house!

MAMIE: Welcome home!

BODIDDLY: To the land of the living!

MAMIE: Amen! Bless Jess!

HOPKINS: Zarita was just looking for you. (*Happily the customers retire to tables with the drinks as Simple remains leaning stiffly on the bar.*)

SIMPLE: Don't mention Zarita, please, Hop! She's near about ruint me. (I.5)

- Before performing this scene, try a short improvisation in which all the participants play Jess in his hospital bed. Lie down on your side. Imagine you have a badly grazed backside, and are cut and bruised from being thrown out of a moving car. Now get up gingerly and hobble across the floor. Take off your hospital gown and put your street clothes on. Feel the stiffness in your legs and arms.
- In groups of six, one actor plays Jess. Perform the scene above, focusing specifically on Jess's entrance. The other characters are already standing or sitting at the bar. Try to carry the feeling of tenderness from the hospital improvisation into the bar. Jess may find it difficult to turn his head to greet his friends, or raise his hand in salute. His ribs may be bruised. If someone slaps him on the back, it will cause great pain. Inevitably, someone will.
- When you have carried out this exercise, perform a silent exercise in which each character from the play enters the bar, one by one. Try to express from the way you enter what you may have been doing immediately prior to entering. Have you been at work? What sort of work? Have you been sleeping? Drinking? Have you been doing your hair and putting on make-up? Bring something of the world outside the bar in with you as you enter.

Character interaction

This exercise draws attention to the heightened emotional states which characterise much musical theatre. In order for characters to move in and out of the stylisation of songs, their surrounding action and expression tends to be slightly larger than life, so the contrast between 'ordinary' interactions and those that are sung isn't too great. The world of the musical play is often a little brighter or a little darker, a little more exaggerated, than that of a purely naturalistic drama.

Look at the following scene in Paddy's Bar. Simple arrives, disconsolate, after Zarita and her friends have so offended Joyce with their wild party in Simple's room that she has now rejected her boyfriend and refuses to return his calls:

Simple enters and gloomily begins taking articles from his pockets and putting them on the bar.

SIMPLE: Hop, you seen Zarita?
HOPKINS: Nope. Guess she's still recovering from her birthday.
SIMPLE: If you do see her, give her this junk . . .

Zarita enters, cool, frisky, and pretty as ever.

HOPKINS: Uh-oh!
ZARITA: Hel-lo! Jess, I'm glad I caught you. I was a little shy about coming round to your place for my things.
SIMPLE: I brought your things here, Zarita. (*Hopkins puts them on the bar.*)
ZARITA: I thought you might, you're so sweet, sugar. Lemme treat you to a drink, and you too, Hop.
SIMPLE: No, thank you.
ZARITA: Don't be that way. Set us up here, Hopkins.
SIMPLE: I'm not drinking no more myself . . .
ZARITA: I meant no harm. I'm just trying to cheer you up. Like that party which I brought around to your house. Knowing you wasn't working, thinking maybe you'd be kinder embarrassed to come to my place for my birthday and not bring a present, I brought the party to you. Meant no harm – just to cheer you up.
SIMPLE: Please don't try to cheer me up no more, Zarita. Hop, I'm cutting out . . . (*Simple starts out*) . . .
SIMPLE: I'm just gonna stand on the sidewalk and look up at her window.
HOPKINS: I hope you see a light, pal.

Simple exits as the Pianist begins to play softly, 'Look for the Morning Star'. He sings, starting with the release.

PIANIST: Look for the morning star
Shining in the dawn.
Look for the rainbow's arch
When the rain is gone.

The remainder of the song he hums. Zarita, lonely, looks around at the quiet bar, then cries in desperation.

ZARITA: I'm lonesome, Hop! I'm lonesome! I'm lonesome! (*She buries her head on the bar and weeps as the piano continues*) I'm lonesome . . . (II.4)

- Work in groups of five. A 'narrator' tells the story of this scene while four actors mime the action. This forces you to concentrate on the essential or fundamental events which show the emotional state of the characters (Simple's dejected entrance; his refusal of Zarita's offer of a drink; her explanation of her actions; his departure to stand under Joyce's window; the pianist's sentimental and dreamy singing; Zarita's lonely tears).

What your character is feeling

- In groups of four, act out the scene above between Zarita and Simple, with Hopkins and the pianist looking on. Whenever the director claps his/her hands, make a specific gesture to show physically how your character is really feeling. Are you hiding your feelings from other characters or openly expressing them? When the leader claps again, continue with the scene as if nothing has happened.

   Note that Simple tends to show and talk about his feelings openly – his words and his actions reinforce one another. Zarita, however, presents a cheerful and carefree face to the world, while in fact she is lonely and unhappy. Can you show the physical transformation that takes place in her when Jess leaves the bar? She may sit awhile smoking, or looking at her possessions scattered across the bar. She may struggle to remain cheerful, or try to divert herself by putting on lipstick, etc. This is an important moment in the play, as it reveals something hidden in Zarita and gives us a deeper and more sympathetic understanding of her character. In one scene she moves from being 'cool and frisky' to crying in desperation. In the heightened world of musical theatre, these sweeping emotional shifts are not unusual, but they must still be convincing within the context of the play. Zarita is a 'lively bar-stool girl' and a femme fatale, but she is still human, and that means she is vulnerable, contradictory and complex as a character.

Where do you stand?

- Choose a scene from the play and find its major event, for example, Jess's arrival at Zarita's birthday party.
- Choose a character, then decide on your character's opinion of this event.
- The director/leader names an event and the different characters go immediately to a designated part of the room which represents a positive, an indifferent or a negative response to that event. For example, when Zarita and the company burst into Jess's room to celebrate her birthday, Zarita and the denizens of the bar would all rush to the positive corner, while Joyce and the landlady would move immediately to the negative corner. Jess might begin in the negative corner, move to the positive and then return to the negative as he realises the trouble he is in once Joyce arrives. If any characters are indifferent to an event, or seem to be, the director might ask them to make either a positive or negative choice. This exercise demands quick, clear and instinctive character responses.

Intention to communicate

Each line of dialogue should clearly express the intention of the speaker and establish a connection with the person or people being addressed.

- Stand in a circle and speak the following lines of dialogue. Every time you speak, point at the person you are addressing. If you are addressing the entire group, point at each of them in turn as you speak. The aim is to signal an intention to *communicate*. This is crucial in a large-cast, ensemble play, and is true of musical numbers as well as ordinary dramatic dialogue.

HOPKINS: (To Mamie) Good evening, Miss Mamie. How's tricks?

MAMIE: (To Hopkins) Hopkins, them white folks over in Long Island done like to worked me to death. I'm just getting back to town.

PIANIST: (To Mamie) You ought to have a good man to take care of you, Miss Mamie – like me.

MAMIE: (To Pianist) Huh! Bill, from what I see of you, you can hardly take care of yourself. (To Hopkins and Pianist) I got a mighty lot of flesh here to nourish.

PIANIST: (To Mamie) Big woman, big appetite . . .

MAMIE: (To Hopkins) Hopkins, gimme a gin.

BODIDDLY: (To Hopkins, Mamie, Pianist) Hey, now, anyhow!

MAMIE: (To Bodiddly) Anyhow, what?

BODIDDLY: (To Mamie) Anyhow, we's here! (To Hopkins, Mamie, Pianist) Who's setting up tonight? (*Dead silence. No one answers.*) (To Hopkins) Well, Hop, I'll take a short beer. (I.3)

These exercises together encourage young actors to inhabit the characters and their world rather than simply learning their lines. As one of the cast members of the young people's production of the play pointed out, 'It made me think that acting as a character isn't just acting. You have to find out about your character. And think as your character.'

Songs

Musicals such as *Simply Heavenly* require the actors to move fluently from naturalistic performance to heightened moments at which one or more characters sing to one another and to the audience. Josette Bushell-Mingo had to adapt the rehearsal process to the demands of a musical play: 'the scenes have to be hot, you have to earn the songs; I think you have to have much more sense of humour to do a musical, much more of a theatricality, I think you have to have much more of a sense of pathos . . . everything has to be lifted slightly.'

The transition from speech to song needs to be justified in the context of the play, and it's important not to lose the lyrics of the songs under the music, especially when the cast is singing together – these words convey the changing mood of the play and help to define its world. Hughes combined traditional verse forms – defined by what he called the 'racial rhythms' of their poetry – with jazz and blues music to create the strongly atmospheric music of *Simply Heavenly*.

The songs in musical theatre are an integral part of the play and can be explored by young people in the same way as any other passage of dialogue. But extra attention needs to be paid to their delivery and directors should focus in particular on creating a solid ensemble, so participants do not feel vulnerable or exposed, especially when singing solos.

Vocal warm-ups such as tongue-twisters, singing simple rounds and singing at different volumes are all important, not only in loosening up the voice but also as ice-breakers. Musical director Stuart Morley, who worked on the young people's version of *Simply Heavenly*, feels 'people are often scared to make new sounds or to be loud and confident – unless they feel they are supported by the other people in the room, and that everyone is not going to laugh at them if it all goes wrong.' (For vocal warm-ups, see pp. 40–43)

Approaching a song

Look at some of the transitions between speech and song in the play, and consider the mood of the character at that point. This will determine whether the song is rousing and energetic, whether the singer calls other characters in, or whether it is a more personal and reflective utterance. The songs are an extension of the character's identity; each has his/her own performance style, and their lyrics reveal a great deal about them, and need to be clearly articulated.

- As a group, read out the exchange below, which includes a transition from speech to song. Don't sing the words of the song, just speak them as though they were prose:

MAMIE: I'm a lone wolf, I runs with no pack.
MELON: I would pack you on my back if you would let me.
MAMIE: I don't intend to let you. To tell the truth, I doubt your intentions. And, Melon, I wants you to know: (*She sings*)

I been making my way for a long, long time,
I been making my way through this world.
I keep on trying to be good
'Cause I'm a good old girl.
I been making my way with a boot and shoe.
In no oyster have I found a pearl.
I trust myself – so I've got luck
Cause I'm a good old girl.
Sometimes the devil beckons
I look at the devil and say, (*Melon touches her hand*)
Stop that!
Devil, devil, devil –
Devil, be on your way!
I been making my way through thick and thin
'Spite o'devilish men in this world.
There ain't no man can get me down
Not even Harry Belafonte,
'Cause I'm a good old girl.
(*Mamie rises and addresses the entire bar*)
I make five or ten dollars, sometimes more a day.
You men what ain't working know that that ain't hay.
Don't let no strange man get his hand on you –
There's no telling, baby, what a strange cat will do.
It takes all kinds of folks to spin this globe around,
But *one* bad actor tears your playhouse down. (II.9)

- What sort of music do you think would best support this song: fast, slow, high, low, mellow, harsh, etc.? The things to keep in mind are the subject matter and mood of the song, and the character of the singer.
- Use the voice and text exercises from Chapter 4 (*Doctor Faustus*) to pin down the important words and ideas in the songs.
- Repeat the lyrics as a group, speaking the words more expressively and emphatically, beating out a rhythm for them as you go. Look in particular for any shifts of focus or changes of mood in the song and mark these clearly. Note that Mamie continues to address Melon when she begins the song, and addresses him specifically when she says/sings 'Stop that!' Then she turns to involve the entire bar – the song becomes a general statement which Mamie delivers to the world. Its delivery

should get bigger as its implications do. Address one another directly as you speak the last six lines.

- Stand in pairs, facing each other, and read the lyrics aloud. With each new idea or sentence in the song, shake hands with the person opposite. The aim is to separate each of the thoughts from one another so that when they are sung the ideas remain whole, and the words do not run into one another.

Style and delivery

- In order to find the most effective performance style for a song, it can be useful, and fun, to explore the limits of exaggeration and 'pantomime acting'. Start by speaking the first four lines of 'Good Old Girl' as quietly and neutrally as possible. Now speak it very loudly in a variety of accents: Australian, American, French, Swedish, Scottish etc.
- Now speak the first four lines together, but imagine you are a passionate preacher. Put as much gusto as you can into the performance.
- Finally speak the lines in a rap version. Actor Rashan Stone, who played Jess Semple in the professional production, saw the songs as 'an early form of rap'.

Consider the different qualities of each version and compare with Mamie's own character. What sort of singing style best expresses Mamie's character and conveys her intentions in the song?

Creating a relationship with an audience

Critic Susannah Clapp said of the songs in Bushell-Mingo's production, 'Hughes' work is like listening to Chinese whispers. A song starts with one character slumped in a corner of the room and is passed, hissed, sung to a host of barflies, so it turns into something else.' Songs in musicals often get 'bigger' as they continue, becoming more public and incorporating more characters into their audience.

- With a single performer playing Mamie, explore the difference between singing/speaking the song
  a) privately to Melon

    b) more publicly to a small group in the bar
    c) to the entire audience in a theatre.

What effect does it have on the way the song is sung? Those who aren't singing can be Mamie's audience. There must be a palpable sense of connection between Mamie and her immediate audience. The listeners should click their fingers at the end of each line of the song, or mutter, gospel style, 'Yes, you are', or 'yes, she has', etc. The aim is to help the actor/singer keep his/her connection with the listener and with each of the ideas or thoughts in the song.

Songs in musical plays are a part of the dramatic action. The play does not stop while the song is delivered; its characters continue to interact with one another; they carry the feelings which prompted the song right through to its finish, and the song and its presentation have an impact on the characters who hear it. Young actors adapt readily to the conventions of musical drama, and plays such as *Simply Heavenly* give them the opportunity to extend the range of their skills and interests. Seize the songs – pass them to one another like a ball in a warm-up game; keep them in the air and throw them, thought by thought, out towards your audience. This sense of energy and spontaneity is vital in any live performance, and is the life blood of musical theatre. Rashan Stone insists that 'every single audience that comes has to believe that it has never happened before. When you talk about acting I'd say that's what it is, it's about being able to repeat something and give the illusion that it's happening before your eyes.'

Staging the world of the play: an example of a rehearsal process

How can a group move from individual workshop exercises that open up the world of a play to a full rehearsal process which requires a collaborative ensemble and gathers together all the diverse strands of the work to that point? When parallel young people's versions of main stage plays are produced at the Young Vic, the rehearsal process is preceded by a workshop week, in which fifty to sixty participants explore the play in question using exercises such as those above. During these workshop auditions the director will cast the production on the basis of detailed work with young people, and even those who are not cast gain a thorough understanding of the play and the techniques used to explore it.

Kate Wild eventually worked with a cast of eighteen young people to produce *Jus' a Little Simply Heavenly*, a one-hour version of Langston Hughes' play. The company rehearsed twice a week for eight weeks before presenting the play over two nights in the Young Vic Studio. Wild's approach to the process recognised at every point the importance of creating and maintaining an ensemble of performers, and of giving the actors the opportunity to contribute their own ideas and expressive energy to the heightened and dynamic world of musical theatre.

Adapting the text

Kate Wild adapted Langston Hughes' play to provide an opportunity for every member of the large company to participate fully in the production. She focused the action on Paddy's Bar, where the majority of ensemble work takes place, and created six new parts (two choruses of singers and dancers) by dividing up existing songs and dialogue: 'I thought it was quite important that the young people playing these created parts didn't feel "tacked on" to the main production.' The resulting play is approximately fifty minutes long – the reduction in length gave the participants more time to explore staging and songs. 'I did like my character,' one cast member recalls. 'Even though it was a made up one, it ended up fitting in the play perfectly.'

Kate's advice in adapting/editing plays is to be bold and imaginative in exposing the main action of the play and to create opportunities for everyone to be actively involved. In training young people in theatre arts, the emphasis is on cooperation, professionalism and participation, rather than on straining for a 'definitive' interpretation of a text. These productions are in a sense works in progress; they encourage participants to take part not only in the production in question, but also in the next production and the one after that; each time gaining in physical and verbal confidence, technical skill and interpretative insight.

Casting

Casting for *Jus' a Little Simply Heavenly* was done during a week of intensive workshops on the play attended by over fifty local young people. The broad aim of workshop auditions is to increase the participants' confidence, give them knowledge of the story of the play, tools to use when exploring plays, to establish the language and methods used by the director in rehearsals and to assess each participant in order to cast the production. 'Our primary criterion,' says Wild, 'was enthusiasm and commitment. We also gave larger parts to older students as we felt they would best deal with the responsibility this entailed. We tried to cast around people's strengths, but also tried to stretch people. We knew for example that one of the participants could sing, but she didn't really want to. We gave her a song, and while making it clear that she wouldn't have to perform it in front of anyone if she didn't want to, coached her through it. She was brilliant and now has gained confidence in singing in public.' The workshop week meant that even those who were not cast in the production gained valuable experience and took part in the same games and exercises which were later used in the rehearsal process.

Creating an ensemble

Around half of the company involved in the production had taken part in previous projects at the Young Vic. One of the young people who had come to the Young Vic on work experience was employed as stage manager. Her primary task was to call the company for rehearsals and to record lighting and sound cues, props and blocking in the 'prompt copy' of the play.

Rehearsals incorporated sessions on voice work and singing, led by Musical Director Stuart Morley, and on dance, led by choreographer Carolene Hinds. Designer Naomi Dawson worked with the company to design period costumes based on the actors' own ideas.

Wild felt the creation of an ensemble was vital, especially in a production where some parts are considerably larger than others. 'I think the best thing you can do is be as egalitarian as you can.' She advises giving special attention during each rehearsal to small parts, and to decisions about individual entrances and exits and action. 'If someone comes up and asks even the most trivial question about their line, give it serious thought. Give them time. I realised that, as director, my attention was very important to them all and I tried to be as generous with it as possible.' She used warm-up games and songs at the beginning of every rehearsal to bring the company together and to remind them of their common objective: to entertain their audience, sharpen their performance skills and enjoy themselves. Sometimes individual cast members lose focus or confidence and need to be privately prodded or reassured; every company is different, and directors will have to be flexible in their approach to the changing levels of concentration. It may be unreasonable, for example, to expect the actors to give their full attention to complex problems at the end of a long day's rehearsal. It's generally better to reassert their group identity with a song, dance or game in situations like this.

The rehearsal schedule

Rehearsals took place twice a week over eight weeks (three hours on one evening per week and all day on Saturdays). Call sheets were handed to the actors every fortnight, with permission slips for parents/guardians. 'Because we were working with minors, we needed to call them well in advance and we needed to sign them in and out and then keep them in the rehearsal room. All the waiting around in rehearsals can be a problem with young people, because if they are feeling impatient they show it! I had to be organised well in advance with my rehearsal schedule. The smaller a group you have, the better, so where possible I called only a few of the cast for set periods.'

Wild did character and scene work with small groups or individuals, calling the entire company only when all the songs were being rehearsed, and for four run-throughs, the technical and dress rehearsals, and the performances of the show. The 'tech' tested everyone; this rehearsal introduces lighting and sound operators to the play on stage and moves painstakingly from cue to cue. The actors are present to illustrate the action for the technicians rather than to hone their performances. These rehearsals can be frustratingly slow in technically complicated shows, but they are an essential part of the process, and of the experience of any young person interested in the theatre arts.

The world of the play

The rehearsal process began with a sit-down read-through of the script. It is useful to clear up any confusion or questions about the script before the actors get on their feet. Professional casts often spend an entire week on this process. Early rehearsals also included discussion and research into the historical and cultural context of the play. Sometimes directors bring specialists in to talk to the company at this stage – voice coaches, historians, etc., who help them establish the world of the play and explore any unusual environments or situations. Kate Wild used sound and music as her way into the world of the play, and as a means of opening up the musical possibilities of the piece. 'Harlem was such an alien world to the participants and I thought it was really important that they had a strong grasp of the place. We did an exercise where I handed out a selection of material, from photographs to poems to CDs of jazz to newspaper clippings: all centred around Harlem. I asked each group to create an easily repeatable sound from the material (for example, jazz scatting, a street vendor's cry, traffic noise). We then built a soundscape of Harlem from each group's sound. With some groups I had time to get them to create an action as well and we staged a street scene.' During rehearsals, stand-in props were used by the actors. The Deputy Stage Manager will be responsible for compiling a list of rehearsal props and ensuring they are to hand when needed.

Scene work

Where time allows, some directors may choose to sketch certain scenes lightly in early rehearsals, to ensure that the actors understand the dialogue and can begin to explore the emotions of the scene. Introductory scene work is followed by more detailed exploration of the play, moment by moment, in an attempt to uncover the desires of the characters, how they respond to one another, and their intention in entering each scene. Some of the exercises in this chapter were used to help the actors to be very specific about the behaviour, style and manner of their characters and how they relate to one another.

Directors may decide either early or late in the process to focus on where the actors will be on stage throughout the scene.

Complicated moves, however, need to be carefully choreographed and their rehearsal should not be left until too late. Kate Wild felt rehearsals were 'most successful when I made the cast make their own decisions. After reading the scene a few times I got them to decide on the stage area and where all the furniture went (it needed to be readjusted once we were in the theatre, but that took very little time). So the actor who was playing Joyce told us the layout of her room, based on a visualisation exercise. Talking this through with them made them realise that they could contribute to the rehearsal, disagree with me and make their own decisions. It also got them comfortable with their surroundings and started them building an imaginative world.'

Song, dance, movement

The musical numbers in the play often involved the entire ensemble and young participants tend to respond enthusiastically to these sections of the rehearsals. Stuart Morley was direct and insistent about the need for concentration, effort and commitment during rehearsals; he challenged the actors to do their best and acknowledged their efforts when they did: 'Young people need to feel they can add comments, ask questions and contribute their ideas on how to develop the material and interpret the lyrics.'

Each full rehearsal included vocal warm-ups and a song rehearsal – usually a song in the scene being explored, or an ensemble song to energise and focus the company. At other times individual actors or small groups worked intensively on the songs. Musical theatre requires a coordinated rehearsal process which ensures that every element of the play – song, dance and the narrative action – is fully rehearsed and explored with equal commitment. Morley focused on creating a stable environment of trust in the rehearsal room, principally by incorporating playful warm-ups and exercises: 'This helps develop the actors' techniques without them really realising and without taking a heavy "singing lesson" approach.' Morley then moved on to explorations of style and delivery, the meaning of the lyrics and the changing voice quality during the course of a song. Finally the song was sung by principals or the entire cast.

In the dance rehearsals, choreographer Carolene Hinds

incorporated dance steps from the 1940s and 50s. She 'gave [the actors] very specific moves which they loved because they felt very safe knowing exactly what they were doing'. These dance scenes were tightly choreographed, but elsewhere, the director 'tried not to choreograph too much, particularly in crowd scenes. I wanted them to take responsibility for their own characters and let them play a part in shaping individual scenes. Rather than saying, "On this line walk over there," I would say, "You need to be here for this line so find the right moment to leave and a reason to come over". Or I would give them the general motivation, "You think this is a party and you are making yourself at home," and then encourage them to do something and tweak here and there to make it more watchable. They always responded brilliantly when I made them do the thinking, and came up with rich and imaginative ideas.'

Diary of a rehearsal

24.3.03. Rehearsal call 6–9pm, Young Vic Studio. Confusion about call times: some arrive late and the start is delayed which fractures concentration. Kate stresses the importance of being on time, taking responsibility for the smooth working of rehearsals, and draws attention to the next call time. Lots of texting, dancing, singing on arrival; Kate settles them with warm-up and games ('balancing the floor', 'trust circle'). Revised draft retains ensemble celebration scenes and four songs. Focuses on community, music, class, race, relationships. Intended audience of sixty.

6.30. Naomi shows model box. Some think it's 'really cool'; some disappointed by predominance of wood in simple set in brown, cream, black, but excited by prospect of playing in the round with audience seated at tables as if in a café. Keen to discuss period costumes. One actor says she likes coming to theatre and having a proper schedule. Kate leads them to casual rehearsal of 'Did you ever hear the blues?' They're immediately focused; enjoying the singing, and the moodiness of the music.

6.50. Walk-through of Scenes 7–9, with scripts. Kate dives in and out, blocking and discussing motivation, encouraging actor playing Zarita to 'home in' on Jess Semple. The simple stage direction 'Zarita enters glittering' needs to be interpreted.

When she finds the moment, they run through it again to nail it. Kate encourages actors to make choices about when to break/hold a moment and when to drive their intention home. Kate takes one of the actors out for a quiet chat – she's been talking, not concentrating, missing cues. Kate discusses aim of each scene with principle actors and leads a walk-through off book of Scene 9 between Joyce and Jess.

7.40. Musical director Stuart runs voice warm-up with entire cast: face and voice exercises, singing a line in ascending keys and different accents; short songs sung together: this is playful ensemble work. Run-through of song, 'Morning Star'. Stuart describes singing style of '50s – emphasis on blues sound. He demands focus from the cast and drives them to fill the room with sound, which they do. 'Scenario' work: 'What would Pavarotti be like if he was born in Harlem?' he asks. They nearly take the roof off. Company works on 'Did you ever hear the blues?' Stuart pushes them to find their characters: 'Act! Act up!' He demands their attention, but responds warmly to suggestions from cast, and insists that 'it's all about having confidence'. He recognises quickly when they're tired and no longer making discoveries: 'Last time, we're bored now.'

8.20. Run Scene 6 to 'Did you ever hear the blues?' Concentrate on precise placement of furniture, entrances and exits, now that the set design is in place. Kate asks all to remember entrances, exits, blocking. Gets company to describe action of scene. Asks them to stay in character even when not speaking, to make sure there are no 'dead spots' in the room. Encourages them to enlarge their performances to be heard over double bass and sax: 'It's your responsibility to make what you're doing big enough to be heard by the whole room.' Explores ways of moving into the song without assembling actors in one place. Decides to bring choreographer in to choreograph actors during song. Find its changing mood: characters sing to one another or to themselves. Their energy flags. Kate challenges them to give it everything, and gets a sudden, electrifying delivery of the song. What they have yet to develop in precision and power, they make up for completely in energy, intensity and total commitment to the world they have created.

'It was marvellous to see how the young people had captured all the life-enhancing joy of the main stage production,' commented a member of the audience at the Studio production of *Simply Heavenly*. 'This is a beacon of hope for the future for everyone involved in the production.' Director Josette Bushell-Mingo sees the play as 'part of our history and part of the arc of black history and art. Langston Hughes is there with Shakespeare as far as I'm concerned and great work should be performed. He was saying that there is hope; within all this grief, ignorance and poverty, people and specifically black people will find a way to exist and rise above it. We need to see people living and loving in an uplifting and dignified way.' Bushell-Mingo responded to a quality in the play identified in reviews of the first production in New York: 'Its great merit is that Mr Hughes contemplates the people he is writing about with a respect that never becomes patronizing or stuffy and always retains its sense of humour.' Almost fifty years later, according to critic Charles Spencer, the effect was the same: 'It leaves you feeling blessed as well as elated.' *Simply Heavenly* captured a mood which energised performers and audience alike, and gave young people the opportunity to work together to create, inhabit and investigate a complete and robust theatrical world, through the play's 'glowing vignettes' of life on the edge in Harlem.

Chapter 7

PUBLIC AND PRIVATE SELVES – PERIBANEZ

The Young Vic's 2003 production of Lope de Vega's *Peribanez* (c.1605), directed by Rufus Norris, restored to prominence the work of this astonishingly productive playwright of Spain's Golden Age. Born in Madrid in 1562, Lope de Vega claimed to have written 1,500 plays, of which some five hundred are still extant. His life was as colourful as his dramas; he wrote twenty-one volumes of poetry, numerous dialogue novels and literary essays; he sailed on the Spanish Armada and was an officer of the Inquisition. He married twice, fathered nine children, had a number of affairs, mostly with actresses and married women (one of which led to eight years' exile from Madrid), became a priest, and was an avid gardener. His lavish state funeral lasted for nine days. He introduced the *comedia nueva* to Spain, which flouted the classical unities of time, place and action, and combined tragedy and comedy in a potent and earthy mix that drew enthusiastic crowds to Madrid's open-air theatres for over fifty years.

Lope's plays represent the flourishing of a culture fed by Spain's plundering of the New World in an age of discovery and costly colonial expansion. The bloom of artistic achievement that followed this period was accompanied, however, by political and economic decline at home. It is not surprising, then, that his plays deal with issues of power and honour – staples of Renaissance drama. What is less predictable, however, is Lope's exploration of these ideas through the character of a peasant hero, Pedro Ibanez (Peribanez). The play's moral and emotional centre is occupied by the agricultural workers of Ocana.

Peribanez opens with the wedding celebrations for Peribanez and his bride Casilda. The festivities are interrupted by the arrival of the Commander of Ocana, who has been injured by a mad bull. Out of his world, half out of his mind, the Commander wakes at the edge of death to find himself gazing on Casilda's lovely face.

Against tradition, convention and even his own better judgement, the Commander determines to win her heart, despite her firm protestation of love for Peribanez.

He enlists the help of his mule-man Lujan, who procures animals and jewels for Peribanez and his wife. The Commander pursues the couple on an expedition to Toledo to join the festival celebrations. He orders an artist to paint Casilda's portrait in secret. He languishes for want of her. His man Leonardo seduces Casilda's cousin Ines, in hope of securing his master's entry to Casilda's house. On a journey to Toledo to repair Ocana's statue of St Roque, Peribanez discovers the portrait of Casilda and is infected with suspicion and jealousy. Mad with desire, the Commander tries to woo Casilda in his absence, but she is steadfast in her love.

In a desperate attempt to remove Peribanez from the scene, the Commander ennobles him by knighting him and making him captain of a shoddy band of local men. He sends them to fight 'the Arab' under the King's orders. Peribanez claims the right to use his new sword, strapped on for him by the Commander, to uphold his honour, and charges the Commander with the responsibility of protecting Casilda in his absence. He leaves for battle but returns secretly on horseback in the night. When the Commander attempts to rape Casilda in Peribanez's house, Peribanez bursts from his hiding place in a sack of flour and mortally wounds the Commander, before killing Lujan and, finally, mercilessly, Ines, whose foolish love for Leonardo has prompted her betrayal of Casilda. Peribanez flees with a stunned Casilda.

The dying Commander recognises the justice of Peribanez's actions and in his final moments forgives him. When he learns of the Commander's death, the King offers a reward for the capture of Peribanez. At this moment the fugitives are brought before him, bloodstained and dishevelled. Peribanez recounts his tale and begs for mercy for his innocent wife. Prompted by the Queen's sympathetic response to the tragic tale, the King pardons Peribanez, who is left with the ruins of his brief happiness and the prospect of an early death in the King's army. (In the original text, the King's decision produces reconciliation and celebration all round, but in Norris's production, adapter Tanya Ronder instead pursued the darker implications of the action through to their bitterly ironic conclusion.)

Like *Doctor Faustus*, the bigger themes in the play are explored through the choices and actions of complex and sometimes contradictory individuals, while the blending of comic and tragic elements make ready moral judgements difficult and remind us of the imperfect humanity of the characters. Rufus Norris's production sought to give physical form to the abstract ideas and emotional dilemmas in the play. He gave breadth and depth to even the small characters, and focused on the emotional narrative created by 'people living the day they will remember for the rest of their lives'.

Lope de Vega wrote the play in polymetric verse (combining several different metres and forms) which gave greater flexibility and depth to the characterisation and allowed for more relaxed and naturalistic dialogue than had previously been possible in plays of his time. This tendency was pursued in Norris's production through Tanya Ronder's prose adaptation of the original. The language of the play is rendered in simple, direct and unpretentious prose: 'We tried to make those issues and the language as clean and accessible as possible without betraying Lope de Vega's intentions.'

Norris sees the play as an 'uncompromising look at the darker aspects of how pure love can get battered . . . It is about the complexities of love and pride and how the two are not good bedfellows.' Actor David Harewood, who played the Commander, claims 'it's about what people will do for love. Everybody in the play is doing something for love – whether it be duty or actually passion. Some people overstep the mark.' Tanya Ronder believes *Peribanez* is about 'the vulnerability of even the strongest of loves'. The Young Vic production of the play, and the workshops associated with it, sought to give physical form and substance to its abstract ideas, to 'embody' remote Spanish Golden Age notions of power, honour, community, public behaviour and private duty, and to make palpable the experience of love and destructive desire for contemporary audiences and younger theatre-makers.

Peribanez is an urgent, energetic, dark and funny play which expresses a contradiction found in much classical drama. On the one hand its characters and their dilemmas seem familiar and immediately accessible to contemporary audiences, and on the other the codes and concepts of their world may at first seem strange and impenetrable. Just as the characters of *Simply Heavenly* express, resist and reflect on the values of their broader society, so the characters in an early modern Spanish drama embody ideas and attitudes particular to their time and their place. We need to approach these characters by standing in their shoes and looking at the world from their perspective. The approaches and exercises that follow offer ways in which young performers can create precise, expressive and confident representations of characters and conflicts. They encourage participants to ask the kinds of questions of the play and of themselves that directors might ask in rehearsal. These exercises, some of which were used by the professional company, grow out of the more detailed approach to play exploration made possible in a rehearsal process. They assume participation over a number of sessions.

The story of the play

- In groups, make frozen pictures which tell the story of the play through its main actions and turning points. Each group should choose a moment and present it to the others (present the frozen pictures in sequence).
  a) Peribanez and Casilda are married
  b) The injured Commander is brought in unconscious
  c) The Commander wakes and is struck by Casilda's beauty
  d) Casilda, Ines and Costanza prepare for the journey to Toledo
  e) Peribanez is given mules and earrings by the Commander
  f) Ines, Costanza, Casilda and Peribanez gaze on the King in Toledo's cathedral
  g) The painter sketches Casilda
  h) The Ocana festival committee votes to install Peribanez as its chairman
  i) The Commander sickens with love for Casilda
  j) The Commander woos Casilda as the reapers sleep
  k) Peribanez discovers the portrait of Casilda in the painter's studio
  l) The Commander knights Peribanez
  m) Peribanez leads his men to battle, waved off by the women
  n) Peribanez hides in a sack of flour as the Commander arrives with musicians
  o) Lujan seizes Ines and the Commander tries to rape Casilda

p) Peribanez kills the Commander
q) Peribanez kills Lujan
r) Peribanez kills Ines
s) Peribanez and Casilda kneel before the King and Queen
t) Peribanez and Casilda are alone together

In a production of the play, each of these moments must be delivered clearly and strongly so its implications are not lost. Your frozen pictures should present the main action in each event and underline the thought or feeling that it produces or reflects.

Social codes

Lope de Vega created Spain's first truly national drama, combining elements of popular theatre with classical forms. Action rather than exposition defines character and situation. Rufus Norris wanted to find a direct, immediate and accessible form for the action, and incorporated live music and movement with elements from different cultures and environments to make the point that Peribanez's story belongs to all cultures and all times. The codes and concepts behind the action spring from sixteenth-century Spain, but as Michael Nardone, who played Peribanez, points out, 'the moral codes of the play and the emotions are the same as those we experience today. Every human being on the planet, once stripped of cultural differences, laws and conditions, is basically the same.' In rehearsals and workshops, the participants tried to give real and recognisable human form to the abstract notions of honour, community, faith and love in the play.

The setting

The play is set in two contrasting worlds: the world of the peasants, with its sun-scorched fields and houses, its grain-filled barns, its church and streets; and the world of the nobility, which includes the Commander's house, the soaring cathedral in Madrid where the King appears, and the King's palace. Designer Ian MacNeil wanted to emphasise the power structure of the play while suggesting danger and watchfulness in the action. So he created a long red bridge or platform, which curves over the simple, unfurnished space below. From this height, the Commander leans perilously out over an abyss as he yearns for Casilda, and the wily Peribanez uses this platform as a means of gaining secret entry to his own house. He kills Lujan on this elevated walkway, symbolising his violation of the Commander's 'territory', and the blood spills on to the floor below. From up here the King dispenses his justice to Peribanez at the end of the play. Height and depth, like the hierarchies of class and social position, are visibly suggested in the staging.

This exercise is suitable for drama students, or for older participants:

- Even without a set, it is still important to suggest the two worlds of the play. How might this be done, using only the materials in the classroom or rehearsal room? Can you create a visual sense of Peribanez's world with chairs and a table? How might you rearrange these to suggest the Commander's world? If you have no props or scenery at all, is it still possible to convey a sense of difference in the way the characters enter and leave the space, and the degree of formality in their movements and address to one another? Would you use two separate parts of the space to suggest the world of the peasants and that of the nobility, or would you have them share the same space, perhaps suggesting that they are subject to the same emotions (love, jealousy, desire) and the same divine justice?

Community

Golden Age Spain had a detailed and highly developed notion of honour. A man's honour (honour was a masculine commodity) was integral to his social status and his identity. An honourable man was brave, obedient and faithful to his word. Once threatened by word or deed, honour could only be restored by a public act of vengeance. Women were considered vessels for family honour, as purity of blood could only be guaranteed by virtue (chastity before marriage and fidelity during it). It was neither uncommon nor illegal to kill an unfaithful wife. Honour was thought to be unique to the noble classes. But the King's response on learning of Peribanez's acts of revenge is 'Your honour's very important to you'. Peribanez's notion of honour comes not from his ennoblement, but from a strong and certain sense of his rights and of the justice of his cause.

What does the concept of honour mean to us today? Rufus Norris acknowledged that 'recent images of Saddam-loathing Iraqis shooting at US tanks gave us an idea of how alive that concept can be, but what about here?' Assistant director Nizar Zuabi described his role in the production as 'helping the cast to open out and find an equivalent sense of community as that which characterises the "shame" cultures of the hot Mediterranean, so that "honour" comes to feel a concept as rooted in the body as the abstract mind. The actors here are not trying to act out Spanishness. It's their sense of community that creates the laws and rituals from inside the production.' In the course of the play, that sense of community is broken by doubt, suspicion, betrayal, violence.

For notions of honour to have an impact on contemporary audiences, it's important to generate a real sense of community, so that we have a sense of what Peribanez stands to lose. Community does not necessarily imply harmony and total integration, but it does suggest participation in shared activity and mutual values which, when disturbed, can destroy the group in question.

A sense of community can be generated among actors through warm-ups and games, and among their characters through ritual activity (song, religious ceremony, shared labour or language – Norris's peasants spoke in Welsh, Scottish and Irish accents, distinguishing them from the nobility by a shared Celtic cultural heritage). Both actors and characters should feel connected for the sense of community within the play to be convincing. Often a director will begin a rehearsal process by teaching the actors a song or dance related to the action of the play or to the period in which it is set, which can be used as a warm-up, and which reminds them that their characters share the same culture and traditions. Song and music, ceremony and ritual are woven throughout *Peribanez* and offer a number of opportunities for ensemble work.

• Clear the space and divide into two football teams. Spend a few minutes devising a name for your team and a two-line chant to accompany the scoring of a goal. Play a ten-minute game – the only word you can speak while playing is the name of your team. With each goal scored, come together to chant your celebratory song. Note that the team is defined by communal action and characterised by its rituals.

Honour

Critic James Fenton claims 'respect is the current street-slang under whose rubric issues of honour are discussed and fought out.'

- What does the word 'honour' mean to you today? Ask the group to sit on the floor. Choose at random from among the group. Point to an individual and say, 'Your honour is very important to you.' The person you have pointed at must stand up and say 'My sense of honour comes from . . .' and think of one or more sources of honour. For example, someone might say, 'My sense of honour comes from the respect of my friends', while another might say it comes from 'looking after my family' or from 'my religion'. If honour isn't important to you, say so, and say what *is* important to you. You might find that the thing you identify – say 'looking good' or 'doing well at school' – is actually bound up with questions of honour and respect.
- Choose a character from the play and repeat the exercise, speaking as that character.

Costume and society

Costume is one of the 'languages' referred to by Peter Brook, which serves to express the director's intention and reveal both surface and hidden meanings in plays. The choices made by directors and designers with regard to costume impact significantly on the interpretation of the work. Even the simplest costumes can change our perspective on a play and they also have a marked effect on the style of performance. Rufus Norris's production was largely in modern dress, though some vestiges of seventeenth-century costume remained. He wanted to stress the universality of the play's tale of passionate love and illegitimacy, while drawing attention to the seventeenth-century social codes which throw its actions into stark relief.

The Commander, for example, insists on wearing a fine cloak lined with gold when he visits Casilda. He refuses to disguise himself and his status or to hide the truth of his intention:

FLOREZ: I've brought your cloak Sir.
COMMANDER: Good. Give me it. What's this?
FLOREZ: Your dark cloak Sir.
COMMANDER: Am I in mourning? What are you trying to say? Everything I look at upsets me.
FLOREZ: Shall I get you another one Sir? A brightly coloured one?
LUJAN: Can I – it's just that – Sir, the discreet lover in these matters of the heart doesn't cover himself in colours – it's the kind of thing that could repeat on you – in court for instance.
COMMANDER: Get me the coloured one monkey! Are you servants or grandmothers? (III.2)

'Villains,' according to David Harewood, 'get a better costume.' Nizar Zuabi thinks costumes help actors to put forward the physicality and emotional lives of their characters. Even a simple thing like the choice of shoes or hat changes the actor's posture, as does a heavy, enfolding garment like a coat or a cloak, or an obtrusive item such as a sword or scythe. The Young Vic's wardrobe manager, Alison Trett, claims that 'Even the simplest costume helps an actor to move towards the character', though they can also overwhelm an actor's performance if they are merely tokens rather than integral aspects of the character. As one of the actors in the young people's production of *Simply Heavenly* noted, 'Costumes really helped us to get into character – we really came alive with make-up and costume.' While many theatres have wardrobe departments and employ skilled costume makers, obtaining simple but expressive costumes is generally easy and inexpensive. Items of clothing that infer status, such as waistcoats, hats, coats, gloves, etc., can be found in charity shops, and theatre companies will often lend costumes from their store to schools and community groups. A scarf or piece of fabric, worn inventively, can lend dignity, mystery or panache to a character, and suggestive use of colour in garments has a powerful symbolic effect.

Costume and character

The Young Vic's workshops with visually impaired young people emphasise the tactile and symbolic properties of costume, and this hands-on approach can be applied to any investigation of costume in theatre. An immediate way to understand the physical effect of wearing a costume is to touch, feel and weigh it in your hands. Different fabrics suggest different things about a character.

- Choose a character from *Peribanez*. As a group, write down single words to describe the characters of *Peribanez*.
- From a range of fabric samples and offcuts (satin, silk, muslin, wool, denim, canvas, etc.) choose the ones you feel best suit the character (there may be more than one for each). What does the fabric you choose tell us about the character? Does it tell us about his/her social status? His/her personality? Peribanez needs two principal outfits: his working clothes and his military uniform. You may choose to create realistic outfits for your character, but you should use your imagination, and the available resources, to create an individual 'look' which tells us something about the character. You may have only a single fabric type to work with; you can still create distinctive outfits using different colours, shapes, lines. You may have no costumes at all, only a few strips of cloth and some belts or hats. What can you do with these to help define your character's journey through the play? The main thing to concentrate on is creating a coherent or consistent look for the character; too many costume changes and too much variety in costumes is confusing for audiences (especially when actors are playing multiple roles) and creates headaches for both actors and wardrobe departments.
- When you have chosen the fabrics for each character, design a costume for his/her first appearance on stage. What is happening in the play at this point? What time of year is it? Is it hot or cold? Is the character in the city or the country? Inside or outside? Decide on the colour, style and any trimmings for this garment.

Costume designers consider the age, social status, wealth, family and attitudes of the characters when creating costumes for them.

They also have to take into account the duration of the action (for example, the story of the play may encompass many years, and the style of dress, or the economic circumstances of the character, may change from beginning to end).

- Think about the effect that wearing or removing a pair of shoes may have on your character and an audience's understanding of the character.

  Imagine your shoes are a pair of heavy, solid army boots. Stand in rows of four and march in step across the room. Let your boots make heavy contact with the floor.
- Now remove your shoes and socks and walk about the room. Concentrate on the feeling of the ground beneath your feet. Line up again and march across the room. Do you feel you march with less power and authority when you march in bare feet? Do you imagine that the Commander is the kind of character who might often go about with bare feet? What about Peribanez? In their rehearsals for the professional production, actor Michael Nardone, who played Peribanez, decided that his character might choose to go barefoot from time to time in order to maintain contact with the earth. He felt Peribanez could only be sure of his purpose when he could literally feel the ground beneath his feet, and so he removed his heavy army boots in order to commit the murders of the Commander, Ines and Lujan.

Seventeenth-century bowing

Seventeenth-century noblemen choreographed their movements and gestures for reasons of practicality and social etiquette. They often wore heavy and obstructive clothing which restricted their movements (doublets, hose, sword, pistol, cape, hat, heavy undergarments, gowns, etc.). *Peribanez* was written around 1605 and its customs and notions of etiquette and public behaviour are drawn from this period of conspicuous aristocratic display. In this, as in any Renaissance play, it is useful to know something of how social conventions influence the physical behaviour of individuals in highly stratified societies.

- Practise a formal bow. Bowing styles have changed through the ages. In the seventeenth century (and thus in many of Lope's and Shakespeare's plays), bowing among the nobility (or pretenders to the nobility) was an elaborate ritual also known as a 'reverence', involving the following careful movements:

- Walk towards your partner. The most fashionable walk of the period was to keep both legs relatively straight and to swing the stepping foot around the other leg, placing the foot, splayed out slightly, directly in front. Imagine you are wearing a cape, hat and sword.
- When ready to bow, take a slightly larger step and lower your weight on to the back leg (usually the left).
- While you are shifting your weight back, simultaneously tilt your torso forwards slightly and remove your (imaginary) hat with your right hand. Removing your hat is an art form in itself. It involves taking your arm down from the top of your head in a long arc by the side of your leg, keeping the inside of the hat facing towards you. Do not take your hat across your torso; everything is facing forwards, not twisting. Present the top of your head and your heart to your partner, and try not to stick your bottom out.
- While bowing allow the head and back to act as one long section. Lower your head and do not look your partner in the eye as this suggests you do not trust him (though you probably don't).
- Never speak while bowing. Bow slowly and precisely.
- Having bowed, raise your torso and bring your back leg forwards. When taking your leave, bow or curtsy again, and continue your journey, walking in a little semicircle around your partner so you do not bump into him.

Women can get away with doing deep knee bends under their long skirts, or they can curtsy:

- Stand feet together, and step back on one foot.
- Bend your knees while keeping your back straight and gracefully lifting your skirts to avoid tripping on them.
- You should spend the same amount of time (around three beats) going down into the curtsey as you spend coming up out of it.

Public greetings

- In pairs, greet one another as:
  a) Two Spanish noblemen
  b) Farm labourers (a handshake, an embrace?)
  c) Military men (a more economical bow?)
  d) A king and a peasant (the peasant prostrates himself at the king's feet, which he might kiss; the king may or may not lay a hand on the peasant's head, as a blessing)
  e) A queen and a nobleman or noblewoman (a very deep and careful bow or curtsy, eyes downcast; the queen may merely tilt her head in acknowledgement – she probably can't move much at all herself)
  f) Peribanez and the Commander at the Commander's house
  g) Peribanez and the Commander after Peribanez is knighted (Peribanez has been ennobled and can greet the Commander more formally, by bowing; try to reflect your hostility to the Commander in the stiffness or brevity of the bow)

The cycle of feeling, image, action

In his work in schools, the assistant director on *Peribanez*, Nizar Zuabi, explored the means by which an actor transforms him/herself using images as a basis for action. Zuabi approaches his work through the idea of transformation, and the freedom and restrictions which character and situation produce. In workshops and in rehearsal, he helped the actors connect with their characters and with the physical environments of the play.

Zuabi's interest is in finding physical forms for 'inner' experience, and contrasting these with the more predictable behaviour prescribed by social codes and conventions. 'For every feeling experienced by a character in a play, you can find images that suggest movements, shapes, postures and gestures which will assist your performance.' Finding and developing these images and feeding them into the presentation of character gives actors a sense of responsibility for their characters and directly involves their instinctive creative responses. Words (and the feelings they describe), images and actions reinforce one another at every moment of performance: by using a word or an image to inform an action, and using an action to support a characterisation, actors can create original, convincing and complex characters on stage and give concrete expression to the ideas of the play.

The aim of these exercises is to remind actors that their bodies and their emotions are constantly reflecting one another. Like a stone thrown in a pond, an image at the heart of a thought produces ripples which generate feeling and movement and give your action meaning and a sense of intention. The image anchors you to the idea or character you are playing, giving you something concrete to think about and represent. It gives three dimensions to meaning in the play.

Physical rituals

The agricultural environment of the play, the courtly environ-ment of the King and the nobles, and the ceremonial space of the Catholic Church (reflected in the wedding scene) are all characterised by rituals and repetitive activity. In the case of the noblemen, these rituals are determined by social convention, which changes with time and the demands of fashion, but in the lives of the labourers, the rituals are dictated by the seasons and continue unchanged year on year.

How can a 'physical language' help to define a character?

- Choose a physical activity which is described or implied in the play (sowing, harvesting, picking grapes, olives or mushrooms, washing your face, sharpening tools, etc.). Mime this activity, using specific images to inspire and direct your action. Try to find simple, repetitive gestures to suggest these activities. You might hum or sing as you perform them, or make sound effects of hay being cut, soil being turned, etc.
- In groups of three, improvise and rehearse a brief scene which physically demonstrates through their domestic activities the relationship between the Commander, Lujan and Leonardo.

On entering his house, Lujan takes off the Commander's boots. Leonardo pours wine for him. Lujan brings food for the Commander and waits for instructions. This is not intimate, mutual activity; it is ceremonious and hierarchical – the Commander is being waited on hand and foot. In this scene, and in any scene in which society dictates hierarchical relationships between characters, a great deal can be suggested about these relationships simply through the physical encounters between characters (but note that a character's place in a social hierarchy may not be the same as his/her status within a scene – the Commander sits at the top of the social hierarchy in Ocana and therefore has high public status, but his private status as a woebegone lover is relatively low, and Leonardo mocks his employer in his asides). See if you can show some of these tensions in the way your characters perform their domestic routines.

Wedding improvisation

Peribanez opens on a scene of festivity – an important communal ritual – which is suddenly interrupted by the bad news of the rampaging bull and the arrival of the wounded Commander. Group scenes such as this emphasise the importance of the ensemble – each actor works as a part of a whole and his/her action supports the group.

Norris cast actors who were also musicians, stressing that music is a natural form of communication among the play's community of farmers. Composer Orlando Gough suggests it may come from the fact that 'they are trying to escape from the hardships of their life through music, like the blues in a way . . . The music supports the emotional state of the characters or can heighten dramatic moments. It can even provide humour'. Gough's music, based on Eastern European gypsy brass bands with an Arab influence, is at times joyful and at other times discordant. The overall effect is of comedy tempered by something darker, less harmonious. The opening moments of the play establish the tone of the rest of the play, and acknowledge the fine line between comedy and tragedy. Norris carried this collision of comedy and tragedy right through to the play's climax, where Peribanez kills Ines covered in flour like a clown and spattered with blood like a killer.

- Ask one volunteer to leave the room. The rest of the group improvise a wedding scene. A bride and groom link arms and turn in a circle together, cheered on by their friends and families.

- After a minute or two, the volunteer must run into the room with an announcement or action that stops the wedding. It should be something unexpected. When they hear the announcement, everyone in the room should freeze – their reaction to the news should be evident from their facial expression and their posture.

Interrupting a ritual can create sudden dramatic tension. It changes the tone abruptly, and the reactions of the characters to the event or announcement can be very revealing.

In Norris's interpretation, the wedding took place behind a paper curtain. The silhouettes of Peribanez and Casilda were visible, holding hands, before a long-bladed knife chillingly slit the paper and the bride and groom popped their heads out like characters at a funfair. The scene was at once comical and disturbing; it immediately introduced the threat of violence even before the bull had run wild.

- Now go around the room, unfreeze one by one as the volunteer points at you, and describe your feelings at the moment of the interruption.
- Can you think of a way to suggest unease in the opening scene? Are other wedding guests eyeing up Casilda? Is there a drunken reveller brandishing a knife or gun? Does someone start a fight?
- What happens next? Play the scene to its natural conclusion.

Finding actions for images

You can use the imagery associated with a particular character to help you create a strong and simple dramatic action for that character. The aim is to explore words, images and actions which you can draw on in a performance to help you remain focused on your character's essential attributes or qualities. Although the following exercises are involved, and are most appropriate for students of drama or young actors or directors, they can be carried out in any workshop as a way of introducing young people to the role of the imagination in creating and sustaining convincing characterisations.

Consider Peribanez's description of his love for Casilda in the wedding scene at the opening of the play:

> What could be more beautiful than you? I can't think of anything. A grove of olive trees, heaving with olives, curling down with fruit? A meadow in early May, first light, when tiny flowers burst open, seeing the world for the first time? Or an apple – shiny and ripe? Thick golden oil, rich and clean in its clay pot? Everything pales, Casilda, next to you. I smell your lips, I can't imagine a better smell. Not even a wine that's been asleep in a tall dark cellar – white, crisp, perfect to drink. I'd compare you to roses if I were a gentleman, but I'm a worker and wine's the thing. (I.1)

- Lie down with your eyes closed and let your body relax. Imagine yourself as Peribanez.
- Try to find an image that expresses something essential about Peribanez in this moment. It may or may not be something he has mentioned above, but it should be real and tangible; an image that symbolises Peribanez's character. It might be a bottle, for example, or a reaper's blade, a stone, an olive pit, a handful of earth, a plough.
- Explore the image; let it develop in your mind. Concentrate on this activity; don't let your mind wander. Try to see every aspect of the image. Think of it as being three-dimensional, not flat. For example, the image of water is qualified by the colour and surface of the water, its movement, the way light shines on it, etc. Michael Nardone explored the image of 'earth' in rehearsal, and used this image in his physical performance as a way of anchoring Peribanez to the land he worked and lived for.
- Now think of a word to describe that image. The word might be, for example, 'dry' or 'stony'. The combination of word and image gives an energy and intention to the actor. As the character develops during the course of the play, the images will change.
- Now find an action expressive of your image and your word. Try to show as much of the character's nature as you can in the action. Say your image for Peribanez is earth, and your word is 'dry'. Try to fuse word and image in a related action (such as

digging hard, dry earth). Try to perform this action as Peribanez would. Think of the detail of his movements. Are they careless, controlled, confident, clumsy? Keep the image and the word in your mind as you carry out the action. Show it to the group. Now tell the rest of the group what your image and word are.

- Look at Peribanez's words when he returns secretly to his house in the dead of night after leading his men to war, only to find his worst fears realised and the Commander attempting to rape Casilda:

(What else do I need? Why am I waiting? I'm a farmer, who works like a dog, that's all I am. Maybe I should talk to him. Or maybe I should just kill him.) (III.4)

Has your image for Peribanez changed at this point in the play? This speech is savage in its intention. Perhaps he is now like a knife. What word would you use to describe the knife? What action brings word and image together (perhaps you see him sharpening a knife or stabbing it into a sack of grain)?

- Carry out the action of Peribanez sharpening the knife, cutting, or stabbing with it.
- Now speak the lines above with the same intention as a man sharpening a knife. He should not actually perform the action, but he should speak the words sharply, keenly, as though with each line he is drawing a blade across a whetstone or plunging it into the sack.

Character image, character action

The exercise above can be extended to include all the characters in the play, even those with smaller roles:

- As you name the characters of the play, ask participants to come up with a characteristic or overall action which expresses the truth of that character. This action should be based on a word or image which, for you, sums up the whole character.

Character detail

Image work on *Peribanez* allowed the actors to create detailed and very precise portraits of their characters. These techniques can bring great specificity to even rudimentary performances, and give workshop participants an infinitely adaptable, personal set of tools for investigating dramatic character.

a) The Commander: Though he brings about great harm by breaking the social order and pursuing his lust at the expense of his nobility, the Commander is not an unsympathetic character. His love is, quite literally, a sickness, which makes him ridiculous in the eyes of others and, at times, in his own eyes. He recognises Peribanez's right to happiness and honour even as he seeks to destroy both. He is misguided, rather than a full-blooded tyrant, and he is capable of grace and magnanimity. But as David Harewood notes, he 'ends up doing some pretty nasty things', and so 'the challenge in performance is to try and keep the audience with you as long as possible and surprise them with what he actually does.'

- Consider the Commander's actions, as described in the stage directions, throughout the play. What characters do is often more telling than what they say: He *'reaches out and tries to hold on to Casilda'*, *'watches her'*, *'stands but falls again'*, *'paces round the room'*, is *'flooded with disquiet and unfulfilled longing'*, *'embraces'* Peribanez, *'watches'* Casilda in Toledo, *'buckles'* Peribanez's sword on for him and *'knights him'* with it, *'places his hand on his heart'*, *'grabs hold of Casilda'*.
- In small groups, create a frozen picture of one of these moments. Are these the actions of an honourable man, the Commander of Ocana?

David Harewood accentuated the Commander's weakness by languishing full-length across the upper platform of his house. The actor pursued the opening image of the Commander as wounded, unable to stand, and transferred this to the physical expression of his heartache. In this interpretation, the Commander is effectively 'sick' throughout the play; he ends as he began, broken in body though finally restored to his moral senses.

b) Peribanez: Lope de Vega's peasant soldier is no straightforward hero. Though he is a man of the soil and his values are simple and true, he is cunning, possessive and watchful, and the justice he metes out to Ines is brutal and remorseless.

- In groups, create frozen moments of individual moments in the play: He *'indicates his chest'*, where his pure heart lies, he *'dances'*, *'brings water'* for the injured Commander, *'embraces'* Casilda, *'goes to kneel'* before the Commander, gazes on Casilda's portrait, *'hides'* from the singing reapers, *'produces'* gifts bitterly for Casilda on his return from Toledo, *'shows'* his sword and banner to Casilda, *'looks at Casilda'* as he leaves with his men, secretly enters his house, *'climbs into a sack of flour to hide'*, *'unsheathes his sword'* and *'cuts deeply into the Commander's chest'*, *'tries to put some of Casilda's clothes back on'*, *'kills Lujan brutally and messily'*, *'cuts [Ines'] throat'*, *'takes his bloody captain's clothes off and returns to his working clothes'*, kneels before the King, and in a final scene (not included in the production) Peribanez silently dons his military uniform again.

Again, Peribanez's journey from simple peasant farmer and newly-wed to wily spy and brutal executioner, and finally to speechless and grieving servant of the King, is graphically presented in these stark and simple actions. He is far more active than the Commander. As Peribanez progresses through the play, his actions become less casual and more deliberate, until the final explosive outburst of his rage which leaves him empty of anger, and of hope.

c) Casilda: Rufus Norris notes that Lope de Vega's female characters are 'as rounded as his men. They are strong, full-blooded, hot-tempered and canny. They are honest and pure-hearted, but fallible with it.' Actress Jackie Morrison, playing Casilda, describes these women as 'tough, realistic and honour-able. They live within the community and they work as hard as the men . . . They are connected to the land they live and work on. Personally, it's nice to act a woman who has guts.'

- In small groups create snapshots of one of the following moments: Casilda *'dances'*, *'prises'* the Commander's hands off her, *'embraces'* Peribanez, *'kisses'* his hands, *'struggles'* with the Commander, *'stares'* at Ines' body, *'kneels'* at the King's feet, *'looks at'* Peribanez and says nothing.

If you were to present each of the snapshots in sequence, they would demonstrate a clear arc in Casilda's progression from buoyant and expressive young woman to silent and broken wife. Emphasising and capturing the essence of the most significant actions in the play draws attention to the *journey* each character makes from the play's beginning to its end. Character is not static – characters continue to develop throughout a play, and grow or are diminished by events and encounters.

What you say v. what you do

The scene below is used to explore the physical expression of dramatic tension between two characters and can be adapted for the exploration of any play. It makes the point that what a character says may be contradicted by what he does. As audiences and as actors, we need to make judgements about the intentions of a character, using the evidence of all of our senses. Acting out a single moment of tension or conflict allows you to put considerable detail into the representation, and, in particular, to explore the dramatic irony of the scene.

This scene represents a major turning point in the play; once it has taken place there is no going back to the life Peribanez has enjoyed till now. This small moment actually triggers the play's violent climax. Scenes like this often involve a *discovery*, which forces the central character(s) into a new understanding of the world. It's important not to miss these moments in a play; they help you to chart a character's changing motivation and help to clarify his/her subsequent choices and actions.

In the scene, Peribanez has come to Toledo at the request of Ocana's festival committee to have the town's statue of its patron saint, St Roque, repaired by a painter. In the painter's studio he discovers a portrait of Casilda. He claims not to know the woman depicted, and quizzes the painter about the image. To his horror, he learns it was commissioned without Casilda's knowledge by the Commander:

PERIBANEZ: How did you make such a beautiful picture? The eyes, her mouth. Her hair. Where was she from, this woman?
PAINTER: Well now I'm wondering whether it's such a good

likeness after all because actually, she's from the same town as you.

PERIBANEZ: Ocana?

PAINTER : Yes, Ocana.

PERIBANEZ : There is someone who looks like this but it can't be her because she's recently married and I'm sure her husband couldn't afford a portrait of her.

PAINTER: Well yes that might be her. I don't really know, I didn't meet her, I had to paint her without her knowing . . . I did her in secret and then expanded it into this painting.

PERIBANEZ: I think I know who asked you to paint her. Will you tell me if I'm right?

PAINTER: Um – I shouldn't really . . .

PERIBANEZ: Was it the Commander of Ocana?

PAINTER: Well – she knows nothing about it, I guess there's no harm – yes, it was him. A very impressive man. One of the best soldiers in Spain of course, and completely absorbed in this peasant girl!

PERIBANEZ: But she doesn't know that? She doesn't know about the picture?

PAINTER: Not a whisper . . .

PERIBANEZ: Can I take it back with me? (II.4)

The tension here is created by the gap of knowledge between the Painter and Peribanez. Peribanez tries to draw information out of the Painter which will confirm his worst fears. The Painter has no idea that Peribanez is the man wronged by the Commander, and cannot understand why Peribanez wants so badly to possess, protect and remove the painting from the Commander's grasp.

How can this tension be dramatised and the importance of the moment underlined in performance?

- In an introductory exercise, explore an equivalent situation which is more familiar to you. You might improvise a scene in which you have an exam coming up. B possesses the notebook with all the information relevant to the exam. You have to try to persuade B to give you the notebook without giving away your real reason for wanting it.
- In pairs, act out this scenario. How do you lower B's defences?

You might praise her intelligence, implying she doesn't need to revise for the exam. You might express a special interest in the design of the book, or claim you want to show it to someone else as an example of good work. This exercise will help you to focus on the tension generated when one character wants something he cannot reveal to another character.

- Now try to bring this insight to performing the scene above. Use a chair to represent the painting. How does the artist stand before his handiwork? Is he pleased with his work? Is he anxious that it may not be good enough? How does Peribanez behave in front of the painting? Is he mesmerised by it, or can he hardly bear to look at it? How does he signal his distress, even as he makes polite conversation with the Painter? Think of his hands, his shoulders, his mouth. Think about the impact of pauses before he speaks. How long does Peribanez gaze at the painting before he starts talking to the Painter? Where else might he pause before speaking? For example, his question, 'But she doesn't know that?' is a painful one to utter; Peribanez is afraid he might learn that Casilda is complicit in this affair. Try waiting for three seconds before asking this question. Note how it lends weight and tension to the moment. Can you think of a word or an image to describe Peribanez's feelings at this moment? Perhaps he is coiled tight, like a spring; perhaps he is about to snap like a stick. Try to give physical expression to this idea as you play out the scene.

Actions speak louder than words

Look now at the scene in which the Commander prepares to send Peribanez to war, in the hope that he may seduce Casilda in her husband's absence. The Commander knights Peribanez, who then insists that the nobleman protect Casilda and preserve Peribanez's honour:

COMMANDER (*he takes Peribanez' sword from its holder and proceeds to knight him with it*): Do you swear to use this sword in service of God our supreme Lord, and the King?
PERIBANEZ: I swear this and more. I swear to wear this sword in defence of my honour – the honour which you are bound to protect as Lord of this land. I'm leaving my house and my wife

in your care while I'm away. I entrust them to you because they mean more to me than my life and, why would anyone harm them? But Sir I'm pleased to know that you'll guard them for me.

You understand honour. Self-respect. You know it's worth everything – beyond riches or happiness.

I'm away fighting at your command but you've put my sword on for me. I take that to mean I have your permission to use my sword to protect my honour.

COMMANDER: Freely. You have my permission freely. I'm sure you'll use it wisely.

PERIBANEZ: So onwards towards war, and to whatever else may come. (III.1)

This scene is full of irony and menace. The Commander does not fully understand the implications of Peribanez's veiled threat, but is uneasy all the same. He has not expected the humble peasant to speak so openly or to claim the right – usually reserved for noblemen – to protect his honour. Not for the first time in the play, the Commander is wrong-footed and later struggles to convince himself that he has not been discovered ('Get out jaundiced guilt – of course he wasn't threatening me! What can he do? He's a peasant').

- In pairs, play the scene, focusing particularly on the unspoken rivalry between the two men. How can this be expressed in your actions and gestures?

In Norris's production, the Commander forced Peribanez to his knees, wrenched the sword from its scabbard and held it at Peribanez's throat before dragging him again to his feet. The image was one of physical threat and deliberate intimidation, as the Commander tried to demonstrate his power over the peasant. Peribanez, in his turn, stayed motionless with the sword at his throat, never glancing at the Commander, leaving him to stew in his own shame. Who do you think is in control in the scene? The man with the sword, or the unarmed man on his knees? Try playing the encounter with the Commander firmly in control, and then with Peribanez controlling the action.

Playing out a significant moment such as this demonstrates that action is everything in theatre; the way words are delivered, the silences and stillnesses that surround movement, and the gestures themselves are all part of the physical embodiment of meaning. As an actor/interpreter you need to be attentive to the implications of a scene and ensure they are made manifest not only in what you say and do but also in how you say and do it. There are many choices available to you, and each moment in a play can be interpreted in widely differing ways. As long as you have evidence from the play itself to justify your choices, they are worth exploring. Try to be supportive of one another's attempts. When individuals comment on the work of others, encourage them to do so constructively ('I wasn't sure why Peribanez stood up at that point'; not 'I think he looked stupid when he stood up'). Some things will work; others will not. The point is to remain open to new ideas and new discoveries.

Further exploration of image, feeling, action: playing a horse or a mule

The ideas and approaches above can be applied to animals as well as human beings. Rufus Norris points out that 'a principal speech in [*Peribanez*] is addressed to a horse, which, in that world of dependence on horses, made complete sense [but] it is hard to stage it here without falling into cliché or warping the sense'. One of the means by which Norris gave shape to the ideas behind the play was through ironic doubling. Nizar Zuabi helped the actors to play horses and mules convincingly and tellingly. David Harewood (the Commander) played Peribanez's horse; the irony of his Commander being bridled and ridden as the farmer's mount draws instant attention to the play's own blurring of boundaries between power and subjection, honour and dishonour. According to critic Paul Taylor, the actors produced 'a simple and penetrating image' which was a highlight of the production.

When trying to express the nature of a horse (for example) on stage, Zuabi advises actors not to strain to copy the movements of a 'stereotypical' horse but to start by imagining a specific horse – preferably one you have encountered – and looking out at the world through that horse's eyes. The search is for the 'rhythm' of the horse – its breathing, its physical presence, its particular movements – rather than for superficial gestures which signify 'horse', such as prancing and neighing. The overall aim is to build up a specific and meaningful physical vocabulary for the animal. The work is identical to the image work used elsewhere in the play; it emphasises the actor's freedom to transform him/herself within certain limits.

The actors' movements were generated by specific responses to particular moments in the play. They were never vague or generalised.

For every movement, and even in stillness, the actor is expressing an energy and an idea. David Harewood's horse often stood still, but would shift its weight on to one leg, or shake its head to dislodge a fly. Harewood imagined himself not simply as a horse, but as a horse resting by a road on a hot, still day. The more detailed your imagining of the atmosphere and environment, of the colour, texture and sound of things, the more detailed and convincing even your smallest gestures will be.

- Stand around the room facing the walls. This work is private and doesn't need to be shared or witnessed by others. It is about imagination and concentration. Imagine you are a horse tethered to the wall. Close your eyes. Picture yourself. What sort of horse are you? What colour are you? How big are you? What sort of temperament do you have? Are you hungry or well-fed; fly-ridden or glossy? Are you tired and footsore, or restless and flighty?

A mule, by contrast, is a cross between a donkey and a horse, but also the name given to an obstinate person. Mules and donkeys in myths and stories are associated with depression, laziness, stubbornness or blind obedience. But they can also represent peace, humility, patience and courage.

A visit to the zoo may be the most valuable research aid of all. Donkeys have heavy heads; they are not easily startled; their coats are thick and messy; they move slowly and seem awkward, but are actually light on their small feet and quite delicate in their steps. Mules have some of the characteristics of a donkey, and some of the features and attributes of a horse. They are predominantly beasts of burden, and this should be reflected in any interpretation on stage.

- Work in pairs. One person is a mule, the other its owner. Try to think of a word or image that describes a mule you have in mind. Tell your partner what this word is.
- Move about the space as this mule. Your partner leads you on a rope. How does he/she treat you? Are you pulled along resisting, or do you go quietly? Do you hang your head as you walk?
- Imagine you are tethered carrying a heavy load on a hot summer's day. Try putting your weight on one foot and lifting the other to rest it. Imagine flies swarming round your ears and eyes. Mules and horses breathe through their noses. Breathe steadily, letting your body move slightly with the rhythm of your breathing. You might stamp your foot occasionally or shiver or twitch to shake off the flies. Your movements are slower than those of the horse.
- Put an actor playing a horse and one playing a mule side by side. Can the rest tell which is which from their movements?

Characters as animals

This exercise, used by Rufus Norris in rehearsal, applies the above approach to the exploration of character. It offers a purely physical, heightened approach to character. The idea is to forget about thought processes, lines of dialogue and what your character would and wouldn't do, and let your body do the talking.

- Get your group walking around the space in a fairly neutral way, relaxed and easy.
- Introduce the idea of animals. What kind of animal is your character? If a bird, what kind of bird, and if a stork, then exactly what kind of stork? Try relating to each other now. Push the portrayal towards an extreme, without pausing for too much thought, and just observe what emerges. This can help to free 'head-bound' actors or performers who tend to intellectualise rather than trust their instincts, and helps to display clearly the essence of the character from the actor's point of view.
- How does the character animal behave when alone, quiet, sleeping, intimate, defensive, aggressive, and so on? With thought and a little research, approaching character through

animals can help actors to give convincing, original and detailed portrayals.

Rufus Norris's production of *Peribanez* effortlessly transported the characters and concerns of Spain's golden age into the present and gave confident shape and form to their lives and choices. Norris gave breadth and depth to even the smallest roles in the play and by doing so created a mutually supportive acting ensemble. This Spanish classic, obscured by time and cultural distance, proved as engaging and rewarding to explore as many more contemporary and seemingly more accessible plays. In all their work, the creative team sought to open the play up to younger audiences and workshop participants and to give them some of the tools to unearth their own potential as actors and interpreters of the action. Lope de Vega wrote, like Shakespeare, for an open-air courtyard theatre that embraced all classes and mastered a mixture of genres. Norris's production, too, brought a diverse and responsive audience into being. One critic commented, 'It gave me enormous pleasure to see an audience of young people . . . I just thought those kids were drinking it all in. That's the audience of the future.'

Chapter 8

A SENSE OF DIRECTION – TRAINING YOUNG DIRECTORS

Directing is in some ways the most comprehensive of the theatre arts, as it requires an understanding of all the other roles and skills involved in bringing a play to the stage. At the Young Vic, the role of the director is defined and investigated in the teaching and participation work with young people, but it is also explored in far greater depth with a growing network of emerging theatre practitioners who have identified themselves as directors and who take part in the company's comprehensive research-based Young Directors Programme. Directors should be proficient and perceptive dramaturgs, able to move fluently between discussion and exploration of a play's content and form and to engage imaginatively with living writers; they should be able to work constructively and sensitively with actors; they should have insight into all the technical requirements of the production process: the use of lighting, sound, stage machinery and properties, and be able to articulate their needs to designers and technicians and acknowledge their requirements and contributions; they should be aware of the responsibilities of producers, publicists and theatre managers, and work efficiently within production budgets. Above all, they must be excellent communicators, with chameleonic flexibility, resourcefulness and resilience.

How can young people, new to the crafts and skills of theatre, know whether or not they want to be directors? Chances are they won't. Directing is not a mysterious profession – or at least it needn't be – but it is a complex one, which is based on an accumulation of technical and intellectual experience. And at its heart there does lie a kind of mystery, which is the original and idiosyncratic vision of the director – the expression of which is transformed by every new encounter between the director and a play.

According to Associate Director Rufus Norris, 'Theatre Directors fall into two distinct groups: single-minded visionaries, who carry the whole production in their minds, and whose only challenge is how best to get others to fulfil that vision; and everyone else. Fortunately most directors fall into the latter category, i.e. they recognise that they are one of a number of creative people in the room and that, in fact, the combined creativity of all those present is the goal. The demands of their craft focus more on the intricacies of communication, collaboration and creative personal management – on feeding, not forcing. As such, it is a craft that can, to an extent, be taught and learned.'

The longer-term goal is to expand the pool of talented and committed theatre artists and foster a profound and long-overdue perspective shift in the directing culture of the UK. 'There's a tendency,' says David Lan, 'for people with power to keep power, and to keep power in their own hands or in the hands of people like them. Our little contribution is to say actually there are many, many other views of the world, and the more complex and diverse they are, the more our lives and imaginations will be enriched by access to them. The dominance of Oxbridge is evidence of how incredibly primitive our lives still are – how incredibly close we are to the tribe, and how any attempts to disrupt those relationships are resisted. If we really believe in democracy then we've got to act on the belief that no view of the world takes priority over any other experience. Everybody's suffering is equal suffering equally worthy of representation and consideration.

'Part of what we're trying to do, too, is to see a much wider and more diverse range of actors given authority on stage. And new audiences come to those plays, and we hope they'll enjoy the experience, and get something lasting out of it.'

Lan sees the director as a Pied Piper figure who brings with him in his passion for a play all the other theatre artists necessary for its staging. The director works cooperatively and strategically, orchestrating a complex interaction of skilled individuals. But he also calls the tune: directing is a 'primary act of the imagination' in the sense that the director brings the play or performance into being as a work of *theatre* – lifts it off the page or out of the bodies of actors and delivers it to an audience as something three-dimensional, complete, coherent. He is, according to Tom Morris, an associate director of the National Theatre, the 'central sensibility' of the theatrical work. But he can only attain intellectual and philosophical insight into theatre through direct experience of the craft of theatre-making. For this, training is essential. This chapter offers some starting points and examples of how to initiate that learning process.

The issue of training for directors has been raised repeatedly over the last fifty years, since George Devine, Glen Byam Shaw and Michel St Denis attempted to tackle it head-on by setting up the Old Vic Theatre School after the war. In the 1970s Frank Dunlop advocated that young directors receive basic training through theatre companies. But director training at that time was described by RSC Associate Director David Jones as 'disorganised, arbitrary and basically amateur'. A handful of bursaries were provided for trainees to work in regional theatres, but most of the best opportunities were, and still are, reserved for an Oxbridge-educated elite.

Change has been a long time coming. In 1999, director Katie Mitchell lamented the continuing lack of effective provision in the UK: 'The debate about directors' training divides, crudely speaking, into two schools: those who claim that it is irrelevant and that either you have the mysterious skill to direct or you have not, and those who insist that training is a crucial prerequisite for the job. Of course, to some extent it does come down to temperament and natural gifts, but there are basic skills, like textual analysis or stagecraft, for instance, which would be of enormous benefit to any director starting off on his or her career. Training for directors here is patchy and mixed, where it takes place at all.'

Some young directors begin their broader theatre training at college and/or university. Others, probably the majority, learn on the job, usually by assisting on productions, but since most work as freelancers they are effectively having to start from scratch in creating a company and negotiating the conditions under which they will work every time they embark on a new project. The splitting of their focus is exhausting, and can be detrimental to the work.

Young directors are currently being hit by shortages of regional theatre funding, fewer cheap venues and a crackdown on actors' welfare benefits. In combination, these restrictions have reduced opportunities for directors to gain valuable practical and professional experience. There is no longer a clearly defined route for young directors to follow, and they are forced to gather experience piecemeal and intermittently. As a result, many emerging directors feel insecure, for example, about technical aspects of their craft: they have had too few opportunities to work with experienced lighting and sound designers, or to develop their communicative skills in working with actors.

The Young Directors Programme at the Young Vic is an evolving programme of practical and theoretical work which aims to bridge the widening gap between the needs of a growing number of young directors and the professional opportunities available to them. 'It seemed to me when I started here,' recalls Lan, 'that the group of younger theatre people who were most in need of attention were directors. Although there are various training schemes and so on, there isn't a place that devotes a large quantity of its time to trying to work out the implications of what being a director in your twenties or thirties in this country means now.'

With the support of the Genesis Foundation and the Jerwood Foundation, the Young Vic is attempting to redress the imbalance between need and provision in director training. The programme provides opportunities for young directors to explore and develop their craft in a number of ways. Through the Jerwood Award, three young directors work with professional actors for five weeks on a play of their choice and present their work-in-progress to an invited audience. The programme also supports a rapidly expanding network of young directors and designers, and facilitates partnerships and collaborations between young theatre professionals; it has set up a mentoring scheme by which emerging directors work alongside experienced leaders in their field; it offers both Studio and main stage productions to young directors and an ongoing programme of process work in the Studio which allows around twenty directors each year to work with professional actors over the course of a week on particular aspects of their craft. The programme also includes workshops, masterclasses and forums, and explores creative partnerships and job opportunities for over 250 members of the Young Directors Network.

The 'three rules'

Lan's approach to training young directors is shaped by his understanding of three principles which inform all of his own work. 'Of course, the idea of rules in directing is paradoxical, because almost the most important lesson that one can teach to a young director is that anything is possible.' However, the openness with which directors should approach plays can only produce coherent and meaningful results when it is anchored to those basic tenets which for Lan lie at the heart of theatre-making.

1. *Thought is movement*

'It seems to me that what you're trying to do in directing a play is take the audience bodily into the mind and the emotional world of the characters in the play. Meaning in the theatre – on a stage – is conveyed in two ways: by sound and by movement. I discovered, and I can't really explain why this should be, that movement of the body – either the whole body or part of the body – in the right way and at the right time and in a controlled way, appears to convey to an audience what is happening in the mind of the actor. When I say "thought" is movement, I've never introduced this idea to a group of people without somebody saying, "Why are you focusing on thought rather than emotion?" It seems to me actually that thought and emotion on stage are almost inextricably linked to each other. All I can say is that I observe that an actor can convey one set of ideas or feelings by what they say and sometimes a completely contradictory but at least always supplementary set of ideas and feelings by what they're doing; by where their body is, and how their body is.

'What is not possible is to convey anything through stillness, except when stillness is felt as a contradistinction to movement. Stillness in itself means nothing – it's only when something happens that meaning is created. And again, the job, or part of the job of the director is to create meaning and to control meaning. So it seems to me absolutely simple and straightforward that the primary way in which that meaning is created and controlled is through movement, and the movement can be just the tiniest movement of the head, for example, or it can be, you know, three elephants cross the stage. It can be very big movement, or it can be the tiniest, most suggestive gesture. But movement within a structure of meaning is how new meaning is created and conveyed.'

2. Whatever you do, you also have to do the opposite

'It seems to me this is absolutely basic. What I was saying earlier relates to this; that stillness is only meaningful in relation to movement. So say, for example, the lights come on, the actor is on stage, the actor does nothing. The interpretation that the audience is doing is in relation to their expectation of what generally happens in a play, i.e. generally something happens when the lights come up. The interesting thing is that the longer that goes on, the more meaningful it becomes; the audience interprets and interprets – but then suddenly, if it's sustained for too long, it loses all meaning for you and becomes boring, because there is nothing to oppose it. It's a good example of where meaning comes from. On stage black is not black unless it's contrasted with white. Meaning comes by contrast. And one of the ways in which you control meaning is by creating the world in which the event occurs and giving information to the audience about the terms of reference. So if something happens very, very fast in a play – if someone runs across the stage very quickly – simply by that action you create a particular kind of a world. And every movement that happens subsequently will be understood in relation to that very fast action.

'That's the simple stuff, but it's also true at a much more profound level. If you're playing Iago, who is a man who destroys without motivation, the only way you can convey that degree of evil or destructiveness is by also seeing the other side. Otherwise it's boring, otherwise there's no interest in the plot at all. And in fact you can convey what you wish to convey about Iago by playing with lightness and sweetness and compassion time after time after time, until you're ready to go, no, but this is what he's really like, or this is the truth about him or this is the deepest understanding of him. But without the opposite being available, you're into melodrama. And in a sense that *is* melodrama – the villain who ties the heroine to the railway lines is simply evil, and it's of interest to a certain degree, but no more than that.

'The more complex and contradictory our understanding of the characters, the more complex and interesting our judgement of them will be. If you're trying to convey that a character like Faustus is a theologian, he has to use some of the language of theology, but actually very little. A couple of lines, and you get the point. But you will only understand that that character is a theologian by contradistinction to the other characters (the fools, the angels and devils and so on) who speak in a different way, so everything works by contradiction.

'The astonishing thing is that it's true of anything on the stage in all circumstances. It's true of emotion, for example. If you want to express anger you also have to express kindness, generosity. You have to find some moment in your performance where the opposite – the negative of your positive, or the positive of your negative – is expressed.

'The useful thing about this, I think, is it is a rule which you can refer to. Have I done this? And if you haven't, then you should. In *Faustus*, if one's trying to convey that he is a man with a deep spiritual longing for self-realisation, you've also got to see that he's very conscious of the pleasure of eating a bunch of grapes. Otherwise it doesn't mean anything. I think to some extent I'm elaborating something which people feel instinctively, and it's probably true of all creativity.

'It's true of movement too; everything you can think of it's true of. Unless of course you're going for a particular effect. I mean, if the whole point is that your canvas is painted completely yellow, then you don't want to put any green on it. But then the yellowness of that – of your canvas – will be understood in relation to the rest of the world, which is not yellow, and also in relation to other paintings which use yellow in a different way. Again, the job of the director is to say, it is within these terms of reference that I want you to understand what we're doing.'

3. The world is as you know it to be, even if it doesn't say so in the play

'So often, time after time, directors approach a play as if there was only one way of doing it, which is very like a similar play which they saw in the past. The greatest directors are the most individual, the most distinctive; everything comes down to *this* moment, and *this* play, and nothing that came before matters. The brilliance of

Richard Jones, for example [director of *Six Characters Looking for an Author* and *Hobson's Choice* at the Young Vic], is that he is concerned *only* with the vitality of the moment. To persuade directors that what I really require of them as an artistic director is *them*, is themselves, is the deepest, most complex, most contradictory, most provocative side of them; that's what one tries to convey.

'On the other hand, and this is where restriction and freedom and the tension between the two is so important, the job is to do that play. Genuinely try and submerge yourself in the mind and the life and the emotion of the writer. But you should also try to convey as much as possible of yourself and your understanding of the world through the play. And through the restrictions of that discover the way in which you express your own self – your relationship to the world that you live in.

'Sometimes I think it's like a football match. What are you doing in a game of football? The thing you're trying to do is get a ball from the middle of a field to the end of a field. And actually the simplest thing to do is to get rid of all the players except two, and then you just carry on. But that's boring, so you introduce some other people who are going to try and stop you doing that and they're governed by certain rules and they can only stop you in certain ways, and you can only respond to them in certain ways.

'In the same way, the objective in a play is to communicate something – for one body of people to communicate something to another body of people. And what we're after is the greatest intimacy of communication between individuals. So we're saying, "Alright, look it's me, David, trying to talk to you over there, whoever you are". And if it happens to be Shakespeare we're doing, "I will do my absolute best to give you William Shakespeare." But I can only do that by using everything I know about the world to convey that – what I think is in the play, or what I think he put in the play – to other people.

'Another way of looking at it is to think the job of the director is to bring to a production of a play the context within which it is taking place. It's the year 2003 in London, and the only way I understand you can do that is by filtering it, as it were, through yourself. So you have to understand everything that happens in the play through your own experience of being a human being, a son, a lover, a brother, whatever else you are, being all the things you are, and really value that experience that you have of living in the world. There is no limit to the richness and depth of experience a director can put on a stage, and the object is to have as complex a relationship with the audience as you're able to achieve.'

The arbitrariness of what the audience actually sees

As part of the research work which developed out of the rehearsals for *A Raisin in the Sun*, the Young Vic brought young people to the theatre to consider the role of the director in making a work of theatre. Three groups of eleven- to sixteen-year-olds had two intensive sessions with David Lan and two of the actors in the production. Most of the participants had already seen the play, and so were able to make their own judgements about the choices made by the company. The workshops examined the role of the director, and the choices directors make with actors when creating a world on stage. They examined the need for a scene to be convincing, and yet to respond to the 'unreal' and imaginative nature of live performance. The students had the opportunity to direct the actors and bring their own ideas to realising a short section of text.

The director is ultimately responsible for the creative decisions made in bringing a play to the stage, even though the process by which those decisions are arrived at may be highly collaborative. It is important, therefore, when young people explore the role of the director, that they are encouraged to take responsibility for the actions and decisions of the group, and to develop confidence in their ability to listen to those around them, and to make informed choices about the shape and purpose of the scenes they are working on.

Most of the plays explored and produced at the Young Vic are classical plays or contemporary classics. These plays have stature, solidity, emotional breadth and resilience which makes them both challenging and rewarding to work on. They are carried forward generation by generation, continually renewed as they come into contact with our changing concerns. 'They are called classics,' according to Rufus Norris, 'because they stood the test of time, they've proven they can work.' David Lan adds, 'People say of the classics that what makes them classic is that they are perennially new, fresh, every time you come back to them you discover something that you didn't expect to find in them. But if you can explain a play's resonance, if you can account for it fully, it's almost an indication that you ought to move on. It's the mystery, the mysteriousness of one's engagement with art, with the play, that is important.'

Perhaps the main reason for working with these plays is that they are strong enough, challenging and fertile enough to inspire and repay creative effort. 'Almost the most important thing you can do,' claims Lan, 'is present people with the challenge of greatness. You can make clear that, in your opinion, there's no reason why the work they do shouldn't be as good as the work anybody's doing anywhere in the world.'

By examining part of a scene from *A Raisin in the Sun* in detail (Beneatha's friend Asagai returns from a trip to Canada with the gift of a traditional Nigerian robe for her) it is possible to demonstrate how even the smallest decisions made by actors and a director can affect the audience's interpretation of a scene or a moment.

> BENEATHA: (*Holding the door open and regarding him with pleasure*) Hello . . . Well – come in.

Lan wanted to show the participants in the most direct and uncomplicated way what he calls 'the arbitrariness of what the audience actually sees' – meaning that dozens of different ways of playing a moment are often experimented with during rehearsals and that a number of those ways work as well as any other (albeit differently). But audiences coming to see the play only see one of these different options. The idea was to show young people the different possibilities available to the director and actor so they wouldn't simply accept the choices they are presented with when they go to the theatre but learn to question them. According to a local teacher, working closely with professional directors and actors 'gives our pupils an insight into the world outside the classroom and helps raise their aspirations'.

'What I was trying to do,' Lan says, 'was suggest to the young people we were working with how meaning is created in theatre. I didn't say this to them, because it was putting something in philosophical terms; instead we demonstrated it to them empirically. We took one tiny little moment – the arrival of Asagai into the room in which Beneatha lives. It's a very charged moment, and in the simplest way I directed the actors – giving them very simple instructions. One of the characters is on the stage, and the direction to the other is, 'Listen to your cue line – the line before which you come in – and then count five before you come in; then count ten before you come in; count fifteen, etcetera.' This was done in a very objective way – and then I said to the group, what does it mean? It's a very, very simple exercise.

'We tried it another way: A calls B's name. B answers immediately. B counts five before answering; B counts ten before answering; then counts *twenty* before answering. One gets the point immediately. Every time you do that, the audience listening to this interprets it. What does it mean if the person doesn't answer immediately? If the person answers immediately that tells you a great deal about the characters – where they are, how close they are, it tells you something about the relationship between the two people. I mean, never mind the *way* in which they answer, it's simply the timing of it – you try to keep everything else absolutely neutral.

'And I ask the actors, "What did you think? How did you feel? What does it mean? What did you think that character was thinking of you?" I guess you build up a sense of what the job of the director is, which is to control those things, to say, "Oh, just wait a tiny bit more before you say that.' The actor asks, "Why?" You say, "Well, I don't know, just do it, just find out how it feels, what you think it means." You begin to build up a sense of what the network of emotions or ideas is between the characters.

'That's simply delaying a response. Now do the same thing in movement. Character A speaks; Character B walks towards Character A before speaking, or walks half-way, or walks quickly or walks slowly, walks in the other direction. There are a million different variations. And just look at what effect this has. Now to some extent, people watching it interpret it in different ways, and that doesn't matter, because what people pick up very quickly is what I feel is a sort of *heat* – the amount of heat there is between the characters, the amount of tension that exists between them, and so on. So, it's trying to find a way of teaching – you don't need a more complex word than that – how one conveys these different feelings and ideas through simple but effective means.'

Alongside David Lan, Rufus Norris works intensively and extensively with emerging younger directors at the Young Vic. He is a passionate advocate of the role of building-based theatre companies as centres of learning and research, where skills and experience can be shared, and where directors and other theatre artists have 'the right to fail – otherwise they will never succeed'. He insists that directors need time and space to develop a strong sense of identity – a crucial prerequisite for the creation of original and stimulating work.

Norris believes that 'the whole nature of theatre is to be unseparated – from an audience, from our emotions or intellect'. One of his aims as a director is to generate immediacy, honesty and directness in live performance, so that audiences as well as actors at once create and share the visceral thrill of theatre.

The approaches and exercises below are based directly on Norris's work with younger directors. They can be applied to the exploration of particular plays (such as those explored in preceding chapters), or they can be employed by young directors and actors as tools for the analysis of the directing craft. These exercises offer guidance in working with actors to help them produce the best and most precise work possible.

The tasks of creative leadership

'To make the necessary investment of creativity, interpretation and participation in each production,' according to Norris, 'a director needs to draw on considerable personal resources and must encourage and sustain an equal creative investment on the part of each of the actors.' The following are some principles which may help you to get the most out of your actors:

- *Create an environment of trust.*
  Convey faith in the actors' ability.
- *Recognise what actors need.*
  Offer active direction with an understanding of their characters' perspective. Do not manipulate.

- *Be direct.*

   Be clear – not bullying or overprescriptive. A vague direction invites a vague response, so be specific. Discovering that an idea does not work is a step on the way to finding the idea that does, and you will find out more quickly if you know what idea it is that you're testing.

- *Listen.*

   Good ideas can come from anywhere. The skill is in recognising them when they appear; the wider your radar, the more you will pick up.

- *It's about the work, not about you.*

   Recognise your insecurities and do not be ruled by them. Directing will challenge all your doubts and defensiveness, but the more they restrict you the less you will listen. The answers are there – the need to find them is greater than your need to know they were yours.

- *Make decisions.*

   Rehearsal is a process, and wrong decisions are better than no decisions. If a decision is wrong you will soon realise and can make a fresh one. If you are in the company of intelligent and creative people (most actors are both) who are allowed to contribute, they will help you find the right one and recognise it when it comes.

- *Trust yourself.*

   If you are moved in rehearsal, then what you are watching is moving. If you laugh, it is funny. If you are bored, it is unquestionably boring. Make moments of theatre that you want to experience, not what you think someone else might want.

- *Know your material.*

   Read and reread the play you will rehearse, and in detail. Understand particularly where potential turning points are, such as where the dynamic in a scene drastically changes because of how characters are affecting each other.

- *Get on your feet.*

   Plays are there to be performed, not talked about or read endlessly. Actors mostly prefer to do their work on their feet, with their bodies engaged and their instincts consequently freer. The ones that don't are usually afraid or lazy. Most people, of course, are occasionally afraid *and* lazy – it's your job not to indulge either.

- *Push your actors.*
  People respond to positive challenges.
- *Praise your actors.*
  People respond to positive feedback.
- *Do not, as a rule, try to show the actor how to do it.*
  They have to have an understanding of what they are doing and why they are doing it, or they will not own it and may lose confidence. Remember that they are probably better at it than you are, and you cannot do it for them on the night.
- *Do not be judgemental in your direction.*
  You want your actors to inhabit characters, not comment on them, so take a second to think before saying anything negative about a character. Very few people think they are bad, and the same is true of characters, so do not call them so, or instruct them to be so. They may go to extremes in pursuing what they want (which may be bad for everyone else) but for them it is justified. Another way of approaching this is that every character should in some way be sympathetic, and therefore convincingly three-dimensional. There is nothing less interesting than being told by an actor what to think of a character. Humans are enormously complex, and their actions speak for themselves. For example:

In a scene of conflict where B is being provoked by A, the direction:
Try to get character A out of your presence (active)
may be more productive than:
Be more angry with A (general)
which is better than:
You're not nasty enough to A (judgemental)
which is certainly better than:
Try waving your arms at A (manipulative)

Or:
Try it again with all your physical and mental energy focused on your objective (precise)
is better than:
Try it again with a bit more intention (vague)
which is almost always better than:
Do it like this (demonstrative)

But even that is preferable to:
Um . . . (indecisive)

The basic ingredients of good theatre

'Going to a boring or plain bad film,' Norris claims, 'is a dis-
appointing but nevertheless fairly stress-free way of spending a
few hours. Going to a boring piece of theatre, however, is
infuriating. Theatre demands a complicity with and from an
audience who are justified in demanding certain things in return,
and these can be termed the basic ingredients of engagement. A
director's basic job is to recognise and achieve these four elements
or qualities.

Action

'Action is the running engine of any play or production. It does
not mean fights and vigorous movement. It means engagement
on the part of the actors in whatever they are doing, and most
particularly in pursuing what they want. It is safe to say that every
character in every play wants something at every point in the play.
It may be that they want to hurt, seduce, look after or avoid
someone else; it may equally be that they want to discover
something, or have a laugh, be on their own, sleep, die, or go to
the toilet. Exploring what they want and how they go about
achieving or failing to achieve it is at the heart of any successful
rehearsal process, and where characters want conflicting things
you find the heart of any good drama. Whether the director
spends the whole time or none of the time focused on it, this is the
case. Much theatre is saved from tedium by good actors, who can
do this work on their own, either by method or instinct. For a
production to be focused and complete, however, the director will
embrace the craft of exploring action and assist the actors with
their wants, needs and desires as characters.'

Storytelling

'Guiding and holding the attention of the audience is one of the
central challenges faced by the director. The craft of telling the

story is simple but by no means straightforward as there are numerous tempting distractions from this, particularly when a director has a certain "take" on the play, or when there is a lot of business, comedy, or other diversions.

'To tell a story clearly, a director in preparation and rehearsal needs to find answers to some basic questions:

- What does each character want? This can and will change during the course of the story, but the more clear, active and dynamic their wants are, the more focus and energy the story will have.
- What is happening in the play or particular scene that is essential in carrying the story forward?
- What are the key moments in any scene, where the central character/s are faced with an obstacle and must make difficult choices?
- When and how do the central characters change their tactics in pursuing what they want?
- Who, in any given moment, do you want your audience to be focused on or aware of? (Often that moment may not be principally about the person who is speaking.)'

Variety in character and atmosphere

'Variety is the spice of life, and drama usually throws light on life's spicier aspects. It must be rich in colour and tone, involving juxtaposition of character and mood.

'There are endless ways to interpret any given character for an actor, and one of the principal roles of the director is to help the actor with this process. In general it is a good idea to pursue the line of most promise. The starting point is to give the character a journey through the play that is plausible and supports the story. Beyond that, however, you should encourage the actor to explore and find a way through that *is* a journey, taking them where they have never been, with as many turning points as possible. When an actor faces a choice about where to go in any given moment, explore the one that is most interesting, or promises the most in terms of drama. If it doesn't work, strains credibility or falls flat you can try something else, but if it does, it will add vitality and life.

'Each character should have a physical or vocal energy about him or her that is in contrast to everyone else. It is very easy for actors to pick up on each other's energy – their speed, optimism, tension or any other aspect in the kaleidoscopic range of human characteristics. The danger of this is that it produces uniformity and repetition. A character's natural pace of speech, temperament, physicality and ways of moving and responding can and should be particular to that character alone.

'Similarly, the atmosphere of any scene should be in contrast to the next. There are endless defining clues as to how that atmosphere may be enhanced and altered within scenes. Location, temperature, time of day or night and other tangible conditions are the first and most obvious clues, but there are many more. Is the scene public or private? How familiar is this place, and how comfortable are the characters within it? What is the atmosphere between the characters? How does the entrance of a new character affect this? What do they bring in with them? How does the introduction of a new piece of information alter everything, the build-up to an argument, to intimacy? And so forth. The variations are countless and the exploration fertile in releasing or creating drama and freeing actors from habitual interpretation.'

Pace

'The performance of a play, like a piece of classical music, can be broken down into scenes and moments, but must also work rhythmically as a whole. Peaks and troughs, lulls, crescendos and climax points are all there to be drawn out and accentuated to make the most of the story's journey to its end, and the drawing of this rhythmic graph is entirely in the director's hands.

'Be aware of where the peaks of the story are, and how you build tempo and tension up to them purely in terms of pace. Earn your pauses. Audiences are quick to understand and quick to lose interest if the action is indulgent or monotonous.

'Keep the ball in the air. Seeing a play like a volleyball match is a useful analogy. Quick exchanges, long looping moments full of expectation and concentration, the killer blow, the fumble. When the ball hits the ground, it's over, and picking it up again is much harder to do. Even within scenes and speeches you should concentrate on pace and dynamism, and vary the rhythm to avoid monotony.'

Exercises exploring stagecraft

The following exercises, devised by Norris, are aimed at groups of young directors interested in learning more about the craft. They develop the skills a director requires in order to control action, storytelling, variety and pace. These elements of theatre are inseparable in performance – each influences and is influenced by the others. The exercises look at these interrelated elements from three different perspectives: that of the actor, the audience and the director seeking to identify an overall structure for the play.

On a purely practical level, here are some tips to help make the workshops run smoothly:

- If possible, work in a large, clear and airy space, preferably with natural light and not too much noise from elsewhere. Additional spaces may be useful if the workshop subdivides.
- Provide enough chairs for everyone and a table or two. Too much furniture is not a good idea – the workshops are essentially about directing people, not scenery.
- In a directors' workshop, the acting is done by some or all of the directors who are not directing. Everyone should do both if possible. This is for two reasons: good actors cost money to employ, and it is extremely valuable for directors to understand, on the floor, what it is like to be at the receiving end of their instruction.
- Start with warm-ups and games to relax the actors and create an ensemble.
- Work with two or three short extracts (i.e. 1–2 pages) of plays, with enough copies for everyone to have one. They should be in contrast to each other, involve only two characters, and should include two or three turning-points. It is useful if the gender balance in the scenes reflects that of your workshop participants. These scenes may come from any well-written and relatively accessible play, such as those explored in previous chapters.

These exercises are not fixed in stone, and should be taken as a guide only. Reduce, expand or adapt as you see fit; the key is that what you wish to explore can be done in the time available, and that everything you do is related to that area of exploration.

Character 'wants': the actor's perspective

These exercises explore the play from the point of view of the actors. 'The premise here is that all drama is driven by the wants and needs of the characters. If the character knows what they want, and pursues that want, need or desire accordingly, they will inevitably come up against the different desires of other characters, and the resulting conflict will fire the drama. The more strongly those wants are played, the greater the conflict; the more inventively and variously they are pursued, the more colour, surprise, humour and vitality will enrich the drama.'

You should allow up to three hours to complete this group of exercises.

Introduction: Taking someone somewhere

- Ask everyone to choose both a person and a place in the room, without telling anyone. Instruct them to take that person to that place. Chaos will ensue, so the exercise is short, but it illustrates immediately the premise of the workshop.

What do you want?

- Choose a scene and read it through it as a group, on the floor or round a table. Discuss what each character wants, and how they pursue what they want. Do they get what they want, and when? When does what each character wants change? When do these wants bring a character into direct conflict with another character?

These moments are the turning points within the scene, and become the structure that actors usually want to identify. If you disagree about individual moments, the exercises that follow may help to bring you to a clearer sense of how the scene works in performance. As a director, the understanding of this structure within the scene is the foundation for any dramatic or rhythmic variation.

- Divide the group into threes, with one as director and the other two as actors. These divisions should be reshuffled for each exercise. Send each group of three away to look at the scene and replace every line with a sentence by the speaking character which begins 'I want to . . .' *or* 'I want you to . . .' In other words, all the dialogue is reduced to a blunt expression of the characters' wants and desires. Give a time limit for the exercise which demands decisions rather than endless discussion. It is important for each group to respect the jobs they are doing (i.e. director, actor), regardless of their true inclinations.

- Reassemble, act out the scene for one another, observe what each group has concluded and come up with. Discuss.
- Using the same text, and still in groups of three, rehearse the scene quickly with the dialogue as written, but with complete freedom from inhibition physically, for example, you don't have to follow stage directions, or stick to what has been discussed. Let instinct inform your actions and try to respond spontaneously to the words. Characters must stick to the words of the text, but can physically inhabit and express what they feel and want.
- Reassemble and observe. Discuss.

Exercises like this are demanding and you may encounter some resistance or requests for greater clarity. Throw the challenge back on to the director of each group, to try and make the exercise work in a way they understand.

How will you get what you want?

- Keep everyone together. Have a volunteer choose a fairly neutral line from the scene. One by one, have everyone in the group instruct the volunteer to do something physically tangible to them. It must not be vague or general: 'hurt me' means nothing, whereas 'pull my hair' is clear. 'Seduce me' is general, but 'gently stroke my cheek' is specific.
- The volunteer should not physically 'do' anything, but must deliver their chosen line to the instructor, meeting their eye, and attempt to follow their instruction purely with the intention behind what they are saying. They should then move on to the next instruction, using the same line.

The first problem will be to stop people from responding

physically, but beyond that notice how the volunteer will get stuck in a rhythmic pattern with the phrase, and how two widely contrasting intentions might sound almost the same. Point this out.

If desirable, the group can be divided into smaller groups in order to give everyone the chance to be the volunteer, and see how difficult it is to be flexible, but how easy it is to fill any phrase with intention.

- Do the same again but in reverse. The volunteer must now choose a physical action, and the group feed him/her phrases from the scene. The volunteer must fill each new line with the same intention. For example, if the action is 'breaking a stick over my knee', the actor must speak each of the lines given to him/her as though each involved the sudden violent gesture of breaking a stick (do not do it literally).
- Redivide, and get each group to rehearse the scene in question, making clear decisions about wants and how characters pursue them.
- Present, observe and discuss.

Visual focus: the audience's perspective

These exercises are about guiding the eye of the audience – 'taking directorial responsibility for visual focus on stage, which too often is unclear or uninteresting'. This work should take one-and-a-half to three hours depending on the size of group and the amount of time spent on discussion.

The camera game

- Divide the group into two halves, A and B.
- Divide Group A into pairs. Each pair consists of a cameraman and a camera. The cameraman walks the blind camera around the room, stopping it and moving it as necessary, then operating it. This means squeezing the arm of the camera (the signal for the camera to open its eyes) and then a second later squeezing it again (the signal to shut the eyes). In other words, the cameraman controls what the camera sees, from what angle, etc.

- Group B, meanwhile, are creating the images for the cameras to record. These may be complex, simple, moving, surreal, distant or extremely close up, but all should be invented silently and spontaneously.
- After a while, change round, until everyone has been a camera.
- Discuss briefly. What images worked? What was strong and immediate, and what confusing, unclear or just irritating? Why?
- Divide the group into threes, i.e. a director and two actors. Instruct them to go away and return in three minutes with one still image that tells a story.
- Observe and discuss. Do the images say what you intended? Why, or why not?

Passing focus

- Redivide the groups into threes. Separate and create a short scene without words where the focus of the scene changes three times in three different ways, from one actor to the other and back again. How this change of focus is achieved is up to the director.
- Observe and discuss. What worked? How do movement and stillness work within this? Is there a difference between sharp movement and soft movement? How does one actor pass focus to another? What is the physical relationship of this scene to the audience? How do you give someone power, or how can they take it? How can you build expectation? What other ways have not been explored? Encourage people to think imaginatively, and to think outside the box – our focus is often drawn to the unexpected or beguiling.
- Divide the group into two or three with five to ten in each, and repeat the exercise, with one director in each group. Set the task of passing the focus once to each actor, in a different way each time. Keep it silent. Try to keep the scenes as real as possible. (It may be useful to set a specific scenario, a bus queue, or waiting room, for example).
- Observe and discuss.

If the craft in this area is controlling focus in as varied a way as possible, the art of it is to play with the rules. Surprise is a great tool in theatre, and this area of work can be as much about taking focus away from where you may later want it to be (to create variety and challenge expectations) as it is about following the action or story.

- Redivide into threes and separate to rehearse a scripted scene with these things in mind. The emphasis is on what you are doing visually, so the delivery of the text should, for this exercise, remain fairly neutral. Tell the story visually.
- Observe and discuss.

Rhythm and dynamic: the director's perspective

The final set of exercises looks at how the director controls the momentum of the play (and keeps it from becoming boring). 'The premise here is that variety and colour within scenes and characterisations can only be achieved through an awareness of dynamics and rhythm in parallel with the emotional life (the wants) of the characters.' Playwright Harley Granville Barker claimed that a script is a score awaiting performance. In his work with young directors, Rufus Norris actively investigates this notion, encouraging them to see themselves as conductors whose responsibility is not simply to guide the actors and deliver the material with clarity and originality, but also to control its rhythm and tempo, the overall pace of its acts, and the changing dynamic within scenes and individual moments.

These exercises can be one and a half to three hours long, depending on the size of the group and the amount of time you allow for each section. Try to keep the group focused and do not allow individual exercises to run on to the point where they are no longer useful or directly exploring the premise.

Rhythm

- A useful warm-up for this area of exploration might involve rhythm. This will depend on how comfortable the workshop leader is with leading rhythm. Seat the group in a circle. First get the group clapping evenly in time, without speeding up.

Now establish a simple pattern for everyone to follow that repeats on itself. For example, if we take the basic rhythmic template as eight beats, try counting them all in your head but only clapping on the following:

Count in your head: 1   2   3   4   5   6   7   8
Clap: 1   –   3   4   –   6   –   8

This pattern can be used ad infinitum. Get the group comfortable with it at different speeds.

- Divide the group into two. Group B starts when Group A is on beat 5.
- Divide into three. Group B starts when Group A is on beat 3 and Group C starts when Group A is on beat 5. The rhythmic pattern is now complex and demanding. One tip with this is to get each group to strongly emphasise their own beat 1, at the start of each pattern.

Develop this exercise as far as you confidently can, without it losing definition. Plays, like passages of music, have a distinctive and changing rhythm. The director needs to find this rhythm and control its shifts within scenes and across the whole play.

Rhythm change

- Split the group into teams of three (one director, two actors) and separate. Each team should prepare a scene (reading only, not on their feet) with distinct rhythm changes at each turning point in the scene. Avoid discussion about the inner workings of the scene in any other respect – get quicker or slower in response to the action changing, and that's all.
- Hear them all and discuss. What worked? How did the rhythm affect the clarity of the scene? Did the different versions have any emotional power?
- Redivide and repeat the exercise above but with the added dynamic of volume. Quicker, slower, louder, quieter – any combination of these but still no emotional direction.
- Hear them and discuss briefly.

'In classical music, the stave is littered with musical dynamics (usually in Italian) such as *forte, staccato, pianissimo, accelerando, crescendo* and hundreds of others. The vast majority of these are simple dynamic instructions deliberately devoid of emotional specificity. In following the dynamic instructions, musicians will instinctively supply emotional content to the passage of music, according to their understanding of it and their response to it. Too much emotional instruction can clog a musician's or an actor's performance, or over-simplify it so that more subtle detail is lost.' For the purpose of this exercise, the director and actors will be instructed to ignore stage directions such as '(*angrily*)' or '(*with tears in her eyes*)' before a line. The task in this workshop is to explore what happens when you follow the musical route.

- Repeat the previous exercise, dividing again and reading through the scene, only this time use as many dynamics as seem possible without making the scene ridiculous. Go to extremes – compete for the most extreme dynamic swings within the scene.
- Listen to the results. What conclusions can one draw? By now the colours and variation, however ridiculous, should at least be colourful and various, and the scene have life and energy. It is very useful for both actors and directors to have these tools at their command. Theatre is a dynamic medium, and participants should understand the power of movement, pace and rhythm instead of simply emoting on stage.
- Finally, redivide and prepare the chosen scene on its feet. Keep the dynamic instruction strong but plausible, and see how it affects the physicality of the actors and action.
- Watch them, and observe to what extent the emotional content is strong and impulsive.

Because directing is such a personal job in that it exposes and draws on every aspect of the director's personality, it is impossible to define precisely what makes a good director. But according to Norris, 'the more directing can be seen as a job rather than a title, as a thing people do because they're suited to it (i.e. working with people) rather than because they want to be it (i.e. in charge), the more likely we are to have better theatre across the board and happier people working within it. A common criticism of directors is 'he/she couldn't direct traffic'. This analogy is not as daft as it first seems. A bad theatre director, like a bad traffic director, tells people where to go. A good one uses the energy and movement people already have to get them more quickly, more smoothly, more inventively to their destination. The result is immediate, fluent, meaningful and dynamic theatre, which is after all the only theatre worth making.'

Appendix

The following notes are based on the Young Vic's comprehensive Child Protection Policy, which establishes safe working practices and procedures for all practitioners working with children, young people and vulnerable adults.

Good Practice guidelines

It is important that all staff and practitioners should demonstrate exemplary behaviour in order to place the participant's welfare at the heart of the practice and to protect themselves from false allegations. It is important to create a positive culture and environment for the participants.

Outside school hours the parents and carers retain the sole responsibility for their children whether they are present or not. Inside school hours the teacher has the sole responsibility for the participants.

Much of the following is common sense but it is important to read these guidelines and adhere to them at all times:

Working with individuals
1. Treat all participants equally with respect and dignity.
2. Always put the welfare of the participant first – before the good of the production or project.
3. Build balanced relationships which enable the participants to share in the decision-making process.
4. Make theatre fun and enjoyable and promote a spirit of ensemble working.
5. Do not allow children to use inappropriate language unchallenged.
6. Do not make sexually suggestive comments even in fun.
7. Do not reduce a child to tears as a form of control.
8. Do not allow allegations made by a child to go unchallenged, unrecorded or not acted upon.
9. Do not do things of a personal nature for participants that they can do for themselves.

10. Do not give out personal contact details. The only exception is for a full-time member of staff at the company or school to give out a mobile phone number in emergencies.

11. Always work in an open environment and avoid private or unobserved situations such as closed offices or dressing rooms. Where possible make sure there are always at least two adults in the space.

12. Spending large amounts of time with a participant alone and away from others is to be avoided. For instance providing transport for a child (i.e. driving home or going in a taxi) should only happen as the last resort, for example when parents forget to pick their child up or a participant is ill and needs to be taken to the hospital. In such instances due care should be taken.

13. There should be a named person that participants can go to should they have any concerns.

14. There should always be a contact person with legal responsibility for the participant. A visiting director should never assume sole responsibility for a participant.

15. Any visiting practitioner should only discuss issues of conduct or behaviour with a participant when a full time member of staff at the host company/school is present.

16. Maintain a safe and appropriate distance with participants. Only touch participants when absolutely necessary in relation to the particular activity. No other contact should be encouraged whether this is active or passive, eg. 'rough-housing' or sitting on knees, etc. Your relationship with the participant is that of professional practitioner and non-professional actor.

17. If necessary seek agreement from participants prior to any physical contact.

18. Make sure that disabled participants are informed of and are comfortable with any necessary physical contact.

19. Never use physical contact as a way of ensuring a participant complies with instructions, e.g. dragging by the arm, pushing, forcing, etc. The only exception is when the action is preventing harm, e.g. avoiding a falling ladder, etc.

20. Be an excellent role model which includes no swearing, smoking, drinking alcohol or taking recreational drugs in the presence of young people.

21. Provide enthusiastic, constructive feedback and encouragement rather than negative criticism.
22. When working practically groups should be made up of no more than 26 participants.
23. An appropriate number of theatre or teaching staff (freelance or full-time) should be present at all times. The ratio should be 1:8 or 1:10 for older groups. It is recommended that a minimum of two members of staff (freelance or full-time) are present at all times and that children under 8 years of age are supervised at all times.
24. Ensure that there is appropriate space for the number of participants.
25. Ensure there is access to a phone in the building or a mobile phone to hand (when outside the building).
26. Risk assessment must be carried out by a member of the host company or department.
27. There should be a First Aid box to hand and member of staff trained in first aid in the building. First Aid should only be administered by trained full-time staff members.
28. Keep a written record of any injury that occurs – in line with the company's Health and Safety Policy.
29. Regular and appropriate food and drinks should be provided/allowed for.
30. The participants should not be allowed to leave the building during breaks (to visit the shops, go for a walk, etc.) unless they are over 16 years of age.
31. No child under 5 should be left at events without a carer/parent/older sibling.
32. The practitioner and participants should be aware of evacuation procedures.
33. Be aware of any participants' particular needs (hard of hearing, physical disabilities, Attention Deficit Hyperactivity Disorder, etc.) so these can be taken into account when developing work. The participants will be asked to fill in details of any needs as part of the registration process. (For pioneering workshop and training programmes for people with physical and sensory impairments, contact Graeae Theatre Company (www.graeae.org). Strathcona Theatre Company (www.strathco.demon.co.uk) runs theatre skills training courses for people with learning disabilities.)

34. No participant is allowed to smoke, take recreational drugs or drink alcohol on the company premises irrespective of their age. Any medical needs regarding prescribed drugs should be discussed with a member of the host company/department.
35. Make sure that all name badges are removed before the participants leave the work space. No name tags must be visible during any photographic or videoing sessions.
36. Each participant must ensure that they get permission before leaving the room to go to the toilet.
37. Particular care should be taken when participants are involved in projects that require the use of dressing rooms for costume changes. Each gender should be provided with a separate dressing room. The only adults allowed in the dressing rooms are directors, teachers, parents/support staff provided with the agreement of the schools and youth workers. Only staff for whom it is essential to have access to the dressing rooms should be allowed to enter. In a theatre building this includes stage management, wardrobe staff, the workshop/rehearsal coordinators and the director. Where possible the team will include a male and female stage manager to ensure that access to dressing rooms is on a same gender basis. Always respect the participant's privacy and be sensitive to different levels of modesty.
38. Each participant must sign in and out at the beginning and end of each session.

References

Sources and quoted texts

Ackroyd, Peter, *London: The Biography*, Chatto & Windus, 2000.

Aristotle, *Poetics* (tr. Kenneth McLeish), Nick Hern Books, 1999.

Barker, Clive, *Theatre Games*, Methuen, 1977.

Barkworth, Peter, *About Acting*, Methuen, 2001.

Brook, Peter, *The Empty Space*, Penguin, 1968.

Brook, Peter, *There Are No Secrets: Thoughts on Acting and Theatre*, Methuen, 1993.

Brook, Peter, *The Shifting Point*, Methuen, 1987.

Courtney, Cathy, ed., *Jocelyn Herbert: A Theatre Workbook*, Arts Books International, 1993.

Delgado, Maria M., and Heritage, Paul, *In Contact with the Gods: Directors Talk Theatre*, Manchester University Press, 1996.

Doty, Gesdna A., and Harbin, Billy J., eds, *Inside the Royal Court Theatre, 1956–1981: Artists Talk*, Louisiana State University Press, 1990.

Drain, Richard, ed. *Twentieth Century Theatre: A Sourcebook*, Routledge, 1995.

Eyre, Richard, and Wright, Nicholas, *Changing Stages: A View of British Theatre in the Twentieth Century*, Bloomsbury, 2000.

Gaskill, William, *A Sense of Direction: Life at the Royal Court*, Faber & Faber, 1988.

Gottlieb, Vera, and Chambers, Colin, eds, *Theatre in a Cool Climate*, Amber Lane Press, 1999.

The Complete Grimm Fairy Tales, Routledge, 1975.

Grimms' Fairy Tales, Puffin Books, 1971.

Hahlo, Richard, and Reynolds, Peter, *Dramatic Events*, Faber & Faber, 2000.

Houseman, Barbara, *Finding Your Voice*, Nick Hern Books, 2002.

Huxley, Michael, and Witts, Noel, eds, *The Twentieth-Century Performance Reader*, Routledge, 1996.

Johnstone, Keith, *Impro: Improvisation and the Theatre*, Methuen, 1981.

Linnell, Rosemary, *Theatre Arts Workbook*, Hodder & Stoughton, 1991.

Littlewood, Joan, *Joan's Book*, Methuen, 2003.

McCaffery, Michael, *Directing a Play*, Phaidon, 1988.

Manfull, Helen, *Taking Stage: Women Directors on Directing*, Methuen, 1999.

Mayfield, Katherine, *Acting A to Z: The Young Person's Guide to a Stage or Screen Career*, Back Stage Books, 1998.

Reid, Francis, *The Staging Handbook*, A & C Black, 2001.

Rodenburg, Patsy, *The Actor Speaks*, Methuen, 1998.

Rodenburg, Patsy, *The Need for Words*, Methuen, 1994.

Rodenburg, Patsy, *The Right to Speak*, Methuen, 1992.

Rodenburg, Patsy, *Speaking Shakespeare*, Methuen, 2002.

Scher, Anna, and Verrall, Charles, *Another 100+ Ideas for Drama*, Heinemann, 1987.

Stafford-Clark, Max, *Letters to George*, Nick Hern Books, 1989.

Thomas, Keith, *Religion and the Decline of Magic*, Penguin, 1971.

Toporkov, Vasili, *Stanislavski in Rehearsal*, Methuen, 2001.

Tusa, John, *On Creativity: Interviews Exploring the Process*, Methuen, 2003.

Tushingham, David, ed., *Live 5: My Perfect Theatre*, Nick Hern Books, 1997.

Warner, Marina, *From the Beast to the Blonde: On Fairy Tales and their Tellers*, Vintage, 1995.

Playtexts

Duffy, Carol Ann, and Supple, Tim, *More Grimm Tales*, Faber & Faber, 1997.

Hansberry, Lorraine, *A Raisin in the Sun*, Methuen, 2001.

Hughes, Langston, *Simply Heavenly*, Dramatists Play Service, 1998.

Lope de Vega, *Peribanez*, Nick Hern Books, 2003.

Marlowe, Christopher, *Doctor Faustus*, Oxford University Press, 1998.

Further reading

Acting

Allain, Paul, *The Art of Stillness*, Methuen, 2002.

Barton, John, *Playing Shakespeare*, Methuen, 1984.

Benedetti, Jean, *Stanislavski & the Actor*, Methuen, 1998.

Grotowski, Jerzy, *Towards a Poor Theatre*, Methuen, 1968.

Lewis, Robert, *Advice to the Players*, HarperCollins, 1980.

Stanislavski, Constantin, *An Actor's Handbook*, Methuen, 1990.

Stanislavski, Constantin, *Building a Character*, Methuen, 1979.

Strasberg, Lee, *Strasberg at the Actors Studio*, Theatre Communications Group, 1991.

Costume

Ambrose, Bonnie, *The Little Hatmaking Book II: Elizabethan*, Drama

Book Publishers, 1996.

Holkeboer, Katherine S., *Patterns for Theatrical Costumes*, Drama Book Publishers, 1993.

Directing

Bentley, Eric, ed., *The Theory of the Modern Stage*, Penguin, 1992.

Bloom, Michael, *Thinking Like a Director*, Faber & Faber, 2002.

Clurman, Harold, *On Directing*, Macmillan, 1972.

Counsell, Colin, ed., *Signs of Performance: An Introduction to Twentieth-Century Theatre*, Routledge, 1996.

Irvin, Polly, *Directing for the Stage*, RotoVision, 2003.

Games and exercises

Dixon, Luke, *Play Acting: Drama Workshops – A Source Book*, Methuen, 2003.

Johnston, Chris, *House of Games*, Nick Hern Books, 1998.

Johnstone, Keith, *Impro for Storytellers*, Faber & Faber, 1999.

Movement

Lane, Richard, *Swashbuckling*, Nick Hern Books, 1999.

Lecoq, Jacques, *The Moving Body: Teaching Creative Theatre*, Methuen, 2002.

Marshall, Lorna, *The Body Speaks*, Methuen, 2001.

Newlove, Jean, and Dalby, John, *Laban for All*, Nick Hern Books, 2003.

Production

Arrowsmith, Keith, *The Methuen Amateur Theatre Handbook*, Methuen, 2002.

Pallin, Gail, *Stage Management: The Essential Handbook*, Nick Hern Books, 2003.

Pilbrow, Richard, *Stage Lighting Design*, Nick Hern Books, 1997.

Warfel, William B., *The New Handbook of Stage Lighting Graphics*, Quite Specific Media Group, 1995.

Voice

Linklater, Kristin, *Freeing the Natural Voice*, Drama Book Publishers, 1976.

Wilson, Pat, *The Singing Voice*, Nick Hern Books, 1997.